The Bloody 85th:

The Letters of Milton McJunkin, a Western Pennsylvania Soldier in the Civil War

ADAMS EXPRESS COMPANY'S
Army and Soldiers' Package Express.

No. _______   Pittsburgh, Pa. _Oct. 13_ 186_2_

Received of Mr. _Thos. A Wrisk_

One Box 39¢

Marked _Morrison E W Lunkin Camp D 85_

Regt. Pa Vol 3d Brigade Pecks Division

Suffolk

Which it is mutually agreed is to be forwarded to our Agency nearest or most convenient to destination only, and there delivered to other parties to complete the transportation, or to the order of the Consignee, or to the order of the Quartermaster or other officer of the Regiment to which Consignee is attached.   It is further mutually agreed, that the ADAMS EXPRESS COMPANY are not to be held liable or responsible for the property herein mentioned, after delivery to the army wagons, or to the order of the officer of the regiment.

Freight, _Paid_   For the Company,   _B. H. Clarke_

Haven, print.

The Bloody 85th:

The Letters of Milton McJunkin, a Western Pennsylvania Soldier in the Civil War

Edited by Dr. Richard Sauers,
with a foreword and additional material by
Patrick A. Schroeder
From the collection of Ronn Palm

SCHROEDER PUBLICATIONS
2002

ISBN: 1-889246-13-1 (Softcover)
ISBN: 1-889246-16-6 (Hardcover)

Printed by Sheridan Books
Fredericksburg, Virginia

SCHROEDER PUBLICATIONS
131 Tanglewood Drive
Lynchburg, Virginia 24502
www.civilwar-books.com
civilwarbooks@yahoo.com

TABLE OF CONTENTS

PHOTOGRAPHS AND SKETCHES INDEX

FORWARD

Given the plethora of Civil War narratives published in recent years, one might reasonably ask, why print another set of soldier letters? Will they tells us anything different than we have read somewhere else? The answer is a resounding YES! The letters of Milton McJunkin are unique and insightful in several ways. McJunkin's regiment, the 85th Pennsylvania Volunteer Infantry, and its wartime service was atypical of the majority of Civil War units. That organization had the distinction of serving in both the Army of the Potomac and the Army of the James. These letters thus provide a different view of the war than the average Army of the Potomac soldier. McJunkin and his comrades served their time around Washington and saw action on the Peninsula at Williamsburg and Seven Pines (Fair Oaks). But they also participated in expeditions to Suffolk, Virginia, and to Goldsboro, North Carolina. In the latter campaign the regiment, being a veteran one when compared with other units on the campaign, provided a reliable backbone for General John G. Foster's force. Creating a diversion in favor of General Burnside in Virginia, Foster's men slashed into North Carolina. The 85th saw fighting at White Hall, Kinston, and outside of Goldsboro itself and performed well capturing an artillery piece during the engagement at Kinston. Boarding steamers at Moorehead City, they proceeded to South Carolina to spend more than a year in operations against the city of Charleston. While the Army of the Potomac was spilling blood on the 85th's native soil, the boys of western Pennsylvania were consecrating the sands of the South Carolina islands--in one week of siege operations against Fort Wagner on Morris Island, the regiment lost 120 men.

Upon returning to Virginia in May 1864. The regiment was part of General Benjamin Butler's ill fated operations in the Bermuda Hundred Campaign, and then in the siege of Richmond and Petersburg. The 85th Pennsylvania was distinguished in the Battle of Deep Bottom on August 16, 1864, where three soldiers from the regiment captured Confederate battle flags and were awarded the Medal of Honor. Although November 1864 signaled the end of the regiment's service, a portion of the men had re-enlisted as veteran volunteers. These soldiers continued with the Army of the James, and were among the force that cut off the Army on Northern Virginia's escape route at Appomattox Court House on the morning of April 9, 1865.

The "History of the Eighty-fifth Pennsylvania Volunteer Infantry" was written by Luther S. Dickey, and if truth be told, is quite possibly the most boring regimental account ever composed. But since the 85th did have a regimenal, however flawed, little more has been penned concerning the service of these stalwart volunteers from western Pennsylvania. Enter Union loving Milton McJunkin, one of if not the tallest man in the regiment, standing 6'1". His letters home permit us to observe the inevitable evolution of the hardy and boastful recruit to the wearied veteran. Many of the letters contain typical soldier compliants about the need for money and the want of treats. But if one wants to know what was truly going through the minds of these fighting men, read McJunkin's letter of January 17, 1864. McJunkin was a steady reliable man, and sadly his one furlough home proved to be his last. Initially ealthy and hardy, like so many of his comrades he was fated to perish not by bullet or shell, but rather a victim of disease. The reader feels his plight, although the severity of his sickness is not realized until the very end. McJunkin dies with less than a month officially left to serve.

It is truly a shame that McJunkin met his demise before the completion of his term of service. The humorous content of some of his letters, such as the one to his sister on August 16, 1863, where he writes using the jargon of the colored troops (54th Massachusetts) on Morris Island, and telling of shooting at the fattest reb he could see. This comical missive does, however, aptly relate what the troops were experiencing on the island, and he signs it "tiddleywink." Such notations leads one to believe that he was of likeable nature, and probably a favorite around camp; except for the malefactors that were suppressed when officers would direct the hulking McJunkin to assist in securing an unruly comrade.

Complmenting the text, are nearly 60 photographs of McJunkin's comrades--most of them from the collection of Ronn Palm, who also has McJunkin's original letters. Underneath each photo is a military biographical sketch of each soldier derived from his compiled service records at the National Archives. After McJunkin's letters is a summary of the regiment's field service in "The Deeds and Sacrifices of the Eighty-fifth Pennsylvania." Then there is an accolade concerning the flag of the regiment, and the postwar handling of the sacred emblem. The book has been indexed, thus making it a useful resource to the reader.

For ten years, while employed at Appomattox Court House National Historical Park, I've portrayed a veteran of the old 85th Pennsylvania stationed as the Provost Guard at Appomattox in the summer of 1865. It is gratifying that this project has come to fruition, and will help perpetuate the exploits of McJunkin and his comrades. This work is an apt tribute to a noble spirit and fine soldier as well commemorating the reputation of a gallant and hard fighting regiment from western Pennsylvania.

Patrick A. Schroeder
Appomattox, Virginia

INTRODUCTION

In 1915, Luther S. Dickey, acting as historian for the veterans association of the 85th Pennsylvania Volunteer Infantry, published his manuscript history of that unit. Relying on letters and diaries of his comrades, Dickey composed a narrative chronological history of the marches and battles of the 85th from its formation in 1861 through its mustering out of service in 1864. Almost one-quarter of the volume was devoted to an analysis of the battle of Fair Oaks (Seven Pines), in which Brigadier General Silas Casey's division of the Fourth Army Corps, to which the 85th was attached, was attacked and driven from its position. Other officers accused the division of cowardice and Dickey chose to respond to the critics, point by point.

Dickey's book is a rather dry account of the daily movements and occurrences in the 85th Pennsylvania. Accompanied by two maps and six illustrations, Dickey's book is a prime example of early twentieth century military writing. Since that time, many of the primary sources that Dickey used seem to have disappeared, perhaps discarded by families or still remaining in attics awaiting future rediscovery. Over the past decades, letters of 85th soldiers and photographs of men long since dead have resurfaced. One such collection of letters and a gallery of photographs form the basis of this supplement to Dickey's history.

The letters transcribed in this book were penned by Milton E. McJunkin, a 24-year-old farmer who lived near the village of Bentleyville in west Pike Run Township, Washington County, Pennsylvania. Like many other young men of his time, McJunkin was stirred to arms by the sundering of North and South. He joined the Union army on 15 October 1861. McJunkin seems to have enlisted by himself; other dates of enlistment of those men living near McJunkin show that no one else signed up when McJunkin did. Captain William H. Horn was recruiting a company in McJunkin's area. The majority of his men came from Bentleyville, Beallsville, Zollarsville, and Fredericktown. Nicknamed the Lafayette Infantry, Horn's command became Company D of the 85th Pennsylvania.

Joshua B. Howell, a 55-year-old lawyer from Uniontown, recruited the 85th in the counties of Fayette, Washington, Greene, and Somerset, to serve for three years. The unit was organized in November 1861 and served until November 1864, when most of the survivors went home. Those who had re-enlisted remained in the field as a detachment of the 85th until consolidated with the 188th Pennsylvania Volunteer Infantry.

McJunkin's career with the 85th is reflected in his letters home. The eighty surviving letters (7 from 1861, 32 from 1862, 19 from 1863, and 22 from 1864) contain much information about the 85th. Unfortunately, little is known about the recipients of his missives. McJunkin was not in the habit of starting his letters with salutations. Occasionally he would do so. At times, it was possible to match the postmarks on envelopes with the letters to identify the recipients. Most letters were sent to his mother, Mrs. Margaret McJunkin. Others were addressed to Melville McJunkin (quite possibly an uncle) and Thomas A. West (probably a brother-in-law). The names of others mentioned in his letters are difficult to trace after a century.

The letters have been transcribed exactly from the originals. No attempt has been made to alter spelling or content. The editor has added punctuation; McJunkin usually did not bother to add periods or commas, nor did he capitalize correctly. These additions have been placed within brackets. The editor has also broken the lengthier missives into paragraphs for ease of reading. Footnotes have been supplied to identify places, people, campsites, or explain background.

Like many enlisted men, McJunkin wrote home more often at the beginning of his enlistment. By 1864, his letters usually were brief and sometimes very sarcastic in tone. He became more and more perplexed and angry at the lack of mail from home. He constantly sought boxes of goodies and complained when he did not get what he requested. There are few letters with good battle content. Such letters describe his participation in the fighting at Fair Oaks (Seven Pines) and the siege operations at Charleston, South Carolina. Even then, McJunkin did not pontificate and proclaim to know all; his battle writing was strictly limited to what he saw and did.

The McJunkin letters illustrate quite graphically the progression from young recruit to battle-hardened veteran by 1864. A cocky, young recruit, McJunkin was already calling his regiment "The Bloody 85th" even before it left the Washington, DC, area. McJunkin usually described his physical condition for the folks back home, sometimes including information about other recruits from West Pike Run Township. He passed along camp gossip and news about the enemy. At times McJunkin provided the folks at home with drawings of himself and things he saw.

He made it quite clear what he thought about the officers of the 85th. He liked Colonel Howell but did not care much about Captain Horn. By the end of the Peninsula Campaign, McJunkin had become anti-George McClellan. He also despised Major General David Hunter, who so thoughtlessly placed the troops from North Carolina under hardships because of his grudge against Major General John G. Foster. McJunkin had much to write about Brigadier Generals William H. Keim, Henry W. Wessells, and John J. Peck. By 1864, McJunkin was counting the days to muster-out; the privations he endured under bad officers made it apparent that he would not re-enlist. Perhaps the best letter of the entire collection is that of 17 January 1864, giving the veteran's thoughts after he found the isolated grave of a fellow soldier.

Sadly, McJunkin never made it home alive. The burden of military service finally took its toll on the young man. On 26 July 1864, an ill McJunkin was sent to the general hospital at Bermuda Hundred, then transferred to Balfour General Hospital in Portsmouth, Virginia. The illness was here diagnosed as consumption. Fearing the worst, McJunkin became more and more agitated when someone from home failed to come take him north on furlough, which he finally received on 15 October. Thomas A. West came to Portsmouth and accompanied McJunkin as far as Harrisburg. Here, at the Soldiers' Rest, McJunkin died on 25 October, of chronic diarrhea. He was buried in the cemetery at Beallsville, Pennsylvania.

His mother, widowed since 1851, then sought a pension because she stated that her son had provided key financial support during the war. After help from the Pennsylvania State Agency, the local House member, and some of her son's wartime comrades, Mrs. McJunkin was granted a pension of $8 per month on 7 July 1868, retroactive to October 1864.

The pamphlet reprinted here, *History of the Old Flag of the 85th Reg't.*, is a rare piece of ephemera that seems to be unique to the 85th Pennsylvania. During its term of service, the regiment carried two stands of colors. One was presented by Governor Andrew G. Curtin in November 1861 and replaced by a second issue in early 1864. As part of the Commonwealth of Pennsylvania's Civil War Flag Collection, both are available for public inspection at the Pennsylvania Capitol Preservation Committee's flag room in Harrisburg.

A second flag was made for the regiment by a group of Uniontown ladies and presented to the regiment before it departed for Washington. It was carried side by side with the state colors during the war and brought home to Uniontown in 1864. Thereafter, it was displayed at regimental reunions, during which the veterans would vote to appoint a color-bearer to maintain the flag each year.

In 1893, John G. Stevens, longtime bearer of this flag, decided to keep it from view because he felt that the flag was being destroyed by his fellow veterans, who literally tore it to shreds for souvenirs. In 1898, a group of 85th veterans took Stevens to court, demanding return of the prized flag. Two years later, a judge rendered his verdict by dismissing the suit, writing that the veterans had never made any official transfer of the flag to the regimental association. Thus, the plaintiffs had no title to the flag. A superior court judge later upheld the lower court ruling, but it was already too late, for Stevens complained that the flag had practically been destroyed during the time it was out of his possession.

However, the booklet does not tell all about this flag. Newspaper clippings found by the Mason-Dixon Civil War Roundtable in Uniontown reveal additional facts about the local flag. At the battle of Deep Bottom (16 August 1864), a minie ball struck the finial of the state-issued color, dented the brass, and remained embedded in it. When the regiment arrived in Harrisburg in November 1864 to be mustered out of service, many of the veterans wanted to keep this emblem of their valor. However, the state flag was required to be turned over to the care of the state military department. To get around this problem, some enterprising soldiers of the 85th simply removed both colors from their staffs and switched poles. Thus, the wooden staff of the Uniontown flag was turned in with the state color, while the state-issued staff went home with the Uniontown flag.

Information from the clippings allows the reader to make more sense of the flag pamphlet, which is very confusing regarding the identities of the color-bearers for the regiment's flags. Color-bearers for the Uniontown flag seem to have been Joseph G. Raeger (November 1861-April 1862), Jacob Deffenbaugh (April 1862-sometime in 1863), and John M. Moore (October 1863-November 1864). Bearers for the state colors were Richard Lincoln (wounded at Fair Oaks), George Orbin (July 1862-September 1863), and Alexander Ross (May-November 1864). Walter C. Craven carried the state color temporarily in August 1864 when Moore was suffering from sunstroke.

Included in this book is a rare newspaper history of the 85th Pennsylvania. Written by Adjutant Samuel L. McHenry, the piece originally appeared in the 3 July 1886 edition of the Philadelphia *Weekly Times*. Edited by Alexander K. McClure, this weekly paper made its debut in 1877. The major attraction of this weekly was the "Annals of the War" series that featured recollections of Union and Confederate veterans. So popular was this feature that the *Weekly Times* published a volume of the best contributions in 1879. The series ran until the late 1880s and included more than eight hundred articles. McHenry's brief history of the 85th is one of several unit histories that appeared in the "Annals of the War" series.

The accompanying photographs of 85th members are principally owned by Ronn Palm, who also owns the McJunkin letters. Copies of McJunkin's letters have been deposited in the manuscripts department of the United States Army Military History Institute, located at Carlisle Barracks, Pennsylvania. Also deposited are letters written by Adam McJunkin, Milton's older brother. Adam had migrated west before the war and enlisted in the Springfield Independent Battery, also known as Vaughan's Illinois Battery. His letters cover the period from November 1862 through May 1865.

Dr. Richard A. Sauers

Milton E. McJunkin, Company E

Author of these letters, McJunkin poses here in a forage cap and overcoat. A watch chain dangles from a shirt button and one suspender is visible. At his enlistment on Oct. 15, 1861, at Beallsville, he was 24 years old, and a farmer with gray eyes and dark hair. Undoubtedly one of the tallest men in the regiment, McJunkin stood 6'3", and was a native of Washington County. He mustered in as a private on Nov. 11, 1861. Present with the regiment until receiving a furlough on May 23, 1863, and had rejoined the regiment by July. McJunkin served faithfully until falling sick on July 25, 1864, and reporting to the hospital at Bermuda Hundred, VA. Transferred to Balfour United States Hospital at Portsmouth, VA, he was diagnosed with phthisis pulmmalis. Finally given a 30-day furlough on Oct. 12, he died on the way home at the Soldiers' Rest in Harrisburg, PA, three days later.   (Ronn Palm Collection)

1861

Camp Lafayette[1]
Oct 28th 1861

We will not be on parade until three o'clock so I thought I would commence
a letter

Camp Lafayette
Oct 29th 1861

Well Mell I guess I will write a little more while they are getting dinner[.] I
am hearty and weigh 3 1/2 lbs more than I did when I came here[.] there is
only 2 or 3 on the sick list in our company and they blame them with haveing
the blues more than any thing else[.] we have not got our uniforn yet and I
dont expect we will for several weeks[.] there is quite a variety of
amusements in camp to pass away the time[:] some on parade[,] some pitching
quates[,] some playing ball[,] some playing euchre[2][,] some writing letters[,]
some reading their bibles[,] some reading novels[,] and everything else you
could think of[.] we have good grub and plenty of it[--] fresh beef or pork all
the time[,] good bread and sea biscuit[,] coffee thickened with sugar[,] beens[,]
potatoes[,] cabbage[,] and butter once a week[.] in fact we have all here that
a man could wish to make himself comfortable[.] we all like a soldiers life
much better than a country life[.] we drill 4 hours a day[--] at 9 am[,] 1 pm[,]
and from 3 until 5 on regimental drill and the balance of the time is our own
except when we are on guard which happens about once a week[.] I must
close for the present and go to dinner[.]
Well I will write some more now before we go on parade[.] you can

---

[1] Camp Lafayette was located in Uniontown, on the old fairground south of
Fayette Street.

[2] Euchre was a popular card game utilizing the 32 highest cards of a deck.
Each player was dealt five cards and the player making trump was required to take at
least three tricks to win.

1

tell mother it is all talk about the officers reading our letters before they are sent[.] I have sent three since I have been here and I <u>know</u> I am the <u>only</u> one that read them[.]

we go to church as often as we please[.] we had preaching in camp last sunday at three o'clock[.] tell mother she can go on to oliver taylor's and get her pay[.] I fixed it up as I came along[.]

Well I have run out of something to say so I must close[.]

write often and tell me All the particulars how that horse is getting along and every thing else[.]

direct your letters to
Union Town Fayette Co Pa Care of Captain Horn
Lafayette Infantry

Camp Lafayette
Nov 2d 1861

Well it is still raining and I have nothing else to do so I believe I will write a letter to somebody[.] it commenced raining night before last and has kept it up pretty well ever since[.] on night before last it blew quite a gale from the ridge[.] it upset several tents[.] it was rather the bigest wind I ever saw around here[.] Our boys are all well there not being one in our company but what is abel for his rations[.] there is some few though in the Regiment on the sick list but it is their own fault[.]

I forgot while writeing the above about our Captain[.] he is on the sick list to day but I think he will be all right against[.] we get our uniforms which the Colonel says will take place on day after tomorrow[.] perhaps it is the case and perhaps not[.] he says it is so though and that we will leave here in about two weeks[.] I hope it is the case for I want to dry up them rebbels fussing against the first of may as I want to marry about that time in the year[.] Well I am tired writeing now so I will close until after dinner[.]

Nov 4th/61

It is not raining to day but it is wet cold and disagreeable and looks as if it might snow before night but I believe I would rather see snow than rain because our quarters will not turn rain very well and I think they would turn snow[.] We are all well[.] the Captain got over his spell last night and this morning was abel to eat as hearty as any of us and for my part I never enjoyed better health that I now do and another thing I feel better contented than I have before since the war commenced[.] I feel now that I am serving my god and my country[.] if I fall in battle I fall in a good cause and my God will be with me but I expect to return in peace in less than a year[.]

Well I am down on these little offices[.] nothing <u>less</u> than Captain will suit me[.] I have just returned from the mountains[.] I was sent out there this morning at the head of a squad of 15 as corporal[.] just as we got through hopwood six of them broke off in to the woods and I saw nothing more of them until I got back to camp[.] there is some that wont obey non commissioned officers[.] that is the reason these little offices would not suit me[.] I took the balance on out through and we attended to our business and came back and found four of the six in camp[.] the other two came in shortly after us[.] we were not out on any very important business and you need not take it that I am in any office yet[.] I was only corporal of the squad for today but I must quit or make a finish of my letter for dress parade comes off now shortly[.] we have not drilled any since friday[.]

I guess our uniforms has Come[.] one of the boys says he sat on one of the boxes that had them in so you see that came pretty straight[.]

we will not go through brownsville when we leave here[.] we will take the cars here and go to pittsburgh and from there I think to Williamsport Maryland[.]

No more at present

M. E. McJunkin

Camp Lafayette

Nov 7th 1861

Well we got marching orders About 10 minnets ago so I just thought I would write you a few lines to let you kno about it so if there was any body in that neighbourhood who wanted to come over before we left they might have an opportunity[.] we are all well in our Company but Alex Mckey[3] and William Lash[.] Mckay had the dysentary and I don't know what ailed Lash but they are both about well now[.] they will be back in camp this evening[.] I had the head-ache yesterday[ ] I thought I was takeing the measels but I am all right again to day sound as a dollar[.] you can judge of my health from my weight[.] I was over in town last night and got weighed and I weighed 187 lbs[.] I weighed 170 lbs that monday we came over here[.] I have cleaned up my ration every time since I got back[.] I sleep very well[.] I am generally in bed before the retreat is beat and I am generally awaked in the morning by the reveillee[.]

---

[3] Regimental history has spelling as McCay.

We have had quite an excited time in camp this week[.][4]
Captain Giler[5] was elected Major and that throwed his company without a Captain[.] they could not make a fuse with another[.] there is two companies split all to pieces and divided in to other companies but it has been noisy times here since the election[.] they have been fighting and jangling a goodeal about what companies they would join[.]

Well I am tired writeing so I guess I will say the rest and close[.] the Colonel told us a while ago that he had just received a dispach from the governor that we was to leave here on tueday for Washington City but he has told us soo many lies that I dont place much stress upon it but it may be so this time[.] I hope it is[.] you never heard such a cheering as there was here when we got the word[.] we had the united voices of about 1000 men[.] you must excuse my bad writeing for I got the worst pen in camp as every body had to write a letter and them that Could not get pens was staveing around here getting ready to start makeing quite a stir[.]

no more at present
M. E. McJunkin

Camp Casey Maryland Nov 25[6]

I received a letter from home yesterday and was glad to hear that you were all well[.] our Company are all enjoying good health at present except 2[.] one of them took the measels 2 or 3 weeks ago[.] he is about well now[.] the other took sick last night[.] I dont know what ails him yet[.] I had not time to finish my letter yesterday[.] I will write some more today[.] I think there is a battle across the potomac today[.] we have heard the roar of artilery all morning[.] I will just write general this time and give you the particulars some pretty day when I have more time[.] Well we left Lafayette last wensday 9 am did not

---

[4] See Dickey, p. 11, for an account of the elections and attendant problems. When a regiment was organized, each company elected its own line officers (captain and two lieutenants). Then, the company officers elected the regimental officers (colonel, lieutenant colonel, and major). At the beginning of the war, elections were usually based on popularity rather than military prowess.

[5] Absalom Guiler, who served until 31 May 1862, when he was discharged on surgeon's certificate.

[6] Camp Casey was located near Bladensburg, MD. The 85th remained in this camp from 23-28 November 1861.

change cars till we got to baltimore[.] arrived in Washington City friday night[.] marched out here to Camp Casey on saturday arrived here about dark[.] we are 5 miles north of the city on an out post[.] there is 3 Regiments of us in this camp[.] soldiers are pretty plenty around here[.] we could if needed have 200,000 men on the ground we occupy in 2 or 3 hours time[.] on last saturday I got up on the steeple of the Capitol[.] it is a level country around here if you dont know it[.] it is about such place as the western reserve in ohio[.] so to return to my story[.] when I was on my elevated position I could see as far as my eyes would carry[.] the landscape was magnifficent[.] as far as as you could see on every side the country is dotted with the tents of our troops[.]

you said mother was in a reverie[.] tell her not to disturb herself about me[.] I am better contented than I ever was before[.] war will invariably make a man better or worse[.] I am not worse[.] it is the best thing any loyal man can do to come to war when our cause is so just and no man[,] woman[,] or child if they go where war has been and see its ravages if they are not traitors but will say go stand up for your country and if need be spill your last drop of blood in defense of your native land[.] haman said tom talked of comeing to the army[.] tell him to stay where he is[.] he has no business in the army[.] he cannot stand it[.]

the surgeon told me the truth when he examined me[.] I weigh almost 200 lbs now and I stand camp life better than 2/3 of the regiment[.]

you cannot write to me until I write again and give you the address[.]

you will hear from the Bloody 85th again[.]

M. E. McJunkin U. S. army

I will write as soon as I can and give an address[.]

Camp Casey
Nov 26th 1861

Well we have got our tents moved and our streets fixed up and all comfortable so I guess I will commence another letter[.] I guess I will give you my address before I go on further lest I fill my sheet and have no room[.] direct to Washington City, D.C. Care of Captain Horn, Co. C, 85th Reg. Pa. Vol. it is nessary to have this full address especialy the number of the regiment and the state and also the Captain[.] I just caution you for fear you think so much is not nessassary and by doing so I not get the letters[,] for you must recolect there is a great many regiments in our army[.]

we left Camp Lafayette last wensday 9 am got down to some town close to pitt against dark[.][7] from there to miflin against daylight to harrisburgh 10 am[.] stayed there till 8 pm[.] had our flag presented by governor along with a first rate speech[.] to baltimore 10 am and changed cars for the first from starting point[.] we marched through baltimore on foot[.] our officers gave us strict orders if anybody insulted us not to answer or resent it but the bloody 85th cannot always obey orders[.] however there was no danger in passing through when we did if we had no arms there was two regimens of cavalry[8] marched before us through city[.] I guess there was about 10,000 troops there on that day[.] we took the cars 7 pm for the capitol[.] arrived about 10 at night[.] marched to the soldiers retreat took supper and stayed til saturday evening[.] marched out here arrived about dark and done the best we could until today when we fixed up things to suit our selves[.]

we are now in the heart of the enimies country[.] there is rebel encampments within 2 hours march of where we are encamped[.] they are trying to cut off our connection with the north[.] one railroad is all that connects us with the north and if they get that destroyed it would cause us some trouble but we have a heavy guard on it[.] there is from 10,000 to 12,000 from the maryland lines to washington city[.]

it done us a heap of good to have the people along the road cheering us as we came[.] everybody cheered until we got into dixie[.] from that through some of the folks would shake their fists at us even among the lassies[.] we saw one seceshion flag in baltimore but we could not get to pull it down[.] the soldiers all get along like brothers[.] they all do all they can to make each other comfortable no difference where they are from[.] they all meet as old friends as soon as they see each other they are well acquainted[.] as for the scarcity of grub I can tell you how that is the regiment adjoining us have sold enough of their rations to buy three stoves to each company[.] you see by that that they were not starved very much and we all fare alike[.]

I dont know yet where we will winter[.] as for them socks I got them[.] I have six pair of good socks[.] you may think strange of that bible but that is easy explained[.] we were presented with a clasp testament and army hymbook[.] I spent half a day in the Capitol and then did not see half of it[.] it only covers 3 1/2 acres[.] enclosed I send a piece of a [?] I got out of the senate chamber to show you what a grand place them divils had to be in while they were bringing about this war[.] I could not describe the big house to you[.] it is the most magnificent sight I ever saw or ever expected to see[.]

---

[7] McJunkin refers either to McKeesport or Greensburg.

[8] Actually, the cavalry numbered two companies, not two regiments.

what it cost to just furnish the senate chamber would buy out I expect two of the richest men in washington county[.] I will give you our mess Hezekiah Horn[,] Elias Horn[,] Oliver thomas[,] Isaiah Jordan[,] and myself.

Laddie[9] likes these frosty mornings very well[.] he is as fat as a hog[.] I guess I will quit writeing now for diferent causes[.] one is my candle is most gone[.] another I am sleepy[.] another we have to have breakfast over against half past seven[.] we go to the City tomorrow to draw our arms and then uncle abe wants to see what every body thinks the best regiment in the service[.]

they have named us the bloody 85th already[.] they say the begining always shows what the end will be[.] I guess it is the calculation for us to winter in charleston[.] they say we are to be the advance guards of uncle abes grand army[.]

M. E. McJunkin
U. S. army

Fort Good Hope, Dec.26th/61[10]
Co. D, 85th Regiment P.R.C.

Friends and fellow citizens I take my seat by the stove this afternoon to let you know how things are prospering in the Bloody 85th[.] they are all getting along excellent so far[.] there is only 8 in the hospital now and the most of them will be discharged in a day or two[.] I have got well of the measels but before I left the hospital my face got bunged up with Erycypalus[11]

---

[9] The identity of "Laddie" is unknown.

[10] Fort Good Hope was an early name of Fort Wagner. Letter of B. Franklin Cooling to Richard A. Sauers, 11 March 1991. The later name appears in B. F. Cooling and Walton H. Owen, *Mr. Lincoln's Forts: A Guide to the Civil War Defenses of Washington* (Shippensburg, PA: White Mane Publishing Company, Inc., 1988), p. 198.

After leaving Camp Casey, the regiment moved to Camp Wilder (28 November-2 December), then broke camp again and marched to set up camp near Fort Good Hope, located east of Washington. The 85th remained here until 12 March 1862.

[11] McJunkin is referring to erysipelas, a strep infection that produces red rashes on the affected area as well as fever. See Gordon C. Sauer, *A Manual of Skin Diseases* (Philadelphia: J. B. Lippincott Company, 1959), p. 102. My thanks to Dr. John H. Persing of Lewisburg for this information.

and the Surgeon put some kind of ointment on to kill it and it made my face a beautiful olive color[.] they call me Indian Chief altogether now so I am staying with them until it comes off[.] the principal part of the sickness that has been in our Regt has been measels[.] I think that more than half of the Regt have had them since I came[.] I was about the last that took them[.] I think they have about run out now for they stayed out on me for more than a week to see if anybody else wanted them and nobody has taken them yet[.] we converted a brick church into a hospital the other day[.] we have a splendid view of Washington City[,] Alexandria[,] and surrounding country[.] from our position we can see several forts and scores of encampments[.] we have not the least idea how long we will stay here or where we will go when we leave[.] as for them furloughs you spoke of I think they will be scarce until we go home to stay which I think will be shortly if England keeps quiet[.]

I forgot to mention before that I received your letter of the 9th and was rejoiced to hear that you were all well and that I had your prayers for if anybody needs the the prayers of the people of God it is the soldier[.] continue to offer up your prayers for me[.] I feel confident that my God will return me safe to my friends and when this Acccursed Rebellion is crushed out I again walk my native hills in peace no longer carrying my rifle and saber[.]

I take the Christian advocate now[.][12] it is a great friend to me in my leisure hours which are few when I am on duty[.] I have not drilled any now for about three weeks and have only stood guard once since I left Uniontown[.] A great many fellows here got nice little boxes of nice things for christmas[.] how I wished for something I knew was clean but then a soldier could not eat any thing clean[.] I want you to have a big plate of toasted bread soaked in cream for me when I come home[.] you might send mell over once in a while with a coffee pot of milk and a roll of butter and a plate of fried mush[.] we can get butter here for 30 cents a pound but it is so strong that it only takes two ounces to weigh a pound and we can get corn meal at six cents a pound[.]

I will have to mention something about Laddie[.] I am afraid he will go home a bad boy[.] Will and I do all we can but he wont take any advice[.] his principle faults are profaneness and he dont care for anything[.] he will not take a cent of money home with him[.] I expect he has given them sharks half his wages already[.] we have not got our pay yet but expect to get it next week[.] you may think strange that a man can spend his money before he gets it[.] I will explain it[.] the sutlers sell out tickets and take the boys notes for it and then when payday comes they take theirs out of the head of the heap[.]

---

[12] The *Christian Advocate* was one of many religious newspapers published for the benefit of men in uniform.

they will only take one dollar out of my pile and they would not have got that only I had to have some butter for christmas[.] I will close for the present and prepare for supper[.][13]

Dec 27th[.] I have had my breakfast and I believe I will finish my letter[.] my health is good at present[.] my face is still a little enlarged from ericipalus[.] I guess I cant think of much more to write so I will just write a little about our officers & men[.] I like all the officers in our Regt except the Adjutant and our first lieutenant but then I dont take any account of them[.][14] I think them beneath my notice[.] I dont think there is a man in the Regt but what likes our old Colonel and I believe he thinks as much of us as though we were his own children[.] he calls us all his boys[.] he comes to the hospital every day[.] I have a heap of fun with him since I got my face painted[.] he has promised me a new years gift[.] Idont know what it will be perhaps my wages[.]

mell told about a man in our company haveing his head took off as we came here[.] there was a man in the Regt got drunk and got his hand hurt going through a bridge was all the accident that that happened as we came[.] there was a man in our company by awkwardness shot of[f] the two middle fingers on his right hand since we came here[.] that is all the accidents that has happened to the regiment since I came to it[.] Well I have got my sheet about full and got about all the knews wrote so I will have to close[.] we can hear the contending armies fireing on each other a little every day[.]

M. E. McJunkin, Co. D, 85th Regt. P.R.C.

[undated 1861]

Co. D, 85th Regt. Penna. Volunteers, Fort Good Hope

Well Mother I guess I will write you a few lines[.] I believe I ought not write

---

[13] McJunkin here criticizes his comrades for buying items at high prices from the regimental sutler. A position authorized by law, the regimental sutler accompanied the regiment and set up his store to provide items not issued to the soldier, such as tobacco, newspapers, candy, shaving kits, extra clothing, and other such items. Many sutlers charged exorbitant prices and were widely condemned for such pratices, which included issuing IOUs to penniless men, to be deducted from soldiers' monthly pay.

[14] McJunkin refers here to Adjutant Andrew Stewart, Jr. and Lieutenant Rolla O. Phillips of his Company D.

Andrew Stewart, Jr., Company I

At age 25, Stewart was appointed adjutant on Sept. 25, 1861. He enrolled on Oct. 1, 1861, at Uniontown. Stewart came down with typhoid fever in May 1862, and received a furlough home to recover. On July 12, 1862, he was assigned to duty on Gen. William Keim's staff. Throughout the summer Stewart was regularly assigned to duty as aide-de-camp in the brigade, being commissioned a first lieutenant. He resigned his commission on Sept. 18, 1862, to receive an appointment as captain and assistant adjutant general of US Volunteers. Stewart then joined Gen. Henry Wessell's staff. On April 20, 1864, he was captured at Pymouth, NC, and held in various prisons including Libby, Danville, Macon, Charleston, and Columbia, before being paroled. He appears on the company muster out roll on Nov. 22, 1864, at Pittsburgh. (Ronn Palm Collection)

home until I receive about 16 letters[.] I have written so many and received no answers[.] the general health is tolerably good here now[.] there is only 9 men out of the regiment in the hospital and all of them except 2 have the measels[.] I am getting well of the measels now[.] I had a light turn of them[.] they have been out on me pretty thick now for 5 days[.] I dont know when I will leave the hospital[.] when the doctors get hold of a man here they keep him pretty close until he gets well[.] I could have performed duty all the time if there had been no danger of afterclaps[.] when a man takes the measels here he is exempt from all duty for 3 or 4 weeks so you see in that time if he takes care of himself he is entirely well[.] there has been 3 deaths in this regt[.]

we have taken 11 prisoners[.] while we were over at Camp Wilder some of the guards in a new york regt shot a cecesh one night[.] when they went up in the morning to inter the poor fellows remains it turned out to be an old cow so they skined her and made a dinner of her[.]

as we passed Fort Lincoln on our way to camp Casey we came very near being cut to pieces by our own men[.] the way it happened[:] right opposite Fort Lincoln was a very pretty place to rest and the officers told the drummers to give the boys the long roll which is invariably to arms[.] it was not 2 seconds until we had 4 pieces of artillery leveled on us and our colors was all that saved us from being tore all to smash[.]

The pluck of our officers and men were tried to a nicety on last thursday night week[.][15] we were roused on said night between 12 and 1 o'clock and there was the fastest geting around for about 10 minets I ever saw[.] we had our ammunition distributed and was in line of battle in ten minets after the alarm was given[.] fellows who was not abel to set up the day before was in ranks as soon as any[.] all were eager for the fray except about one half of the officers[.] some of the officers were either so badly skared or excited that they did not know what they was about but it all moved off and we had no fight[.] it is the talk now that when we get this fort done we will all go home and drill one week out of every month and be at home the balance of the time[.] we are to be ready for a call though at any time[.]

No more at present[.]

No more until I receive a letter or two from home[.]

M. E. McJunkin

---

[15] The incident here referred to took place on the evening of 15-16 December 1861. See Dickey, pp. 15-16. The incident would date this letter 13 December.

1862

Jan 1st 1862
fort good hope

As I was delayed in getting my letter started I thought I would put a note in it[.] I have been acting as hospital nurse for a few days and had no chance of getting my letter over to camp[.] I came back to my quarters yesterday the hospital being too confineing[.] I will have to tell of two more deaths[.] one boy was buried yesterday[.] another will be buried today[.] the health is generally good in camp[.]

I must close for the present[,] wash the dishes[,] and have some New years[.]

M. E. McJunkin

Fort Good Hope
Jan. 9th 1862

Well friends I guess I will still write a little if you wont[.] I have only received 3 letters from home since I left Uniontown and one of them was forwarded[.] I received a letter from libby on new years day and your last day after[.] I will write a big letter this time and if you dont do a little better I will forsake you and write to somebody that will answer not only what I write but will write 2 or 3 to my one[.] you must recolect that a soldier in a No one Brigade dont have much time to write and therefore you ought to expect to write about half a dozen to his one[.] But I have said enough on this subject[.] you can now use your pleasure about writeing[.] I will go to work and give some of the knews[.]

to begin we enjoy pretty good health in our Brigade at present[.] We are still stationed up here on top of the hill ready and willing and even enxious to go over and bring in jeff davis[,] beauregard[16][,] and all the rest of them southern pigmies for they certainly are pigmies in understanding or they never would try to fight against 600,000 soldiers who are soldiers and men in every respect[.] I will have to boast a little on our brigade[.] it is counted the best on the potomac; our regiment is given up by everybody that has saw it to be the most moral and christian like regt in the service[.] if we _are_ out on the tented field in arms slaying our fellow men and hurrying them into eternity it does not stop us from trying to serve our God. we know our cause is just and we can ask Gods protection and his blessing on our arms when we go on the bloody battle field.

Well I have had my diner so I guess I will write some more[.] I expect you will see the exploit of Colonel howell's 85th penna regt in the papers before you get this letter but for fear it becomes exagerated by the time it reaches you I will give you a description of it[.] you need not suck all you see in the papers. the papers say that McClellen[17] makes the army on the potomac keep the sabbath[.] I have not saw a sabbath since I left Uniontown[.] I will tell you our sabbath work. we get up in the morning[,] get our breakfast over[,] clean our arms[,] pack our knapsacks[,] brush our clothcs[,] black our shoes[,] and clean up our quarters and be ready for inspection at ten oclock[.] then at 1 we go on dress parade[.] at 3 we attend preaching and then if it is a nice day and we have time we go on dress parade again[.] I see I have got of my subject[.]

on last monday night[18] about dusk Companies A, B, C and D, got orders to prepare rations to last until the next evening and and pack in their haversacks and to emty their knapsacks and strap them on and be ready to march by 7 oclock but I missed getting to go[.] I have not got very strong yet and the Captain would not let me go so I contented myself with going up to the prayer meeting tent to preaching, but the rest went[.] they marched 18 miles[,] captured an old cecesh[,] got into his store and drank all his whiskey and port wine[,] took all his dried beef[,] sugar[,] and cheese and other little articles they thought would be useful[,] took him and them and marched back to camp[.] arrived pretty much all day[.] the first came in about 9 oclock in the morning and from that they came dropping in until almost night[.] so now

---

[16] General P. G. T. Beauregard was in command at Charleston when the first shots were fired at Fort Sumter, and so gained notoriety in the North.

[17] Major General George B. McClellan, Union general-in-chief and field commander of the Army of the Potomac, to which the 85th was attached.

[18] Night of 6-7 January. See Dickey, p. 19.

Joshua B. Howell, Colonel

Founder and commander of the 85th Pennsylvania. At age 55, this beloved officer organized the regiment at age 55. He was born on Sept. 11, 1806, at the family mansion "Fancy Hill," near Woodbury, NJ. Howell came from strong military stock–his father serving as a colonel in the War of 1812, and his great-grandfather was a colonel in the Revolution. He did his schooling at the academy in Woodbury, he studied law in Philadelphia, and there was admitted to the bar. Howell set up practice in Uniontown in 1828. He was enrolled as colonel of the regiment on Aug. 2, 1861. Well-respected in southwestern Pennsylvania, Howell had no formal military experience, yet through his influence he succeeded in raising the regiment although Pennsylvania's quota had been filled at the time. Naturally smart and insightful, Howell steadily rose from command of the regiment, to a brigade, and ultimately a division. He is shown here as a colonel. (Ronn Palm Collection)

if you see any other description than what I have give you can believe it or not[.] I have given a true statement of the case[.] my statement is different though from what I saw in the paper yesterday[.] one load of the provender came into my mess[.] it consisted of about 10 lbs of very nice loaf[,] sugar[,] 7 or 8 lbs of cheese[,] and one bucher knife. some feched in dried beef some filled their canteens with whiskey[.] they differed in opinion about what was most worth carrying home but they all got back safe if the most of them was pretty well yorked[.] Well I guess I have said enough about that battle[.]

I pass to something else[.] Will Allman I believe comes next in order[.] he is getting quite ferocious[.] the other day he put two balls and a buck shot through a fellows cap[.] you see that was cutting pretty close[.] he is in better health than he has been for a number of years[.] Laddie is in perfect health[.] he has not been sick a minnet since he left home[.] he likes soldiering very well[.] I think that we will fech him out all right and make a fine boy of him yet[.] he has begun to listen to advice[.] Jim Watkins and Hartmans boys[19] are enjoying good health and I dont hardly think you would know them now[.] Capt Purviance[20] has not got 3 finer looking or finer <u>men</u> in his company than just them three boys[.]

Now I want to tell mother about the grades of society in the army[.] there is just two grades[.] one part of the army try to serve god and live as they would at home[.] <u>that</u> is one grade[.] another class is those who think that as they are away from home they will act as bad and be as ornry as they can as their friends are not here to see it and likely will never find it out[.] that is another class[.] those two classes do not associate together[.] there are rich and poor in both classes[.] here it is not regulated like it is at home[.] society here is regulated by the conduct not by the purse[.] for instance there is Watkins and hartmans boys[.] they are now looked up to by people that looked down on them at home[.]

Well I suppose mell will want a page[.] well I am getting along fine so far[.] day before yesterday I took a small rabbit hunt not knowing but I might stand a chance of getting my name up by captureing an old cecesh or two[.] well I went out across the country a few miles and saw a couple of fellows jukeing around in the bushes but before I got slipped up I saw 40 or 50 other fellows not very far off so I just thought it would likely be supper time against I would get back to camp so I did not seek an interview with them at that time[.] I thought I would put it off untill a more convenient season[.]

I want you to put a good many chestnuts and some of them big hickrey

---

¹⁹ McJunkin refers here to friends in Company E.

²⁰ Captain Henry A. Purviance of Company E.

nuts in that box uncle milton is goeing to send me[.] I wrote in my letter to
libby for a box and I want several nice little things sent in it[.] tell mary to fix
up something to put in it[.] tell haman to fix up a little honey so it will cary
without spilling and mother and sis can fix up something to help fill up the
box[.] if uncle milton dont send one you folks can get a nice little box about
2 ft square and let mary haman and nicholson's help you fill it[.] I will tell you
what I would like to have[.] I would like to have some butter a few chestnuts
and hickory nuts[.] you can fill up the balance with good cakes or what ever
you have a mind to put in[.] Tell whites Laddie is stout and hearty[.] Tell
Nicholson's our Chaplain is in good health and doing his duty and is well liked
by most of the Regiment[.][21] Tell Millie to answer that letter I wrote her while
at Uniontown[.] Tell every body to pray for the welfare of the soldiers and for
their country[.]

      M. E. McJunkin, Co. D, 85th Regt P.R.C.

                              Fort Good Hope, Jan 24th 1862[22]

Well I received that box day before yesterday evening but it is a pretty big job
to find out who it belongs to[.] enclosed I send a note I found in it this
morning[.] Icant understand how it is no other note in the box said any thing
about any body but myself[.] the last letter I received from you told of the
sausage[,] cheese and sugarcakes for will[.] he got the cheese and sugar but
I found no sausage in the box[.] I also saw Laddies name on the can of apple
butter which I gave him the same evening and then today I found this note and
from the way it reads I thought it was likely his box and a mistake in direction
so I thought I would write and see who it was for[.] if it is for me I want you
to write soon and let me know and if you should send any more To me I would
rather have them sent to me and not to the whole company unless you tell who
the things belong to[.] Billy Lash got his box and was very much pleased with
it[.] he wrote a letter to millie last sunday[.]   I was very much pleased with
that tobacco[.] it excelled any thing I have saw since I left old Pennsylvania[.]
I was glad you thought of that horseleg[.] it is the first I saw since what I
brought with me run out and I always liked it the best[.] I wish the half of the
box (that is if the box is for me) had been filled with horseleg and butter[.] I
dont care near as much about cakes as I used to[.] my appetite for them will

---

²¹ Chaplain John N. Pierce of Greene County.

²² Sent to Melville McJunkin.

likely come back when I get right well again; you need not think by this that I am sick or any thing for I am abel for duty now[.]

I was on guard yesterday and hada fine time of it[.] I had to keep 10 drunk soldiers in the guard house all of them bound to be out[.] I soon got all under my control except one waggoner[.] I had to prod him several times with the bayonet before I could convince him that I was boss of the shanty but I got him to see that he had to do as I told him[.] I had orders to put the bayonet through them if they tried to break out past me so you see we use people pretty rough when they get drunk here[.] the guard house has been full ever since pay day[.]

here I have a chance to speak a good word for Co. D. there has not been a man in our company under guard yet and only 2 or 3 on double duty[.] but I must return to my story as my paper is most filled[.] my health is still improveing but I cannot eat very strong victuals yet[.] I have eat no meat except fresh beef for a good while[.] there has been no death in the Regt since the day before Newyear's[.] it froze up last night and is pretty cold today but much more pleasant than it has been for some time back[.] I must take Laddie a roll of butter and a lot of cakes to do him until I hear whether the box is for him or me[.] if I live and keep my health and we stay here I expect I will send for a small box in a month or so to be sent to me so I will know what to do with the contents[.] I have not much to write this time only all our boys are well and most of them doing well[.] I expect we will stay here until the war is over[.] I wrote in my other letter about some money I sent home but for fear it dont get there I will mention it in this[.] I sent $20[.] you will get it from Tommy Johnston about next week as it goes to him with a good bit more[.] when you write let us know who sent that box[.]

   M. E. McJunkin

Fort Good Hope
Feb 14th 1862[23]

Well I guess I will write you a small letter today if Review and dress Parade dont come off too soon[.] To begin we are all enjoying pretty good health at present[.] the Pikerun boy's[24] are all hearty except Will and me and we are able

---

[23] Sent to Melville McJunkin.

[24] McJunkin refers here to West Pike Run Township, Washington County.

for duty[.] I have been bothered with dispepsia ever since I have been sick and just worked along with it until a few days ago[.] I went to the doctors and he mixed up a bottle of stuff for me and I hadnt been takeing it two days until I could eat fried beef and a little butter[.] I was sorry then that I had not gone sooner but I feel pretty well now[.] I am most as big as ever[,] dispepsia and all[.]

about three weeks ago we commenced to throw out pickets[.] we have them out about 4 1/2 miles[.] we go on picket duty by Companies[.] our company goes out every tenth day and is out 24 hours[.] almost every day the pickets fetch in a prisoner or two[.] they examine them and let some go and send some to the City[.] they was fighting on the other side of the creek yesterday and last night but I have not yet heard any more about it[.] we could see the smoke and hear the guns from here[.] I have now been in the service about 4 months and have the first General to see[.]   Brigadier General Keim[25] took command of this Brigade a few days ago but I have not seen him yet[.] he quarters in a dwelling house about a mile from Camp[.] two of my mess was over to guard him last night[.] he has to have 7 men there every night[.]

we have not drilled any of any account since December until this week[.] if the weather keeps favourable we will be put through from this out[.] there is 50,000 troops ordered from here to kentucky[.] some think we will form part of it[.] if we do you can all go down to Pittsburg and see us march through with our austrian rifles and saber bayonets[.] if we do go there about   3/4 of our officers will go home and be replaced by west pointers as there is about that many pretty green[.] our Captain is to green to be this far from his mammy if it could be helped[.] about 3/4 of his men are down on him the bigest kind and there has some jawed him more than I would like to be jawed if I were in his place; him and I had a little round the other morning and he has not spoke to me since[.] but one consolation[,] I made out to get in the last word as usual[.] he has found out that he has several men in his company who were born with tongues of their own and who are not afraid to use them when necessary[.]

but I have said enough on this subject[.] I will commence on

---

25 Brigadier General William H. Keim took command of the brigade on 9 February. A Pennsylvanian by birth, Keim was educated at a private military academy, became mayor of Reading, and spent a term as a House member from Pennsylvania. He was a major general in the state militia and commanded the Second Division, Department of Pennsylvania, during Major General Robert Patterson's 1861 Shenandoah Valley Campaign. Keim died of disease on 18 May 1862, probably from contracting fever in the swamps of the Peninsula.

something else[.] the weather for a few days has been much more pleasant than Common[.] it is a Camp report that we will be taken to the City for city guards in a few days but I dont know how it will be[.] You need not send that box until we know what we are goeing to do[.] besides I have enough of the other to last me for sometime yet[.] I had the disppsia too bad for cakes to be of much account to me[.] I eat most of the pound cakes and some of the little ones but the doughnuts was of no account atall[.] there was too much grease in them for the way my stomach was; but I would not have taken 50 cts a quart for the chestnuts[.] I could not divide the nuts[,] sugar (that is my share of it)[,] butter[,] apple butter[,] plumbs[,] and tobacco[.] I have the 3/4 of the tobacco left[,] about half the butter and a little apple butter[,] about half the plumbs[,] and all the dried apples[.] we draw dried apples as part of our rations[.]

I believe I have no more to write about except what to end in that box[,] only I shouldnt wonder much if I were discharged pretty soon after we begin Brigade drill on account of my being too short winded for as much double quick as we will have to go through[.] they tell me here though that I will when I get fairly over the spell be better than I ever was before[.] o yes I forgot to tell you I had a man from the 12th Pa to visit me[.] he came over last tuesday and stayed all night with me[.] it was nelse mathews[.][26] he looks better than I ever saw him[.] he is in good health[.]

as it is getting dark I will have to close and tell you what to put in the box the next time I write[.] I want you to write once a week after this[.] If you have got that money just keep it to pay for the box you did send and to pay for the other that is if I dont come home on a furlough after it myself and if I do come home I may not have enough to fetch me back again[.] no more at present but remain uncle sams boy for the present[.]

    M. E. McJunkin

The reason I have sent no pictures home is because I have not been to the city yet and dont expect to for some weeks[.] I will send a few when I get them if I dont come home[.] No more at present[.] I want you to answer them other three letters[.]

---

[26] Nelson Mathews, Company F, 12th Pennsylvania Reserves.

Fort Good Hope
Feb 16th 1862

Well Mell you do the most writeing so I will write you a few lines to rectify some mistakes and one thing another[.] I wrote a letter last friday but did not get it in the office but I got it sealed and the stamps on so I will send it and this one too[.]

about that rabbit hunt[--]I did not tell you that the body of men I saw was one of our companies who had gone down to a big meadow for the sake of level ground to drill on[.] there is bush whackers here but they are not bold enough to come out in such bodies as that[.] I just wrote that that to let you see how easy it is for fellows to deceive without lying[.] so you see by a little lying a fellow in the army can make his company appear a goodeal morer than it is[.]

I used to think when I was at home that we did not get half the truth but we got more than the truth[.] everything that is published about the war is exagerated[.] sometimes you get it 2 or 3 times as bad as it realy is[.]

I guess I cant think of much to write to-day[.] I want that horse took care of right and not spoiled for I want him to ride next fall if I am spared[.] I expect if things move on right and I live and keep my health to be at home about next may or june[.] as you are pretty good at drawing I want you to draw that Ugly Little Redheaded Things Likeness And Send It In Your Next Letter[.] I want Mother to get her likeness taken for me[.]

No more at present[.]

Melvin E. McJunkin

You can let that box rest until we find out where we will go to[.] I think likely we will go to the City of Washington to remain dureing the War[.]

Fort Baker, March 2nd 1862[27]
Co. D, 85th Regiment, Pennsylvania Volunteers
P. R. C., Invincibles, 2nd Fire Zouave Regt.

Well I guess as we dont go on dress parade until three oclock I will try to write a few lines but I dont know hardly where to begin as there is nothing much to write about at present[,] but as I have begun I suppose I will have to say something[.]

well to begin with I am well at present and all the pikerun boys are in

---

[27] Fort Baker was located north of Fort Good Hope.

good health as also the Regt[.] we have been underr marching orders for several days but the old Colonel went to the City yesterday to try to get the orders countermanded as it would be very apt to be as fatal to the Regt to move out of our winter quarters and go to sleeping in the mud as it would be to go to Manassus and I heard last night that he got it put off 20 days and thought he could get 10 days more added to it but I dont give this as a fact[.] it is only a camp report with me[.] it may nevertheless be true but I for my part dont take much account of anything I hear unless I know it to be a fact[.]

I expect my next letter will be wrote on Meredian Hill and perhaps in Richmond for the Stars and Stripes will certainly float both at Richmond and Manassus inside of three weeks[.] Well I am pretty tired writeing so I think I will not write much today[.] so I close for the present and perhaps rite some more after a while[.] for the preent I must go to Church[.]

March 2d 1862

Well as I am on guard today I guess I will write a little more[.] there is still not much though to write about[.] there was some very heavy fireing on the Blockade last night[.] Gen Lander is dead[.][28] McClellan and Banks are taken[,] Marlborough was surrounded yesterday and I suppose e'er this is taken[.] while on dress parade yesterday a dragoon came in to Camp and gave the old Colonel a hand-full of general orders which he read to us[.] general orders always come on a bad day to be out so far[.] we have quit goeing on picket as there is some 4 or 5 regt in advance of us[.]

if our officers had have known their business we would have got our pay about today but I guess we will get it this week anyhow[.] as for two kinds of money I never heard of it before[.] we only keep one kind here but you need not bother trying to get anybody to take it[.] you can just keep it[.] it will be as good as long before there is any land in the United States so you can make use of it to pay my dets and pay yourselves for what you have been doing for me[.] you can pay Dan Snyder for them boots as they were worth the money[.] the balance on them is 75 cts[.] I am still wearing them and expect to wear them home when I come to stay[.] they are the best boots I ever had[.]

Well mell I expect you to keep Colonel[29] Clean unless you want a complete dressing whcn I come home[.]

I must tell you how McClellen and Banks are taken[.] they are takeing

---

[28] Brigadier General Frederick W. Lander, commanding a division in the Shenandoah Valley.

[29] Name of McJunkin's horse.

21

a trip over into Dixie[.]

I think we will go to the city next week but I cant tell anything for certain[.]

No more at present[.] My best respects to those brave and patriotic young men who stayed home to serve their Country[.]

Mary Eliza West

Fort Baker March 9th 1862[30]

Well as I have got tired of laying in bed and dress parade dont come off until 5 oclock I thought I would write a little letter[.] I am enjoying pretty good health at present[.] I only weigh 180 lbs[.] The pickerun boys are all in good health[.] the Regt in general are in good health[.] I guess we move to Calarama hights this week[.] it is close to the city[.] I have to go over tonight and guard the General[.] it has been nice weather for a few days and we have been improveing it in way of drill[.] we have two Battalion drills every day if it keeps good weather[.] we will be put through from this on[.] I have not much idea that we will ever be in a fight[.]

I guess I have told all the knews; only Will Allman I guess is mad at me from some cause[.] he has not spoke for more than a week and I guess as I gave him no cause to get mad I shall not bother myself to ask him what it is about[.] the Capt has got as friendly as ever[.]

About that box[.] I would like to have some little things but I dont know whether it would hardly pay or not to have one sent as we get plenty to eat here[.] I guess though I will resk a small one; one a foot square is plenty big enough[.] just put in 1 roll of butter[.] go to Hamans and buy some sugar cakes and some honey if you can get a small enough can to put it in[.] put in a little poke of elderberries and fill out with what ever you please only make better cakes than you did before if you send any and dont send any dough-nuts[.] put in about a pound of homemade cheese and send the box by express[.] pay the postage there[.]

---

[30] Sent to Melville McJunkin.

Meridian Hill, Camp Keim
March 15th 1862[31]

Well I guess as it is too wet for them to have us out on inspection I will write a few lines to let you know how we are prospering[.] we are in good health at present[.] I think there is only 3 of our regt in the hospital now[.] I cant doubt but that our regt has been favoured by providence for we have lost but 6 men and the 86th New-York that moved with us from Camp Wilder to Good hope has lost 75 men and most of the Army on the Potomac have lost pretty much in proportion with the 86th New-York[.]

on last wensday we left Good Hope and came over here and was a little surprised[.] we thought that there was so many had crossed the river that there was nobody left on this side but we were a little mistaken[.] there is from 10 to 15,000 in this Camp and I expect there is 50,000 in sight of us[.] as I was saying we came here last wensday[.] we happened to have a nice day to come and dry ground to pitch our tents on but I happened to have the pleurisy for the next 2 days after we came which was not very pleasant but yesterday we all marched down to the Arsenal and traded off our old Muskets for Austrian Rifles[.] they are calculated to kill a rebel 900 yds and if all reports are true they will likely do it before long[.]

it is the talk now that we are ordered to help Burnside out of a scrape but I cant write any thing for fact until I know it to be so[.][32] we may leave here monday and we may not[.] it is thought here that if we have no bad luck the war will be over in less than a month[.] it is our calculation to follow up the rebels now and wind things up[.] as we go they think they think they are goeing to baffle us around until hot weather so we cant follow them and then by that time they will get some foreign power to help them but I guess we are as sharp as them[.] I think we will likely come in on both sides of them now pretty soon[.] I believe it is too disagreeable to write to-day so I will stop[.]

M. E. McJunkin

---

[31] Meridian Hill is located just north of Washington. The 85th remained in this camp from 12-28 March 1862.

[32] Brigadier General Ambrose F. Burnside had taken his division to the North Carolina coast in January 1862. After capturing Roanoke Island in February, Burnside moved on Newbern and captured the city after a hard-fought battle on 14 March.

Sunday March 16th 1862

March 17th 1862

Well as I guess I did not get this letter started today I will write a little more[.] I was on guard yesterday and it was a pretty cold day and as we have got our tents pitched on the ground and cant have fire in them we have to take moderate days to write[.] today so far is very nice[.] we have just got our streets cleaned up and had 40 rounds of cartriges a piece distributed[.] we always have our camps laid off in regular order[.] it would pay any body to come to the City just to see things; it is said that there is 75,000 of us going to leave the city to go over on James river to Newport News[.] we were ordered to be ready today but I dont think we will leave here for sometime[.] we may leave in a few days[.] we are ordered to be ready to march at an hours warning but it is not likely we will go from the City except in a pinch[.] the health of our regt is good[.] there is but one sick man in our campany[.]

I guess I have said all that I have to say at present[.] as I am cook today I have not much time to write[.]

I would like for mother to get her picture taken and send it to me unless the war is likely to end pretty soon[.] I would like for you all to get your pictures for me when I come home as I dont expect to make Penna my home when I come back[.] we have not got our pay yet[.] I dont know when we will[.] I will send a few pictures home when we do get it[.]

M. E. McJunkin

Since writeing the above I received yours of the 12th and was glad to hear from home[.] if mell has the measels just let him keep in the house and take no medicine as medicine is unnecessary for that complaint[.] I did not take a drop of anything for them when I had them[.]

March 18th 1862

Well as my letter is still on hands I guess I will put in a little more[.] it is the talk now that we leave here tomorrow morning at 7 o'clock[.] the Potomac is black with vessels today but I dont know whether we will compose part of the fleet or not[.] we are the best drilled regt on this side of the Potomac but I will not believe we are going until we start[.] we are doing some big drilling this pretty weather[.] all the regts around here were target shooting today[.] we have a regt of flying artillery just joining us[.] it looks nice to see them drilling but the nicest sight we have is when a Brigade or a Division gets together on a clear day and march in columns enmass with fixed bayonets[.]

24

I guess I will have to quit now and get ready for inspection[.]

Camp Keim, Meridian Hill
March 21st 1862

Well as it is still a little damp I thought I would write a few lines[.] to commence I am enjoying pretty good health at present[.] all the pickerun boys are well[.] the health of the regt is good[.] I received a letter from will daybefore yesterday[.] they are pretty near all sick[.] will has the liver complaint[.] Aunt Mary is buried[.] he has not heard from ad[33] since he left there last fall[.] he has not heard from you for 2 or 3 months[.]

daybefore yesterday we thought we were going down in Dixie[.] the day before we boxed up everything that it was not realy neccessary to carry along and sent them to the patent office to be kept for us until we came back so by 7 o'clock day before yesterday we had six days rations in our haversacks[,] our knapsacks packed[,] our tents struck and ready to march to Alexandria to go on the fleet[.] so we waited a while for the General and when he did come he told us the orders was countermanded[.] there is 80,000 troops laying at Alexandria now[,] 40,000 without tents[.] it would astonish a country clodhopper to come here and run about a week or so[.] we have about 200,000 troops here more than we have any use for at present[.] perhaps we can make use of most of them as soon as we can get transports[.]

March 22d 1862   Camp Keim, D.C.
Well as we have got off of inspection and dress parade dont come off until half past 3, I guess I will write a little more[.] to begin with we are all well at present[.] it is a little cool today but I guess if they dont find too much for us to do we can write a little[.]

I will have to go now and help clean the street[.]

Well the street is cleaned and I have got back to my writeing again[.] I guess though I have not much to say after all[.] we have been drilling a little here lately[.] daybefore yesterday we had a little review[.] there was some 10 or 12,000 of us out[.] there was a lot of country codgers from your parts here[.] they said there was from 50 to 60,000 thousand on review[.] so you see how little the fellows knows who have stayed at home[.] yesterday we were practiseing a little with our guns[.] there is 3 batteries of flying artillery here with us[.] there is about 30,000 troops around the city at present and I

---

[33] Adam McJunkin, Milton's brother.

25

guess they have no place to send them to except they disband them and send them home[.]

Gen. Casa[34] I understand has said that if we dont leave here by tuesday that we will be disbanded[.] Casa is Majr. Gen. Commanding this Division[.] Gen. Wm. H. Keim Commands this Brigade[.] we are in the 2nd Brigade in Casa's Division and the first regt on the Right Wing of the Brigade and the 3d Co on the Right Wing of the Regt so you see we are right in all points[.]

it is acknowledged by everybody that the Bloody 85th is the best drilled and most moral regt in the service[.] when I say the best drilled I mean among the Volunteers[.] this has been a hard winter on the morals of the soldiers[.] they have had nothing to do and you can see the effects of idleness very plain in the army[.] I did not think that it was possible for men to retrograde as fast as the greatest portion of the army has[.] Well I guess I will quit writeing and begin to get ready for dress parade[.]

March 24th 1862.   Camp Keim

Well we have got in from general Review and got our supper so I guess I will try to finish this letter[.] I have nothing new to write about[.] you all hear what our troops are doing as soon or nearly so as we do[.] of course as we are at head quarters we hear a little sooner[.] we have no idea what we are going to do[.] we may be disbanded before a month and we may stay the full term of 3 years[.] the latter though is not likely[.]

I have been at a loss to know why I get so few letters the last 3 or 4 weeks[.] I have been in the habit of getting from 2 to 6 or 8 a week but the last 3 or 4 weeks I have hardly got 1 a week[.]

as soon as we get our pay I will get libbie and the rest of you a likeness[.]

Will calls his boy Milton Elmer[.]

for myself and Ellsworth I would like to be on pickerun a few days but 8 or 10 days is the longest I could get and I dont think that will pay for going so far[.]

---

[34] Brigadier General Silas Casey commanded a division in the Army of the Potomac. This division eventually became the Third Division, Fourth Army Corps. The First Brigade, led by Brigadier General Henry M. Naglee, consisted of the 52nd and 104th Pennsylvania, 56th and 100th New York, and 11th Maine. Keim's Second Brigade included the 85th, 101st, and 103rd Pennsylvania, and 96th New York. The Third Brigade, commanded by Brigadier General Innis N. Palmer, was composed of the 81st, 85th, 92nd, 93rd, 96th, and 98th New York. Four batteries of artillery were attached to the division.

Friday night April 4th 1862[35]
Camp near New Port News

Dear friends[:]

as I have got another day's work done and have our shanty to myself I thought I would try to write you a short epistle to let you know how we are prospering[.] we are getting along extraordinary well takeing every thing into consideration[.] we have but one man in our regt in the hospital at present[.]

since writeing to you last we have had some changes[.] when I wrote last we were comfortably fixed in our tents on Meridian Hill (with plenty of the best of grub)[.] we are now camped in a swampy wilderness in the heart of an enemies country where our supplies are uncertain and none of the best[.] but for all that we are all better contented than while laying around the city[.]

on this day week Hezekiah Horn (one of my mess mates about my size) and myself went to the city to see the sights (I will tell about our visit in my next as I will not have time in this one)[.] while there I traded off a pair of shoes that I did not need for a likeness for Mary which I will send the first oportunity[.] but to return to my story[.]

when we got back to Camp we found our Division packed up and ready to march so we started off and marched until half past 11 when we stoped for the night[.] we stayed in that neighbourhood until sunday when we marched to Alexandria and took ship for fortress Monroe[36] where we arrived on tuesday (by the way Chesapeak is a pretty large stream as we got out of sight of land on the route)[.] as soon as we got landed we marched out here where we are now in camp[.] there is now about 150,000 troops here and are daily comeing in[.]

last night we put a Pontoon bridge across the James river and today the first Brigade in our Division under Gen. Keys[37] started for Richmond or that is the suposition[.]

I received that box yesterday week and was very well pleased with it all except the ginger cake but I made out to get it eat by soping it in the homemade molasses[.] Well I guess it is bed time[.] I will mention here that

---

[35] Written to Melville McJunkin. See Dickey, pp. 24-26, for details of the movement to the Yorktown Peninsula.

[36] Fort Monroe was a brick fort at the tip of the Yorktown Peninsula. It remained under Union control throughout the war and was a base of operations for many expeditions.

[37] Brigadier General Erasmus D. Keyes commanded the Fourth Army Corps.

all my mess are on picket tonight[.] I was on guard last night and have to stay alone tonight[.]

April 5th 1862

since writeing the above I am told that our letters will be opened at Fortress Monroe and if there is any knews about our movements or anything else they will stop there so I will not give you any more in this[,] only we have heard the big guns all last night and today at York Town[38] and we are looking for orders every minit to go and reinforce them[.] I have just put enough pills in my box to cure secession in 60 of them if I get them down all right[.][39] it only takes one pill of the kind I have to cure cecession in its worst form[.] all that is necessary is to get them down right[.]

That I believe is all the knews I will give you this time[.] I could fill a dozen sheets with stuff that would interest you but I guess I will not this time[.]

I am enjoying good health at present[.] the greatest trouble I have now is I have not had any tobacco for a week and cant get any[.]

Dixie is the most barren country I ever saw[.] I wonder the half the people dont starve in good times[.] the rebels did hold big bethel but they heard we were comeing and so they took to their scrapers[.]

No More At Present[.]

M. E. McJunkin

his hand and pen With Many a whack Will bear the back And send the rebels howling back[.]

Virginia Swamp April 29th 1862

Well mell I guess I will try to write you a small epistle to keep you posted on war matters[.] to begin there has nothing taken place here yet except skirmishing[.] there is a goodeal of that though day and night[,] more than

---

[38] The Confederate troops on the Peninsula were entrenched across the Peninsula at Yorktown to contest McClellan's advance. The Union troops halted before the entrenchments and brought up siege artillery in preparation for a siege of the town.

[39] McJunkin refers here to his cartridge box, which he has just filled with 60 rounds of ammunition.

night though than day as night is the best time to steal marches on each other[.]

April 30th 1862

Well I had to put up my portfolio yesterday and shoulder my rifle as we expected an attack last night[.] by the way there is 4 companies of us from our brigade out here on picket since yesterday morning[.] we will be relieved in an hour or two though[.]

Well we are back at camp again[.] I quit writeing this morning to go out and take a look at the manoevres of the rebels and when I got back to where we were stationed our company had been relieved so I had to sling my knapsack and trot back to camp alone but I expect you would like to hear of some of our performances as we go along[.]

well to begin where I left off[.] as I was saying we was out yesterday and part of today on picket in front of two rebel forts and a large encampment so close that we could easily fire into them with our rifles[.] in the afternoon the divils got pretty sassy as they used a couple of pieces of artillery pretty freely in flinging shells and ball over at us but they did no harm[.] the worst feature was when we would climb the trees to take a better view of them[.] they would make use of a swivel in flinging pound balls at us and they rolled them in pretty close generally[.] we gathered some of them and fetched into camp for curiosities[.]

yesterday our division was out reconnoitering in force[.] we had two batteries of flying artillery and 5 regts of infantry[.] they got to the forts we were laying before in the evening and got to throwing shells and grape at each other for a while but did not do much execution as we were in the swamp and they had to shoot at random[.] we had 1 capt and 1 private killed and several wounded[.]

we had a good joke on some of our company last night[.] ever since we have been in the service until since we left Washington they were very brave and was bound not to go home without a fight, so last night we expected a general tare up and so of course give them all a chance of showing their bravery[.] standing picket is the most dangerous part of war[.] our 3d sargeant took sick yesterday morning and was not abel to go out and about the time the guns opened in the evening our first sargeant took sick very suddenly[.] our Captain is also unwell[.] he has not been well since we came to Yorktown[.] our 1st and 3d sargeants are enjoying good health today and I am glad to see it for we dont like to see people get sick where men are needed as they are here[.]

this though is a very unhealthy place[.] this spring there has been several very suden deaths here since we came[.] more of our hospitals is filled with wounded than sick[.]

I guess I cant think of much more to write so I guess I will try to show you how we stand picket[.] well I think I can show you the picket line of our division so here goes[:]

show you the picket line of our division so here goes

picket   line

now you will want to
know about sos many
reserves and squads
those two supports are
to relieve the men on
their posts at regular
intervals   in case of
an attack the pickets
are to fall back fireing
on to the reserve and
if they are not strong
enough they are to
continue tos retreat
fireing and by the
time they get to
the last reserve
the line to camp
. . . . . . with the fireing

May " 1st " 1862
well I have a half
an hour to myself
this evening before
inspection so I
guess I will
try to finish
my letter to
begin I am

3d Brigade   Camp of Cass
             First
Division   Brigade
    2nd
  Brigade

two supports
reserve
picket line to camp
Reserves
enjoying bet[ter]
health since we
came to York
Town than I
have since I lef[t]
Union Town la[st]
fall; you never . . .
me near as fat as . . .
am now . . .

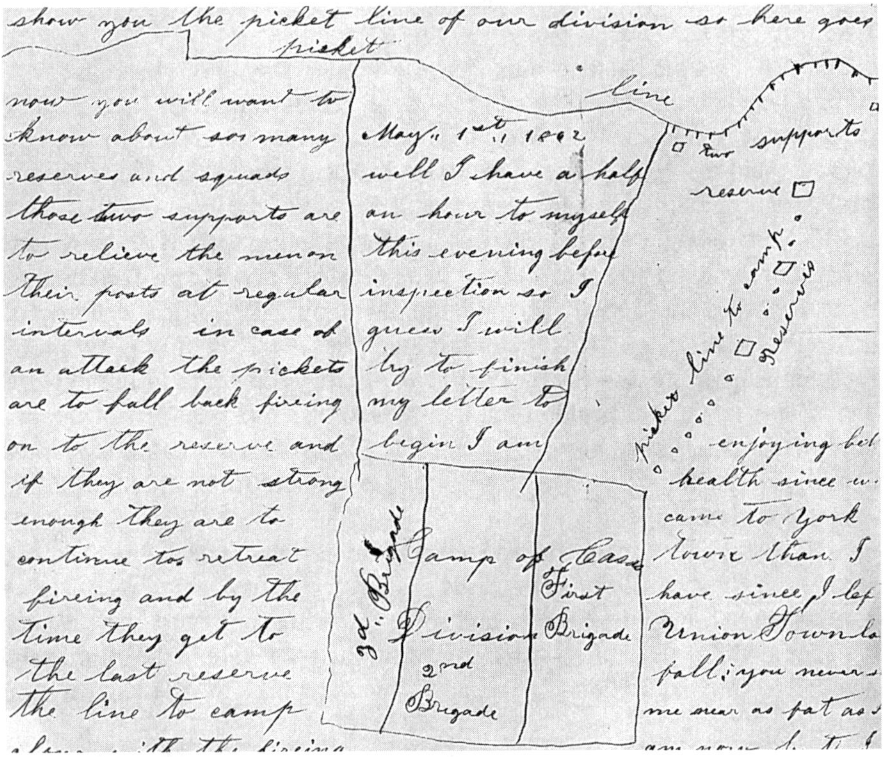

now you will want to know about so many reserves and squads[.] those two supports are to relieve the men on their posts at regular intervals[.] in case of an attack the pickets are to fall back fireing on to the reserve and if they are not strong enough they are to continue to retreat fireing and by the time they get to the last reserve the line to camp along with the fireing has the camp alarmed and reinforcements on hands[.]

  May 1st 1862
well I have a half an hour to myself this evening before inspection so I guess I will try to finish my letter[.] to begin I am enjoying better health since we came to York town than I have since I left Union Town last fall[.] you never saw me near as fat as I am now but I am not as heavy by 30 lbs as I was when I left Union town[.] you cant tell anything about what a man can stand until you see him tried[.] you know every body said I could not stand much[.] there has not a man in the regt stood more than me since we came out and the majority have not stood as much[.] I have been on duty all the time since we came out except the two months I was sick last winter[.] but enough of this[.] I will try to think of something else[.] the folks at home write to the boys that the war is about over but it dont look that way to us[.] we are looking every day for the hardest fight on record to commence[.] I must close for the present and finish some other time[.]

  May 2nd 1862
Well we have just come in off fatigue duty so I guess I will write some more[.] I could fill 40 sheets of paper with knews but I guess it is not necessary[.] I can tell it when I come home if I am so fortunate as to get there[.] I still live in hopes that I will be at home before harvest[.]

  the rebels are very much afraid of Casey's Division[.] they are all Pennsylvanians and New Yorkers except one regt which is the 11th Maine[.] the rebels hate Colonel Howell's Pennsylvania Tigers as they call us[.] they call our guns the d----d canary birds[.] they are much longer range than theirs[.] they fling ounce balls with certainty 900 yards[.]

  Halt in the woods, between
  York town and richmond
  in hot pursuit of the enemie, May 9th 1862

Well friends as there has several things taken place since I last wrote I guess I will scratch a few lines to let you know that God in great mercy has spared my life until now for which I am thankful[.]

on last sabbath morning[40] we were called out for a kind of reserve[.] we started off expecting to be back in camp before night[.] we only took one days rations and what clothes we had on our backs[.] we went out about 5 miles and pulled down the secesh flag from two forts and planted the stars and stripes and marched on in hot pursuit of the enemy for 15 miles before we halted for the night[.] about 12 o'clock it begun to rain and rained on until tuesday morning[.]

on monday morning we heard the roar of battle about 5 miles in advance of us[.] we started off and halted in a valey about 1 1/2 miles from the battle ground[41] to wait on our grub but before it came up the word came that our forces were falling back before the enemy so we started off double quick through the mud and rain[.] when we got up we formed in line[.] the second shell that the enemy threw wounded Capt. Morris[42] in the head but not dangerous[.]   we advanced steadily[,] falling to the ground when we heard the shells comeing[.] when we got to the woods we started off double quick to charge the infantry[.] when we got to the scene of action we met our brave troops comeing back[,] their faces blackened with powder[.] they told us to give them H--l[,] that that they would be back to help us as soon as they got some more ammunition[.] we formed in line under their fire of the enemy and poured in a volley and kept up a continued fire for about twenty minets when the rebels gave back[.] they formed[,] came up again when we poured in a deadly fire and gave a tremendous cheer when the rebels said it was the damed sharp shooters and took to their scrapers[.] so we held our position until morning when there was not a rebel to be seen[.]

I walked over part of the battle ground[.] I tell you it is a hard sight to see men torn and mangled on the battle field[.] you can see death in every form[.] the loss in the 85th was two wounded[.][43] one has since died[.] the 85th went into battle as cool as though it had been dress parade[.] our loss in killed[,] wounded[,] and prisoners in the whole affair up to the present is about 3,000 men[.] the rebel loss is from 6,000 to 7,000[.]

I guess I will close for the present[.] this is enough to keep you from being uneasy about the pickerun boys[.] the pickerun boys are all enjoying

---

[40] 4 May 1862. See Dickey, p. 36.

[41] Battle of Williamsburg, 5 May 1862.

[42] Captain John Morris, Company F.

[43] Captain Morris and Sergeant Daniel F. Miller, Company K. Miller died on 5 June.

good health and are in fine spirits[.] I weigh 180 pounds so you see I am in pretty good order[.] I have not received any word from you since I left Washington[.] give my love to all enquireing friends[.]

    M. E. McJunkin

McClellen says we will be home in this month[.]

Halt in a Wheat field about
thirty miles from Richmond May 11th 1862[44]

Well friends as we will likely remain here until tomorrow I thought I would write a little as you will likely be uneasy until this war is wound up and so I thought as we are chaseing the enemy and in skirmishes most every day I would write as often as I could to let you know how we are still getting along[.]

the Pickerun boys are all well except Oliver Thomas[.] he has been sick for about a month[.] he was not abel to advance with us[.] he is in the artilery is the reason I always forgot about him when I said the pickerun boys were well[.] I for my part have enjoyed better health since I left Washington than I have since I first took the measels[.] in spite of the hard duty and marching which we have had to go through along with the scarcity of grub I have gained flesh faster than ever before[.]

I received your letter of the first yesterday and was glad to hear that you were all well but I think you are giveing yourselves too much trouble about us[.] you must recolect that we are Union soldiers fighting in a good cause and going to keep on God helping us until the Stars and Stripes shal float from every Battlement in this republic[.]

you never saw such a looking set of human beings as the rebels are[.] of course there is exceptions but in general they are dirty[,] greasy[,] ragged fellows[.] they are the most blood thirsty[,] yet the most cowardly demons I ever heard of[.] they have shells buried along the road fixed so that when they are trod on they will explode but we have been sharp enough to look for them so they have not done much harm yet[.][45] along the first there was some

---

[44] To Melville McJunkin, from near New Kent Court House.

[45] McJunkin refers to the use of "torpedoes" by the Confederates. Artillery shells were buried in roads and set to explode when walked on, similar to today's use of mines. However, the devices were widely considered to be outside the bounds of civilized warfare and their use was stopped.

33

bursted and killed and wounded some of our men but their contrivances to destroy us have proved more destructive to themselves than to us[.] before they left York town they burned all the houses but one and fixed an infernal machine in it to kill our men but some of themselves that did not know about it went to go in when it went off and killed about 100 of them[.]

you talk about not getting to stay there[.] I reckon you will stay there until I come home and I think as I am the only representative of the McJunkin tribe in the 725,000 Northern troops who are fighting for their country that you have a right to a portion of that property for your own[,] but I guess we can live without it[.] I would send some more money home only I have no way[,] only in letters and so I thought I would just keep it[.]

no more at present[.] direct as usual[.]

I think God willing I will be at home in a few weeks[.]

M. E. McJunkin

Halt in the woods about 25 miles from
Richmond Va. May 14th 1862

Well as Col. Mcgiffin[46] is going to start home today I thought I would send you a little money[.] I will send fifteen dollars; I could send more if we would get payed as we ought[.][47] there is 2 1/2 months wages due us now but I dont know when we will get it but enough of this[.]

the Pickerun boys are all well[.] we are still chaseing the rebels[.] they are badly whiped now but I guess they are not goeing to give up until they are all killed[.] the divils dont appear to have a bit of sense[.] every few miles they make a stand and get cut up and taken and then take to their scrapers again[.] we have got 100,000 of them penned up so that they cant get away without cutting a road through the federal troops[,] which if they do they will have to show more bravery than they have ever done yet[.]   the best of the

---

[46] Lieutenant Colonel Norton McGiffin, discharged on surgeon's certificate, 12 May 1862.

[47] McJunkin here criticizes the chronic lateness of army pay. According to Army Regulations, each company was to be mustered for pay on the last day of every other month (February, April, June, August, October, December). Muster rolls were updated and every man's activities since the preceding roll were recorded. Privates like McJunkin were paid $13 a month, which was generally more than a man could earn as a laborer or factory worker. However, owing to the large number of units and limited number of paymasters, army pay was usually late.

Norton McGiffin, Lieutenant Colonel

McGiffin was born in Washington, PA, on Jan. 23, 1824. He attended Washington College, where he graduated in 1841. He then began employment at Judge Nathaniel Ewing's law office in Uniontown. At the outbreak of war with Mexico, McGiffin joined the Duquense Grays, which became Co. K of the 1st Pennsylvania Volunteers, and campaigned from Vera Cruz to Mexico City. McGiffin proved a gallant and efficient soldier. In 1849, he was elected treasurer of Washington County, a post which he held until being elected sheriff in 1859. In 1861, he was elected a representative of the county legislature. At the commencement of the Civil War, McGiffin recruited a three months' company which joined the 12th Pennsylvania Volunteer Infantry, and he was made lieutenant colonel. Upon completion of service, he returned home and busied himself recruiting when offered the rank of lieutenant colonel with the 85th. He enrolled and was commissioned to date Oct. 20, 1861, and mustered in on Nov. 7, at Uniontown. McGiffin fell ill in Jan. and Feb. 1862, and requested a furlough to recruit his health. He never recovered sufficiently enough to retake the field and he resigned on May 12, 1862. Captain Samuel L. McHenry said of McGiffin: "His undaunted courage and self-possession gave confidence in his leadership, which was never misplaced." (Ronn Palm Collection)

rebels fell at Williams Burgh[.] out of 600 of their far famed Lousianna Tigers that went into that fight[,] 110 got out and some of them has since been taken[.] it is said they had three regts of indians there[.] I dont know how many there was though but they were strewn pretty thick over part of the battle ground[.] on another part the rebels were all shot in the back[.] the loss was heavy on both sides but the reb's lost 3 to 1[.] our loss as near as I can find out in killed[,] wounded[,] and prisoners in that battle was about 3,000[.][48] we lost a good many dureing the siege[.] if we succeed in captureing those we have in the pen think they will certainly give up[.]

I was amused at the darkies all along the road[.] they are all glad to see the yankees comeing[.] they wont work a bit any more[.] they bake all their meal up in hoecake to give the soldiers but we always pay them big prices for all we get from them[.] there is any amount of corn and beans at every house and a good bit of wheat[.] we have found as high as 2 or 3000 bu of corn on one plantation but we never take any thing more than we want at the time[.] we have seen but very few whites yet and they are all of the poor class[.]

I asked an old slave if he was a secesh[.] he said[,] no he was an old side baptist[.] the darkies all think we can whip the rebs if we can catch them but they say we will have to do some fast runing if we catch them[.] the other day as we come along I got into conversation with some slaves[.] I asked them how the rebel army looked as they went along[.] they said[,] oh your men can easy whip them[.] there is so many of them poor worn out creturs[.] they dont look pert and lively like your men[.] I asked them if there was as many of the rebels went along as they had seen of our men[.] they said good lor amihty no not half so many[.]

I guess I have said enough now so I think I will close[.] I got a letter from will the other day[.] they are all well again[.] he has bought a house and two lots in newcastle and is getting along fine[.] Mclellen says we can all go home in this month[.] I hope he is correct for I hate to see so many men butchered if they are enemies[.] I want you to write all the knews of the day[.] we have reptiles[,] insects[,] and wood ticks in abundance here[.]

M. E. McJunkin

Margaret McJunkin

---

[48] Losses at Williamsburg totalled 2,283 Union troops and 1,560 Confederates.

Kent Court House Co Va May 16th 1862

Well Col Mcgiffin got off before I gave him my letter so I guess I will not send any money as several of the boys have sent money by mail and the letters got there and the money did not[.]

us Pickerun boys are all well[.] Co D are all present or accountet for except one[.] I guess he is helping guard knapsacks of his own accord[.] some of co D are sick of fever and some have a disease that cannot be cured <u>now</u>[.] there is but one thing that will cure it and we haint got that at present[.] it is the declaration of peace[.] when it is read in the hospitals it will call many a sufferer to health and vigor again[.]

we have 30,000 rebels penned on an island and 5 brigades more fastened in a swamp[.] I guess it is the calculation to commence <u>shelling</u> the <u>swamp</u> today[.]

we have the rebs in a bad fix in this neighbourhood[.] if they dont surrender they will be in a worse one[.] I guess it is the idea to show no quarter's[.]

old abe and mcclellen are both here[.] I guess though it is not worthwhile for me to write much knews for you see it in the papers before my letters get there so I guess I will close for the present[.]

Bottom Bridge Chickahomanie Valey May 20th
Richmond 16 Miles[.] Mcclellen onward to Richmond[.]

Well as I have a little time this morning I thought I would write a few lines to you to let you know how we are getting along[.] I am well at present but pretty tired but I cant say any more that our regt is all present and in good health[.] we had when we came to Va 930 men[.] we now can only muster between 4 and 500 effective men[.] our Co has 89 men[.] yesterday we left the cross roads with 42 in ranks[.] a good many though followed as fast as they could who were not willing to be left behind[.] our Co has been highly favoured as it is the only co in the regt that has not had a death[.]

Lincoln is here with Mcclellen[.] he says we must be in Richmond before a week[.] I think if I am spared that I will go home when we get richmond[.] it is the talk that we all will be disbanded when we get there but I dont know how it is[.] I have got that I dont believe anything I hear and only about half what I see[.] I think though if I am spared to help take richmond I will get a discharge and go home anyhow[.]

we have had some right warm days down here this spring[.] there is right smart of rattle snakes[,] copperheads[,] and moccasins here along with

a great number of scorpions and wood ticks[.] since we got to marching we
have got into a more hilly country where we can get good water[.] it is more
settled up also[.] i dont think the people expected to see the yankees this side
of york town for they had their corn all planted and oats sewed[.] some had
worked their corn once[.] we have destroyed a greateal of wheat as wheat
fields is generally our camp ground[.] I think if the northern people was to go
and see those states where war has been they would be more resigned to their
friends absence but I think that all the volunteers that are alive will be home
in time for harvest[.] I guess I cant think of anything more to say[.]

      the Pickerun boys are all well except will Allman[.] he has not been
abel to march in ranks for 2 or 3 days[.] I think they sent oliver thomas to
Philadelphia[.]

      in the battle of Williamsburgh Col Howell acted Brig gen[.] I did not
see very many officers until after dark but it did not make any difference[.] we
knew how to do[.] Lieutenant Micheoner[49] was running around among us all
the afternoon[.] he carries a gun[.] he took aim at five rebs that day[.] he is
the only officer in co D that they put much confidence in[.] his enemies are
as scarce in co D as some mens friends are[.]

      no more at present[.]

      M. E. McJunkin

Camp in the Woods Near the Chickahominy
June 6th 1862[50]

Well friends as I have not written since the fight I thought I would drop you
a few lines to let you know how we are getting along[.]

      I suppose you have heard how our Division disgrased itself[.] I will
try to give you a statement of facts[.] our company was on picket at the time
so you see I saw the whole performance[.] about 1 o'clock the rebs fired 3
shots into our camp to give Casey warning[.] at the same time we[,] that is us

---

[49] Lieutenant John E. Michener.

[50] In this letter, McJunkin describes his part in the Battle of Fair Oaks
(Seven Pines), 31 May-1 June 1862. Casey's division was attacked in force on 31
May and driven from its entrenchments and camps. Many soldiers lost all their
personal belongings when the camps were sacked by Confederate troops. Casey's
men were lambasted by other officers and the press for the retreat. In actuality, the
division did quite well and was forced back by weight of numbers. See Dickey, pp.
65-172, for an extended treatment of Casey's division at Fair Oaks.

38

pickets[,] were attacked by 5 Brigades and nearly surrounded[.] our company was in the centre of the line and was cut in two so you see we had to retreat[,] as it was useless for 200 pickets to try to check 5,000 of the best troops Jeff had so we scattered and got to camp the best way we could[,] still poping over a reb when we got far enough ahead to shoot before they would be on us[.] we were all very nearly taken at the start as we had orders to hold our ground but they did not expect a general attack[.]

but as I was saying[,] I retreated about a mile as it was that far to camp[,] under a perfect shower of balls with men falling on all sides[.] I never saw hail fall faster than the balls fell around me while I was in the cross fire[.] when I got out of the woods there was the rebs behind me only about 100 feet and on my right and one of our powerful batteries and two regts of infantry in front[.] more of the pickets were killed by our own arms than by the rebs[.]

our artillerists poured in voley after voley of grape and canister[,] mowing down rebs by the hundred[.] never since the world began was as many men killed in the same length of time and by the same number of men as caseys Division killed in that bloody field[.] we dont deny that we fell back[.] we had to fall back or be surrounded and taken[.] there was 5,000 of us held our ground for nearly two hours against 50,000 of the rebel army and not until we were attacked on three sides and about one third of our men killed and wounded did we retreat and the majority of our officers retreated before we did[.]

lindsey hartman was shot through the head[.][51] he was the only pickerun boy that was hurt in that fight[.] I will close for the present and give you the particulars some other time[.] I give God the honor of my escape for it was a miracle that I am alive[.] there was several shells exploded close around me[.] there was one hole through my pants leg[.] I dont see how I came off so safe[.]

I am enjoying good health at present but am like all the rest[,] pretty tired[.] we have worse times now than we ever had while Gen keim was with us[.][52] I would rather have lost all the officers in the Division than him[.] he was a <u>man</u> and the <u>majority</u> of the rest are only <u>things</u>[.] the paper states that some of the officers lost their lives trying to rally the men[.] it is false[.] they ran away some of them and left their men[.] Major Gazzon[53] of the 103 run

---

[51] A member of Company E.

[52] Keim had died on 18 May. His place as brigade commander was taken by Brigadier General Henry W. Wessells.

[53] Major Audley W. Gazzam, commanding the 103rd Pennsylvania.

John Patterson, Company A

Shown here seated, wearing a frock coat, Patterson enrolled Sept. 13, 1861, at Thompsonville. He was 22 years old when he mustered in as a private at Uniontown on Oct. 16, 1861, as a member of Capt. Vankirk's company. He was present until wounded at the Battle of Seven Pines (Fair Oaks) on May 31, 1862. Records show he recovered in a hospital at Annapolis, MD. He was back with the regiment by July 1862, and remained on duty until the end of Aug. 1864, when he was detached to serve with the ambulance corps and posted to the 1st Division, 10th Corps, headquarters. In July/Aug. 1863, a deduction from his pay was made for "one metallic figure"–probably for his cap. He mustered out with the regiment at Pittsburgh on Nov. 22, 1864, then 25 years old. (Ronn Palm Collection)

his men up on the enemy with no loads in their guns and but mighty little amunition in their cartrige boxes and got them cut to pieces so of course they could not do much execution[.]

Picket on the Charles City Road June 15th 1862

Well as I am on picket today I guess I will scratch a few lines to let you know how I am getting along if the rebs dont interrupt me[.] they have a passion of causeing the Austrian rifles to belsh when our company is on picket[.]

to begin I am enjoying good health at present[.] I am several pounds biger than ever I was at home[.] Lew Rimmel[54] and myself are the only men in the regt who have held our own in spite of col howell[.] the officers in one way and another have got this Division pretty well used up[.] we landed 13,000 troops on the peninsula on the 1st of April[.] we can now muster 3,000 men able to walk[,] not over 2,000 that I would consider fit for duty[.]

God has blessed me with good health so far for which I am thankful[.] the harder times we have the stouter I get[.] I dont know how to write about the rest of the boys[.] Laddie is in good health[.] he has not been sick an hour since he left home[.] Wm Hartman and Allman are still unwell but they are still on duty[.] Jim Watkins is not well[.] I am afraid he will not make the landing if he stays here[.] I have not heard from O. Thomas since I left York town but I think he is getting well[.] Lindsey Hartman fell at his post in the late battle by a minnie ball through the head[.]

you have seen the lies in the papers about our Division but I stated some facts in my last letter so I will not write any more about it now[.] two thirds of the rebs that fell in the whole affair before richmond fell before cascys division[.] you can see sights here that will fech tears to the eys even of the stern soldier but we cant expect to be engaged in a civil war without seeing a great many strange things[.]

june 16th
Well the rebs did not bother us yesterday but I was too lazy to write and it is about as hard a job today but I guess I will write to let you know that if you dont think my letters worth answering that I will quit writeing[.] I have wrote about 20 I guess that you have not answered[.] I got 2 out of them 3 that you wrote so you see you have no excuse[.] two letters is all that I have got from you since I left Meriddian hill[.] If I knowed mother was at wills I would

---

[54] Corporal Lew Rimmel, Company C.

write there instead of home for I think she is all that cares about hearing from the way the letters comes[,] for out of the two she wrote one[.]

but I guess I have jawed enough now[.] for all I care if I could hear from Mother and Colonel I would not care whether I got any letters or not[.] I hardly ever think about the rest of you anyhow so you can tell Mother to take Col and go to Will's and I will write there once a week[.] she can help mag get ready for that wedding if she has found me a woman[.] the last letter I wrote to them I gave orders for her to look up one for me against I come but I have not heard yet whether she has found one or not[.] if the rebs dont get me and I can get a furlough in a few weeks and live and keep my health I think I will go to wills and see about it[.]

But if I keep on this way you will think I put in any foolishness as you wrote about ad[.] the next time I want you to give me Jim Pattersons address and also ad's as I should like to hear from both of them[.]

Camp Wessells Va. July 12th 1862[55]

Well Mother as I hear you are at home again I thought I would write you a few lines to let you know how we are getting along[.] I cant write as I used to[.] I cant say the pickerun boys are all here and well[.] Hartman's boys are both gone[.] I still think though that Will is not killed but prisoner[.] it appears to be our best men that we lose nearly always[.] Linsey Hartman was as good a soldier as ever walked and was the only one killed in his Co[.] it is no doubt all for the best but it seems hard[.]

I cant see why more men are ordered out[.][56] I think there is enough out now for the officers to kill[.] I can say truthfully that the officers by neglect and ill treatment have killed 5 to where the rebs have killed one[.] I dont see why the authorities dont look into it[.] I have known men[,] sick men[,] to be dogged along and kept on duty until they just naturally droped down and died in their tracks while hearty men[,] favorites of the officers[,] have been hauled along in the ambulances because too lazy to walk[.] the doctors are as much to blame as the officers[.] if God dont in great mercy

---

[55] Camp Wessells was located near Harrison's Landing on the James River. McClellan retreated to the landing after the Battle of Malvern Hill.

[56] McJunkin refers to President Lincoln's 2 July call for 300,000 additional volunteers for the army.

convert the soldiers before this war is over the fate of the majority of the officers is undoubtedly sealed[.] we have great and good men in office but that kind of men cant get very high offices with a few exceptions[.]

but enough of this[.] I for my part have had no reason to complain for myself for God has in great mercy blessed me with good health but it grieves me to see my brothers in arms so badly treated[.] the pickerun boys[,] all except Hartman's boys[,] are present and getting along very well at present[.] Lieutenant Crawford[57] is in command of our Co at present and I hope he will be our Capt[.] I am useing all my influence to get him in[.] if I only succeed we will have an officer over us that is worthy of being over a whole corps but he is too good a man to raise much[.] it was laughable yet outrageous in these battles to see commissioned officers with their backs to the foe[,] their coattails straight out and waiveing their hands at some of their men who had followed their example crying go back boys go back boys and stick up to them[.] I dont know whether it is right to tell on the divils or not but I reckon if I mention no names it wont matter much for it will all come out when the war is over[.]

it is no use talking[.] the rebs will fight[.] they can stand everything but cold steel[.] all we get off them we have to get at the point of the bayonet[.] they can beat us standing up and being shot at or chargeing on batteries but when it comes to a charge bayonet we are irresistable[.] in all the fighting here we nearly always just pour in one volley and them charge[.] old abe rode along our lines the other evening which caused quite a noise[.] I guess I have given all the knews of importance[.] no more at present[.] give my love to all enquireing friends if I have any in that neighbourhood[.] I want you all to write all the particulars[.]

Camp Wessell Va july 19th 1862

Well friends I guess as we got paid off the other day I will write a few lines and send Mell 20 dollars to speculate on until I come home and when I get more time I will send Mother 20 more as that is as much as I care about resking in a letter at a time[.] it takes so much to do a fellow here or I might have had 75 dollars to send this time[.] I used to hear it said that no matter where a man was if he had money he could buy any thing he needed but I have found it to be a mistake[.] we have been 2 and 3 days without a bite to eat

---

[57] McJunkin apparently refers to Lieutenant John M. Crawford of Company G.

frequently since we got into active service marching and working all the time[.] I will give you a list of the prices of some of the articles we buy[:]

	$$	cts
2 lb can of honey	1	00
pt can apples	1	25
pt can syrup		50
qt can veal mutton or chicken	1	25
pt can condensed milk		75
dried peaches per pint		25
cheese per lb[,] from 40 cts to 1		
ginger cakes[,] two and 3 cts apiece		
figs[,] 2 for 5 cts		
oranges and lemons[,] 2 for		25
raisons per lb		50
soda sugar or butter crackers per lb		30

and everything else in proportion[.]

I felt a goodeal relieved the other day while looking over the list of prisoners from Fair oaks to see the name of my mess mate Hezzekiah Horn[.] I am now the only man of mess No 11 on duty[.] Thomas is at home[,] Jordan is in the hospital at Ports mouth[,] Hezzekiah is prisoner at salisbury N.C[,][58] and Elias is sick in Camp[.] I have not missed any duty since last January[.] here it is like it is there them that will do may do not[.] over half the men that go to war are ever in a fight[.] out of 90 men in our co 43 have done all the fighting and most of the work[.] there is a good many in our co like there is in all others that make it a rule when there is any danger to take sick and not get well until the danger is over[.]

if I had mell here I could soon get a mule and caryall from the rebs and start him in the sutler business and in six months he could buy the best farm in that country[.] if I was free I could[,] if I had the consience[,] make from 50 to 100 dolars a day just as easy as I make 50 cts but I am not free and not likely to be for sometime[.] I did think I would get a furlough but things are too owley here at present for men who are always at their post to get away[.]

Watkins and allman are under the weather a little at present[.] Laddie is well[.] I must say for him he is as good a soldier as we have[.] true he has not been in any hard battle but he kept out honorably[.] he has been in several skirmishes and showed that he would stick to it as long as the rest and then he

---

[58] The Confederate government opened a prison camp in Salisbury, NC, in December 1861.

is always ready for duty[.] I suppose you have seen our old Capt before this[.] he did not like this business any better than the rest of us[.]

after the right wing of this army had fallen back cos C[,] D[,] & E of our regt were detached as guards at Mcs Headquarters[.]
the 3 cos mustered 88 men[.] we were put under Major Haller[.] so the morning the fight closed Haller got us out in line and told us if there was any cowards among us for them to leave ranks then for he would shoot the first man that wavered after we got into battle so Capt Wm H Horn sloped and was the only man who did[.][59]

M. E. Mc.

[July 20th 1862]

Well I have got that other sheet full so I will begin on this one[.] I must hurry too and finish my letter and go and get a pass to go to the 8th P.V. tomorrow as I want to see some of my old friends[.] you can tell the folks there that George Deems is enjoying good health[.] his Regt is camped about three miles from us[.] the whole P.R.C. arrived here on the Peninsula last week[.] while I think of it I will show you the difference between playing soldier and acting soldier[.] on the last of march the 8th and 85th Pa met at Alexandria[.] the 85th had the most men on duty and the most rugged robust men[.] we met again last week[.] the 8th had 960 men on duty and the 85th 200 so you see the contrast[.][60]

it is a nice thing to set in the corner and talk about soldiering but it is not quite so nice to be in a hot climate acting soldier[.] now for instance our company musters 30 effective men since the Battle[,] that is 30 on duty[.] there is not that many fit for duty though and we perform the duty of 101 men[.] I shouldent wonder if we done even better than that the day of the battle[.] I think if every 200 in the Division had killed as many as the 200 pickets did the rebs would have had to walk over more dead boddies than ever was walked over before[.] the artilery fixed them up about as fast as the

---

[59] Companies C, D, and E of the 85th were detached from the regiment on 29 June and sent to guard Jones' Bridge over the Chickahominy River, some twenty miles from camp. The companies returned to the army on 1 July during the fighting at Malvern Hill. Instead of rejoining the 85th, the detachment was sent to guard General McClellan's headquarters, remaining there until 5 July. Major Granville O. Haller of the Regular Army was one of the officers on duty at army headquarters.

[60] McJunkin writes about George Deem of the 8th Pennsylvania Reserves. The Pennsylvania Reserves were a division in the Fifth Army Corps and suffered heavy losses during the Seven Days' Battles. The 8th Reserves lost 230 men, and did not have 960 men on duty as McJunkin claimed.

infantry[.] they would throw in double charges of grape and canister and often you could 2 or 3 rods of the enemy fall from a single shot[.] on monday when we got the battle ground back you could count 50 or 60 on as little as a rod square[.] Caseys Division as near as I can learn killed over 2000 rebs and you know there is generally about 10 wounded to 1 killed[.] at least that is the way it was in our division[.] no doubt we had more wounded according to the number killed than them as we shot minnie balls altogether and they used buck and ball[.] we drawed the loads from some of their guns and found as high as 19 buckshot in a gun[.] they are to wound as you do as much good in wounding one man as killing two[.]

I wrote you a letter just a few days after the battle and gave som knews so I dont know how to write now not knowing whether you got it or not[.] I guess I will close for the present[.] I would like to write some more knews but it is getting dark and I must go and get my pass to the 8th as I shall want to start pretty early in the morning[.] I must tell you before I stop that you will likely have to pay the postage for a while as the rebs got my knapsack and portfolio which contains all my paper[,] envelops[,] and stamps and I can get no stamps in this country[.] it is not because I have no money though I still have some money[.] tell Mary I reckon some good looking secesh lady in Richmond has that picture I was goeing to send her[.]

if any body there wants to go to war just tell them if they want easy times and dont want to do much for their country to go in the cavalry but if they do want to be of any account to go in the infantry or artilery[.] one regt of infantry is worth at least 2 of cavalry[.] all the cavalry is fit for is scouts[.] they cant fight infantry or lancers any one[.]

July 21 1862
Col J. B. Howell
I respectfully ask leave of
absence to visit friends in the 8th Pa Vol[.]
approved by
J. W. Crawford
Lieut Com Co D

Respectfully approved
forwarded
Joshua B. Howell

George Ketchem, Company D

This 1862 or 1863 photograph shows Ketchem with his corporal stripes on a frock coat, military vest and dark blue trousers. One of the taller men in the regiment, he stood 6'13/4", when he enrolled at age 20 at Jefferson on Oct. 10, 1861, and mustered in at Uniontown, five days later. He had a fair complexion, dark eyes, light hair, and was a carpenter before joining the 85th. A native of Greene County, Ketchem rose through the ranks being promoted corporal on July 6, 1862, and sergeant on Mar. 1, 1864. He re-enlisted on Feb. 29, 1864, as a veteran volunteer. Ketchem sustained a gun shot fracture of the left thigh at the battle of Deep Bottom (Run) on Aug. 16, 1864. He died of exhaustion from his wound on Sept. 26, 1864, at Fort Monroe, VA. (Ronn Palm Collection)

Camp Wessell Near Harrison's Landing Va
saturday July 26th 1862[61]

Well folks it's right warm today[.] Nevertheless I guess I will try to scratch a few lines for the sake of sending Mother a little snuff money[.] I wish I could get into her snuff box this evening[.] I was dreaming last night of comeing in at the back door and getting hold of her box but when I waked I found myself laying behind the breast work here on the peninsula[.]

Well we are getting along pretty well at present[.] Allman is well[.] he is off duty with rheumatism in back & leg[.] Watkins is still off duty but I think it is homesickness more than any thing else[.] I have not heard anymore from Hartman[.] Wilson is still hearty as a buck and the best contented man in the army[.] he never even enquires about the folks at home[.]

I am getting along fine as a lady[.] I sometimes get out of humor and jaw some of the blamed officers just to hear them snort[.] I failed in getting Crawford in for Capt but Phillips[62] makes a very good one[.] I want you to keep me posted on how that thing than ran away and left us gets along and what he says about us[.] I mean Capt. Wm. H. Horn of Co. D 85th Regt. P. V. I must tell the truth[.] he went home despised by every man in Co. D except me[.] I liked him well enough[.]

Well mother I reckon you are satisfied now that I came into the army when I did[.] I am now seasoned to a soldiers life[.] I can now fight three rebs with the bayonet easier than I could have fought one when I left home and that is the way we do most of our fighting here[.] and another thing[,] I have been with the boys every time and none can say they ever saw me excited[.] at fair oaks George Kechem[63] and myself were the last to leave our posts[.] we were stationed behind two large pine trees blazeing away in the direction the rebel balls were comeing for we could not see a man ten steps in front of us[.] the first thing we knowed we were alone[.] the rest of the pickets was about 50 yds in a full run and the rebs had got clean past us on the left[.] the thick groth of under brush is all that saved us from being taken but God alone saved us from the missiles of war for we were exposed to all kinds of implements to kill from both sides for about 20 minets[.]

after I got out of the woods and was goeing through the fallen timber I caught my foot on a limb and just as I fell a 12 pdr whistled along over my

---

[61] Sent to Melville McJunkin.

[62] Captain Rolla O. Phillips, promoted 6 July 1862.

[63] Corporal George Ketchem of Company D.

back and plowed up the ground a few feet in advance[.] if I had not just triped the instant I did I would have been torn to attoms and many other instances similar show plainly that God is present even on the bloody field[.]

Sunday July 27th 1862

Well I guess I will write a little more today[.] I could write a goodeal but I guess I will fill this sheet with little acts[.] at fair oaks a niger was carrying a wounded capt off when two rebs came up when he snached up a loaded gun and shot one and plunged the bayonet through the other and succeeded in carrying off the capt[.] a boy in our regt but very little larger than mell has done as much duty as any man in the regt and at fair oaks when the regt was in the pits he stood on top laughing and makeing his remarks every time he shot[.] a little new yorker about the size of mell was shot through the mussle of the arm in the start and stayed until he fired 13 rounds after[.] in these last battles after the yankees would make a charge I think anybody would have to laugh to see the rebs running in every direction and the yankees after them yelling like injins for every one wanted his prisoner but the rebs can beat us running in this climate[.] at the battle of malvern hills we had quite a noise[.] we were in between the gun boats and rebs[.] for several hours there was one continual roar of artilery[.]

tell Tom not to go to the army by any means & tell jake not to go unless drafted and I dont want you to send any body to the army that is of no account there for they are of less here and make it that much harder on us[.]

I understand mary is dangerously ill[.] I dont know why you never mentioned it[.] I might have got a furlough before these fights if I had known she was so poorly but now furloughs have played out for a while[.] we started a bible class here today but there was not a lady out[.] I will send ten dollars this time[.] I sent 20 in my last if you ever got it[.]

give my love to all enquireing friends[.] tell aunt mar that I was at McCalls Division the other day and saw Charles todd[.] he is all right[.]
M. E. McJunkin

July 30th 1862

Col. J. B. Howell

I respectfully ask leave of absence to visit the landing[.]
M. E. McJunkin

Approved Respectfully

49

forwarded
By order Joshua B. Howell   Respectfully approved
     Col Comdg 85th P.V.   & forwarded to Col. J. B. Howell
     S. L. McHenry   R. O. Phillips Cmg Co. D
          Adjt

Well I got a pass the other day to go to the Landing to get some pictures taken
but before I got started the word came that the rebs were advanceing so I had
to stay close to the breast works so now I will have no chance to get any for
I dont know when so I will draw one myself[.]

Camp Near Harrison's Landing Va
August 8th 1862[64]

I received your lengthy and interesting epistle of the july 20th some days ago but on account of fatigue and picket duty I have been unable to answer it so I have got my breakfast and I thought I would commence a letter while the rest of the boy's are getting their breakfast[,] for we are goeing to strike tents and rearrange our camp today which will occupy most of the day[.]

I am enjoying good health at present but I am begining to grow old[.] there is some gray hairs in my head and whisker's already and sometimes my legs are a little stiff but I guess anybody will be a little old against they go through what I have[.] I have done more though than I need to have done but I would sooner do half a dozen mens work than see my friends on duty when I knew they were not able[.] Wilson is in good health[.] Allmon & Watkins is both under the weather[.] they have done but very little since fair oaks[.]

we were surprised as well as pleased yesterday morning to see some of our boy's that we lost in the last fight step into camp[.] they were taken to Richmond the 1st of july and the other day there was 3,000 exchanged[.] Will Hartman is one that come back[.] he looks better than he did when the rebs got him[.] they report that they were used well[.] there was only one of our company got back[.] the rest are in N. C. at sallisbury[.]

you say mother is uneasy for fear I get in trouble with the officers[.] you can tell her she can rest easy on that score[.] if a soldier attends to his business and does his duty he is not goeing to have any trouble with officers unless the doctors are the principal cause of it[.] Capt. Wm. H. Horn and me had two rows last winter[.] the last was the night we embarked at Alexandria[.] I think Capt. Wm. H. Horn would have went into the Potomac that night if he had not shut up and scampered into the boat[.] that was the last trouble I have had with officers[.] Horn after he found out for certain what I was attended to his own business as far as I was concerned[.] at fair oaks I kept him from being taken prisoner for we were in a large swamp and he was not very well and when we were attacked he got bewildered & did not know what direction to take for camp[.] all the rest just tried to save their own bacon[.] I stayed with the Capt until I got him past our first battery and showed him our camp & then I thought it my duty to help my comrades all I could[.]

I have missed no duty since last january[.] there was a week the first of july I was unfit for duty but we had lots of it to do and I could not stand back and see others not any more able than I was at work[.] I still feel the

---

effects of the measels and suppose I always will but my health is better this summer than it ever was before[.] I can eat hearty when I have it or when I have nothing to eat[.] I can do without 2 or 3 days without eating without any trouble[.]

one night not long ago the rebs got to shelling us and by accident a shell hit in a squad of niggers and killed a few but our officers soon showed them that it wouldent do for them to go to killing niggers[.] they give them to understand if they wanted to kill any body that they must kill soldiers so the other day they took 50,000 troops & between two & three hundred field pieces & went up to malvern hill and killed a good many rebs[,] took a few prisoners[,] and drove the rest back to Richmond[.][65]

I believe it is the calculation to plant the stars and stripes in Richmond before August is gone[.] it created quite joyful sensation in the army when the word come that 300,000 more troops was ordered and the sooner they come the better for their country and themselves[.] I advise all that can to get into old regts[.] there can 5 or 600 get into the old 85th as long as Howell and some more that have resigned was here[.] I could not ask any body to come to our regt but we are now pretty well officered[.] Col Purviance is a good officer and Capt Vankirk in my opinion will soon be Lieut Col[.] Major Treadwell is a first rate fellow & not afraid of rebs or anything else! our pitch on malvern hill was to keep the rebs away from Pope until Burnside got to him[.] it hit the nail on the head[.] our Chaplain got back today[.][66]

you write very interesting letters from home and lots of them you tell the knews how things are goeing[,] on the general feelings of the people on war matters[,] how recruiting is comeing on[,] and in fact you leave nothing untold that can interest me here[.] I often wonder how you can find time to write so often and such long letters[.] now there has never yet been over three months between your letters[.] I know it must worry you to write so much so I cant ask you to write so often in the future[.]   you tolld about getting my letters but did not say anything about the money[.] I sent 20 dollars in one and 10 in the other[.] you have not heard from will[.] I hear from him every week or two[.] I heard about Hopkins a month or two ago[.] if I heard nothing but what I get from home I dont think I would hear very much[.]

---

[65] See Dickey, pp. 197-99, for details on these incidents.

[66] McJunkin mentions Lieutenant Colonel Henry A. Purviance, Captain Henry J. Vankirk of Company A, Major James B. Tredwell, and Chaplain John N. Pierce. Major General John Pope commanded the Army of Virginia. Major General Ambrose E. Burnside, with the Ninth Corps, was moving from Fort Monroe to reinforce Pope's troops in northern Virginia.

Henry A. Purviance, Lieutenant Colonel

Purviance was born in May 1831, and began work in a printing office at the at age 13. He mastered the trade and developed a fine taste for reading and study. This led him to the field of journalism. By the spring of 1861, he and Colonel James Armstrong published the Washington, PA, *Tribune*. In April 1861, he enlisted in Capt. Norton McGiffin's three months' company that was assigned to the 12th Pennsylvania Infantry. Upon his return, Purviance began recruiting for the 85th. He enrolled Sept. 12, 1861, at Washington, PA, at age 30, to command what came to be Co. E. He was sworn into service on Nov. 12. Purviance was promoted to lieutenant colonel on May 15, 1862, upon the resignation of Norton McGiffin. He was wounded at the Battle of Seven Pines (Fair Oaks) on May 31, 1862, and absent by authority until Aug. 5, 1862. He fell sick in late Feb. until Apr. 16, 1863. Well thought of and even loved by the men of the 85th, Purviance was killed by the premature explosion of a Federal shell in the advance trenches in front of Fort Wagner on Aug. 30, 1863. (Ronn Palm Collection)

we throwed a heavy force across the James last night[.] I suppose they are going to act in concert with Pope & Burnside[.] I still say as I said before that Tom has no business in the army[.] they cant make him come and I am doing enough for him and my self both[.] if all the army had done as much as I have the war would have been over long ago[.]

Direct your letters in future to the
3d Brigade, Peck's Division[67]
instead of Caseys but dont take up too much of your time writeing[.]

Camp Near Yorktown Va
August 22nd 1862[68]

Another strategetical movement of the Grand Army of the Potomac[.] Well to begin I am enjoying excellent health at present[.] I have as big a belly on me as old Peter Cleaver[.] Laddie & Will Hartman are both in fine health and spirits[.] Watkins & Allmon were both sent north from Harrison's Landing[.] they both had the rheumatism and as homesick as anybody I ever saw which made them feel worse than they otherwise would but it would make them mad to tell them so[.] I dont wonder much at people getting tired of this business though[.]

you say Tom's name is on the militia roll[.] they cant compel him to come & I advise him to stay at home[.] if he is drafted it takes men to have the constitution of the united states & sound in every respect to <u>work strategy</u> and you know we are doing all by strategy in this war[.] Mell appears to think he would like to come but he would like to get back worse before he was here very long but there is plenty of less boys than him here and they are some of them of as much account in battle where there is no chargeing done as anybody[.] but if we get someplace where we will be likely to lay to lay for sometime I want him to come on a visit and fech me a box tobacco and other little things and see some of the world[.] I would liked for him to have been at harrison's landing while we were there[.] he would have seen 100,000 men in a bunch there[.] As near as I can judge it was only 16 miles around our encampment[.]

there is a greateal of growling at Mcclellan in the north I discover[.] now just look at the matter right and see if there is anything to growl at[.] he

---

[67] Brigadier General John J. Peck superseded Casey shortly after Fair Oaks.

[68] Sent to Melville McJunkin.

has only lost 98,000 men in killed[,] wounded[,] missing[,] and sick since he came to the Peninsula and he is in possession of Yorktown which the rebs occupied when he came[.] so if the people of the north think that a town containing 9 or 10 log houses could be taken with less loss they will just have to think so is all I have to say on the subject[.]

now I guess I will say something about our skedaddle from our breastworks at the landing[.] well we started about two o'clock last saturday morning[69] and hoed it down pretty lively until we got past Williams burgh[.] I am just speaking of our own division now as we covered the retreat on the middle road[.] well to begin we halted as soon as we got out of the breast works and loaded our pieces and marched at quick time until noon[.] we then halted and made a dinner on green corn and peaches which we confiscated in spite of our humane officers[.] we then marched on till evening and halted near some more cornfields which we trimed decently[.] s u n d a y morning we took up our line of march at break of day and forced our way through to the chickahominy[,] crossed on a pontoon[,] and never halted for dinner or anything else until about 4 o'clock when old Peck looked around and saw his division looked very small so he ordered a halt[.] our company numbers 46 men at present[.] I will just name the men that was with the company when Peck ordered a halt so you can judge what kind of a march it was[.] there was myself[,]George Kechem[,] Alex McKay[,] Steve Clandaniel[,] Enoch Brooks[,] & jugger Dale[,] so you see there was only 40 of our Co fizzled out between the Chicahominy and our camping ground for the night[,] three miles this side where we trimed some more corn fields and orchards[.]

bright and early monday morning we started off again and by 3 o'clock we had left Williamsburgh some 4 miles in the rear[.] so there we halted two nights & a day to let Heintzelman[70] pass us[.] he came down the long bridge road[.] while there we eat all the corn[,] potatoes[,] cattle[,] pigs[,]poultry[,] apples[,] pears[,] peaches[,] and every thing else we could find for five miles around[.] the army of the Potomac is fast growing unmanageable[.] it is my opinion if there is not less fortifying and guarding rebel property done from this out and more done towards putting down the rebelion that the soldiers will

---

[69] 16 August 1862. Here follows a description of the division's march to Yorktown. The Army of the Potomac was being evacuated and sent north to help General Pope. Some units marched to Yorktown before embarking for northern Virginia. Peck's troops remained behind on the Peninsula

[70] Major General Samuel P. Heintzelman commanded the Third Army Corps.

be very apt to dismiss the officers and put down the rebelion in short metre themselves[.] we had force enough to have wound up the whole thing last may[.] M'clellen could have taken Richmond with Johnston's whole army and Halleck could have taken Corinth and Beauregard's army and it would not have taken long to finish up the ballance[.][71]

you say all the boy's are going in the cavalry[.] they might a goodeal better stay at home[.] one regt of infantry is worth half a dozen of cavalry[.] just give me my bayonet and no three cavalrymen can take me[.] no more at present[.]

Camp Hamilton Va. Sept 7th 1862[72]

Well Mother I guess I will write a few lines today as I have a little spare time[.] to begin I am enjoying good health at present[.] you will see though by my weight that I am not very fleshy as I only weigh about 190 lbs at present[.] but I must hurry on as I have not much time to write at present[.]

Hartman & Wilson are both in good health[.] I have not heard from Allmon since he was shiped from the Landing[.] I got a letter from Watkins a few minnets ago[.] he is getting better[.] he states that he heard that I wrote home that there was nothing ailed Allmon & himself but homesickness & that they were only playing off[.] now I never wrote such stuff as that & I dont want any more of it to be comeing here[.] they are both good soldiers[.] I received a letter from Libbie day before yesterday but I have not time to answer it at present[.] tell her I will get my likeness the first oportunity and send it to her[.] if I had money I could get it taken here[.] it has happened eversince I have been in the army that whenever I was where I could get it taken I had no money[.] I expect before we get payed off again we will be where there is no ambrotypes establishments as usual[.] I dont look to be payed off for a couple of months yet[.]

we will likely remain here several week's yet[.] the health of the troops here is generally good[.] they are dying off very fast in the hospitals though[.] almost all hours of the day you can hear the muffled drum's and the

---

[71] Major General Henry W. Halleck led a Union army against Corinth, Mississippi, in May 1862 against General P. G. T. Beuregard's Confederate defenders.

[72] Camp Hamilton was located near Fort Monroe. The 85th remained at this site from 24 August through 18 September 1862. This letter is written on the back of a letter Milton received from William S. McJunkin, dated 24 August 1862.

Oliver McVay, Company D

At age 19, McVay enrolled in Capt. Horn's company at Zollarsville, on Sept. 15, 1861.
Mustered into to Co. D at Uniontown on Nov. 11, 1861, McVay had been born in
Washington, PA, was 5'51/2", with blue eyes, dark hair, fair complexion, and employed
as a farmer. McVay was present with the regiment until July 26, 1862, when he was
sent to the general hospital from Harrison's Landing, VA. He was discharged on
surgeon's certificate for disability (chronic pleurisy) at Philadelphia on Sept. 18, 1862,
by order of Brig. Gen. William Montgomery. (Ronn Palm Collection)

dead march & the salutes fired over the graves of the departed[.]

in the last few days there has been some epidemic broke out among the negroes[.] yesterday there was 40 buried in one grave across the river[.] I have written 3 or 4 letters home since I received an answer but from this out it will be just the reverse[.]

tell Tom I want him to go to Dan snyders if he is still shoemakeing and get him to make me a good pair of no. 10 hip boots[,] legs to reach to the knee[.] I want them fashionable military boots to wear outside my pants[.] if snyder is not there get some other shoemaker and I will send the money as soon as we are payed off[.] sometime in the course of two or three months when we get permanently settled for the winter[,] I will want a box from home and they can be sent in it[.] you need not be in any hurry about it as I will not need them for 2 or 3 months[.] I want them large 10's[.] I want Mell to send me some stamps[.] I have had no stamps since I came on the Peninsula except what was sent me[.] I had the honor of eating a piece of wedding cake the other day that came in a letter[.] I would like to hear from Jim Patterson[.] I have not known his adress since I left Uniontown[.] I have written home for his adress several times but you have never given his address or told anything about him either[.]

Camp Hamilton Va
Sept 16th 1862

Headquarters Mess No 15 Sept 16th

As I have nothing of importance to write about I thought I would fill a sheet with foolishness if I dont have to go at something else before I get it done[.]

Well to commence I am still blesed with excellent health[.] I have plenty to eat and plenty to do as I put in half my time guarding and the other half drilling[,] so you see I have not much time for writeing or anything else[.]

it is settled now that we dont go into the Fort as the 3d New york has been assigned that[.] I think it is very likely we will remain here until spring if the rebs dont get to useing our boys too bad elsewhere but I think it would be no more than right to leave us here as I think we have done our share of fighting[.] Houcker's Division is the only one in the service that has done as much as us[.] Genl. Meagher's Irish Brigade can take down the world at a charge bayonet[.] in the fall of the gallant Kearney the Federal army lost one of its best General's although Kearney had nothing to do with our Division[.] yet when the tideing's came that he was among the killed they could not have taken it harder had it been their parents[.][73]

I have not saw such a feeling among our troops since the Death of our beloved Genl. Keim[.] if he had been spared you would have heard a different account of our Brigade from it[.]

now is 17th[,] but Keim did not get his share of praise at the Williamsburgh fight[.] it was <u>him</u> instead of hancock that gained the day[.][74] we had been two day's without a bite to eat and had marched about 24 mile's through
the mud and rain when we halted to wait for our grub to come up[.] the word come that Hooker was being drove back so our Genl got out of bed although scarcely able to set on his horse[.] as soon as we saw him we forgot that we was almost starved and worn out and was ready to follow him to victory[.] under the circumstances we would have followed no other liveing man[.] you will recolect that we had never smelt powder then and had not become familiar with a battle field[.]

well we moved off double quick until we got on an open field joining the woods[.] the rebs were trying to get possession of where we formed in line of battle under fire from fort magruder[,] so we marched in line of battle over to the woods and halted to take wind[.] Col. Howell at that time had command of the Brigade as Keim was in advance looking for a good position for us[.] while standing there Genr'l Sumner[75] rode up in great haste and hollowed Col. have you a regt you can rely upon[.] the old Col without takeing time to give him an answered yelled out forward 85th[.] so we started off double quick down the road to the scene of action[.] the old Col was rideing back and forth along the line with a smile on his face[,] saying now me boys give them the bayonet[.] I thought of the change one short month made at william's burgh[.] I dont think he had an enemy in the regt and at fair oaks I dont think he had a friend[.]

---

[73] McJunkin mentions Generals Joseph Hooker (commanding a division in the Third Corps), Thomas F. Meagher (brigade commander in the Second Corps), and Phil Kearny (division commander in the Third Corps, killed at the Battle of Chantilly).

[74] Brigadier General Winfield S. Hancock led a brigade at Williamsburg.

[75] Brigadier General Edwin V. Sumner, commanding the Second Army Corps.

Suffolk Sept 20th 1862[76]

Well I have got back to my letter but knews is still scarce and time scarcer so I will hurry it through and try to get it off with today's mail[.] to begin I am enjoying good health[.] Wilson & Hartman are in excellent health & spirits[.] I got a letter from Watkins the other day[.] he is not much better[.] I have just read a letter from Allman[.] he is on Craney island[77] and not much better either[.] they both have been worn out in the service of their country and ought to have their discharges but it is not likely that they will get them as neither are Mason's[.]

We are under Major genl. Dix at present[.][78] we were ordered to Washington but last thursday the word came that the rebs were advanceing in force on Suffolk so all the troops that could be spared from about the fort were immediately shiped[.] by 12 o'clock we were on board the S. R. Spaulding[,] wending our way up to Norfolk[,] where we landed and took the cars at 11 o'clock at night and ran up here where we are at present[.]

when we got here the scouts came in with the knews that the rebs were at Peters Burgh and still goeing the other way[.] I think they must have heard of us comeing and did not fancy a collision with the Austrian Rifles[.] the Rebel prisoners say they all dread the Austrian rifles more than any other gun's we have got[.] I dont know what we will do now[.] I think though if the rebs dont come back we will go to Washington[.] the fighting will be done inside of two months[.] it is the talk now that Mcclellan has got the rebel army almost anihilated[.] I hope it is so for we are all mighty tired of this business[.]

I have no time to write any more at present[.] I have got two letters from home since writeing Maria's and the one since that told about her[.]

---

[76] The 85th, together with Peck's division, was part of the Suffolk garrison from 18 September through 5 December 1862.

[77] Craney Island is located near the mouth of the Elizabeth River, and was a major Confederate defense facility for protecting Norfolk. It was occupied by Union forces when Norfolk was abandoned by the Rebels in May 1862.

[78] Major General John A. Dix commanded the Department of Virginia, which embraced the Yorktown Peninsula, Norfolk, and Suffolk.

Joshua B. Howell, Colonel

From the first time he led the 85th Pennsylvania into battle at Williamsburg, VA, on May 5, 1862, Howell was always in the midst of the fighting. In operations against Charleston in the summer of 1863, Howell commanded the 2nd Brigade of Gen. Alfred Terry's division. His troops served at various posts at different times in the campaign including the islands of Hilton Head, Folly, St. Helena, Morris From Feb. to Apr. 1864, he commanded the Hilton Head District. During the siege of Fort Wagner, on the night of Aug. 16, 1863, Howell suffered a concussion from the explosion of a shell, which bruised his head and injected him with numerous splinters. And though he was sent to Uniontown to recover, he longed to rejoin his men in the field. With time still remaining in his furlough, he wrote: "I am very anxious to return to my Brigade, and if well enough, I shall leave here tomorrow . . . ." Howell distinguished himself in leading the brigade in battle at Ware Bottom Church on May 20, 1864–driving the enemy from recently captured rifle pits, and capturing Confederate Gen. William S. Walker. He was absent only one more time, in late July and early Aug. 1864 still feeling the effects of the concussion and general debility from the fatigues of recent campaigns, he received a 20-day furlough. He returned to command of the 1st Brigade of the 1st Division of the 10th Corps, in mid-August. (Ronn Palm Collection)

Well I received your letter of the 14th & 15th yesterday evening[.] I wrote finished one yesterday but I thought I would answer this one right away as I want to know more about some things than it suited you to write[,] but I will talk about things as they come[.]

in the first place you think it strange I dont get all your letters I can answer[.] I have got every letter you have written up to the 15th of this month so now I am goeing to catch you in a lie[.] you said you had answered every letter I wrote and sent some between times[.] now I know that is not the case as you have not averaged over two letters a month since I have been in the army and I have averaged as you will see by refference to my old letters at least four[,] but it is no difference about that now if you do better in the future[.]

you think you have wrote a goodeal about patterson's[.] you never even wrote about them being moved and now you did not tell where they had moved to[.] you told in one place that you had heard jim was shot in the hand and in another that they were looking for him home as soon as he was able to move[.] now I cant understand that[.]

now I will tell you some little I saw at the battle of Turkey Bend[.][80] I saw men there that was shot through both legs[,] through the arms[,] and some through the breast[,] and one man that had his whole privates shot off that walked five miles from the battle field to the hospital[.] now if they could do that[,] how is it that jim was not able to move home if he is only wounded in the hand[?] I have saw several wounded men since I left home but I have not saw any that was only wounded in the hand or arm that was unfit to move[.]

I want to know whether bill griffith is activally raiseing a company or only recruiting[.] you wrote a long time ago that jout was killed and not very long ago that he was sick in the hospital[.] that's a pretty way aint it[.]

Sept 26th 1862

Well I have got to my writeing again[.] Well to begin with since we left the landing we had nothing but salt water to drink[.] it was not very salty when fresh[,] but to let it stand a little while it could not be used so you see as a natural consequence we had the diarrhea worse than common[,] and then when

---

[79] Sent to Melville McJunkin.

[80] An incident during the stay at Harrison's Landing. See Dickey, pp. 198-99, for details.

we came here we found the worst water I ever saw[.] so last monday I was with several 100 more down at one of the railroad bridges working srategy in the woods and of course did not get my letter finished[,] so on tuesday I reported myself on the sick list & was not in good order for writeing again until today[.] I thought I was either takeing the ague or some fever but it turned out to be just a little brash[.] I reported myself for duty again this morning[.] I dont feel altogether right yet but I think I will soon be as fat as ever if I keep on improveing[.]

I have nothing to say about the boys more than I wrote in my last[.] we are 10,000 strong here at present[.] it is reported that there is 50,000 rebs up at the black swamp some 18 or 20 miles from here[.] we are very busy fortifying here at present but I hardly think it will amount to much as I dont anticipate an attack here atal[.]

I got them stamps last saturday and have been useing them in place of money as I unexpectedly got 10 stamped envelop's and a quire of paper but they come mighty handy as I have no time or chance here to do my own washing[.] I can get the darkies to do it and take stamps for pay[.] they wash at 5 cts a piece[.] everything in the grub line is cheap and plenty here as troops are rather scarcer than any place else I have been for some time[.]

you say you are very uneasy about there for fear the rebs would gain the day[.] it is very different with us[.] we have never thought any thing about the rebs goeing any farther north than to get into our trap[,] but I guess old stonewall is too old a fox to be caught very easy[.][81] if we had had as good military men as him at our head this war would have been over last june[.] Mcclellan is undoubtedly a good genl but the most of the under Genl and congress have been working against him[.]

but enough of this[.] Direct your letters to Fortress Monroe instead of Washington but dont change any of the rest of the direct as they will come quicker to the fort than by Washington[.] for fear you haint sense enough to understand anything I will just give the direction in full[:]

Mr. Milton E. McJunkin

Co. D 85th Regt. P. V.

3d Brigade Pecks Division

Fortress Monroe Va

I would like you to send me a dollar in your next as money is a scarce article here at present[.] tell mell to ride Col as much as he pleases but I dont want anybody to put harness on him as I want that job myself[.]

---

[81] McJunkin refers to Stonewall Jackson.

William E. Beall, Company H

At age 27, he enrolled as a private in Captain Tredwell's company at Simerfield, on Sept. 1, 1861, and mustered in at Uniontown on Nov. 12. He was appointed commissary sergeant on Nov. 16, 1861, then on June 3, 1862, he was appointed regimental quartermaster and first lieutenant. In Nov. and Dec. 1862, Beall oversaw the moving of the regimental baggage from the camp at Suffolk, VA. During May 1863, Beall learned that his father had been seriously ill for some time and that his only brother had suddenly died, and was granted a furlough to return home to attend to matters. In forwarding the request for furlough, Colonel Howell noted: "Lt. Beall is a very meritorious officer . . . ." On June 18, 1863, Beall was appointed the acting brigade commissary by order of Colonel Howell. On Aug. 26, 1863, while in the Siege of Charleston, he was detached to serve with the commissary department on Folly Island. Starting June 30, 1864, Beall took the post of acting commissary of subsistence for the 1st Brigade, 1st Division, 10th Corps. On Oct. 13, 1864, Beall was put under arrest and returned to the regiment on Oct. 31, while awaiting sentence of the court martial. Apparently he was found not guilty or sentence was never passed as he was discharged on Nov. 22, 1864, with the regimental field and staff for the expiration of his term of service. (Ronn Palm Collection)

Camp Near Suffolk Va
Oct 11th 1862[82]

Well I guess as I have nothing else to do this afternoon I will begin a letter[.] I have been waiting some time for an answer to some of the others but I guess I will write a little today as I may not have as much time when I get them as I have now[.]

    to begin I am well at present[.] Wilson is well[.] Hartman is in the cooking business in his co and fatter than I ever saw him[.] I have not heard from Allman or Watkins since writeing before[.]

    our fortifications are begining to look pretty formidable here but we are not half done yet[.] we have put up several forts and several miles of breast work[.] I guess it the idea to keep this as a military post after the war is over[.] since writeing we have had two little brushes with the rebs up at Black Water[83] but not to amount to much[.] in the first place the 101st pa and 96th N.Y. a few day's after we come here went up and drove in their pickets but found the enemy in too strong force to do any more and so of course retreated back to camp[.]

    so last or yesterday week about 5,000 of us started up in the evening and got there about 3 o'clock saturday morning and drove 7,000 rebs across the river without much trouble and very little loss on our side[.] they tore up the bridge to keep us from following them but I guess we had no notion of that anyhow[.] all we wanted was to get them on the other side so we layed there all day saturday[,] eating everything we could find and started back to camp in the evening and got here about the middle of the night[.] Black Water is 22 miles from here so you see what a soldiers life is[.]

    we was away from camp only about 30 hours[.] the Army of the Potomack what is left of them is men fhisically[.] we had 2 or 3 new regts with us and about half them give out goeing up and scarcely any of the Peninsula men got behind[.] after we had made the round and was comeing into camp saturday night[,] they all with their extra load of sweet potatoes and chickens was able to come singing and dancing along as if goeing home from a frolick[.] while the new troops without these extras were hardly able to drag along[.]

    I will give you the least load the soldier has[,] just his skirmishing load[.] first is his gun[,] cartrige box and ammunition[,] 25 lbs[;] gum blanket

---

[82] Sent to Melville McJunkin. See Dickey, p 206, for details about the actions mentioned in this letter.

[83] The Blackwater River is approximately twenty miles west of Suffolk.

65

and overcoat[,] 15 lbs[;] haversack[,] canteen[,] and 2-3 days rations[,] about 15 lbs[;] makeing in all 55 lbs[,] which is the least load he can start out with on a march[.] I generally carry about 100 lbs[.] I guess I will quit until the mail comes in and see if there is a letter for me tonight[.]

12th[.] Well I got your letter last night of the 7th with the dolar so I guess I will finish this letter today[.]

it is the first sunday for a long time that I have had nothing to do[.] I intended to get my likeness taken with that dollar but the man left the other day[,] but it wont take me long to spend it for something else[.] I want you to send me one of ad's photographs[.] I want you to nit me a pair of wooly mittens to send when I call for my boot's[.] I want you to have a dried beef liver if you can get it handy but I will enumerate what I want when I call for the box[.] perhaps I will come after it if I get a chance[.]

Well I gues I have no more to write so I think I will stop for the present[.] it is a wet disagreeable day[.] I want you to tell Jim to write me a long letter[.]

I have often heard it said that a man would get used to anything but the longer I soldier the worse I hate it[,] but I think the business will be settled before long[.] I will put some cotton in[.] it is just as it grew[.] I got it when I was up at Black Water[.] there is paches of cotton everyplace I have been yet but I just thought I would get some up there to send home[.]

Fierce Encounter Between a yankee and three rebs. You see he has shot one in the head[,] pierced another with the bayonet[,] and about to fix the other in the same way[.] you see the 1 1/2 oz ball just fired at him missed[.]

Camp Near Suffolk Va
Oct 16th 1862

Well I guess I will scribble a little before we go on drill[.] we have got pretty well through with our fortifications so we have to drill twice a day[.] we are not quite as bad as ad[.] we only drill three hours a day at present but we make it up in working[,] standing picket[,] and skirmishing[.]

the reason of my writeing so soon[:] I got a kind of picture taken today and I thought I would start it at once[.] I was in quite a hurry and therefore did not get a very good one but it resembles me some[.] you will see that I forgot to reverse my accoutrements and so of course in the picture they are just wrong[.][84] when we get paid off if I have a chance I will get a lot of good pictures taken in full uniform[,] armed and equiped[.] I have not time to write much today as we go on drill in a few minnets[.]

I have good health at present[.] I have not heard from Allman or Watkins for sometime[.]

I guess before I start this letter I will give you leave to send me another dollar to buy sweet potatoes and apples with[.]

we are looking to go out on another reconnoisance before long[.] we will likely get some sweet potatoes for nothing if they dont happen to be all gone[.] they was begining to be a little scarce the last time we was out[.]

this is a hard place for a man to live a christian[.] Crouch[85] and myself are all of our company that makes a practice of attending meeting[.] nobody can be promoted in the army except he can drink[,] swear[,] and gamble so you see I have a good chance to put in my other two years in the ranks but I dont want offices as bad as I did[.] I can enjoy myself better as a private[.]

Tell Laddies friends that I command them in the name of Abraham Lincoln and Cabinet to write to him whether he writes or not[.] he has been in the service a year and never missed an hours duty and is just as good a soldier as they make now day's and he has never got but two or three letters yet[.] they must recolect that the boy dont have much time to write here and when he is off duty he feels more like resting than writeing[.]

in that picture I expect you will think I have a sword[.] it is not a

---

[84] McJunkin's photograph was either a tintype, ambrotype, or dageurreotype, for in these photographic processes, the image was reversed. The collodion process used for the more prevalent cartes-de-visite corrected the reversal. Some photographers used stage props, such as reversed belt buckles and arranging the accoutrements on opposite sides of the soldier, to counteract the reversed image.

[85] Hiram W. Crouch.

sword but a saber bayonet[.] it is about two feet long and fully as heavy as a cavalry saber[.] the reason I have it in my hand I was not dressed to have it taken standing and you could not see the saber setting[.] the next pictures I get will be somewhat fixed up[.] I guess I have said all I can think of now so I will quit[.]

17th[.] Well I guess I will write some more this morning just for the fun of the thing[.]

Well to begin Hezzekiah Horn[,] one of my old mess mates that the rebs got up at Fair oaks[,] steped into camp the other night[.] he was pretty well used up but is about well now[.] Jordan got a letter from Thomas the other day[.] he is in Baltimore[.]

now I will give a discription of my messing since I came to war at camp Casey[.] we formed in messes[.] my mess was composed of H and E Horn[,] A. Thomas[,] J. Jordan[,] and myself[.] well we stuck together until we got to Newport News[,] where Thomas was detached and went into the artilery[.] the rest of us kept together until we got to New Kent[,] where Jordan went to the hospital[,] and at fair oaks the rebs got Hezzekiah[,] and at Harrison's Landing Elias went to the hospital[,] so you see I was left alone[.] comeing down the Peninsula there was Hiram Crouch[,] Alex Mccay[,] and myself together[.] now Billy Lash is in Mccay's place[.] Hiram Crouch is a brother of Nate's[.] our's is now and alway's has been the best mess in the company[.]

Camp Near Suffolk Va
Sunday Oct 26th 1862

Well I received your letter of the 17th day before yesterday but a good bit of the knews was old[.] I knew what was in the box the day before for I had eat part of it[.]

to begin I am enjoying good health at present[.] Hartman & Laddie are in good health[.] I have not heard from Allmon for a long time now[.] I get a letter from Will every week or two[.] they are all doing very well[.] I guess it is pretty certain that we will winter here but soldiering is very uncertain business[.] we may be sent to the Shenandoah at any time[.] the old Genl said the other day that it layed between us and the rebs to decide who should winter here so we decided if that was the case to winter here ourselves[.]

Wednesday Oct 29th 1862

Well I did not get much wrote the other day so I will try to finish today[.] we have been very busy for about a week putting up winter quarters when we was not drilling or guarding[.] I will have to hurry my letter through and so of course you wont look for any partickulars[.]

I mention something about that box[.] it came to Suffolk this day week and I went out the next day and got it[.] everything was in it but there had been oil spilt on it and scented some of the thing's but they were not spoiled[.] the lid was off the can of cherries so they were not worth much[.] tell mrs Patterson I am very much obliged for the tomatoes[.] them and the honey make the best liveing I have had for the last six month's[.] the berries are very nice to stew when I am on picket[.] but the painkiller is worth all the rest[.] I have been troubled a greateal with diarhea since we left the landing and about 2 or 3 weeks ago I took a severe cold which settled down in my breast[,] causeing a pretty good chunk of pain[.] but when I got the painkiller I begun to go up right along[.] the pain has left entirely and my bowells are more regular than they have been since I had the meazels[.] the tobacco is the best I have had since that last winter[.]

two Brigades of us started up to Blackwater at half past two o'clock last thursday[.] our brigade was commanded by Col. howell and the other by genl farry[.][86] we had a regt of cavalry[,] a couple of parrot guns[,] two howitzers[,] and 3 or 4 swivels[.] we traveled on until 5 o'clock friday morning when we were fired into by some rebs that was concealed in the woods[.] we soon routed them out of that[,] takeing a few to see if they would pet[.] we then shelled the town of franklin for about half an hour when our ammunition ran out[.] by that time the gunboat had got up and opened on them[.] there was one of our men shot by a citizen so we just strung him up on the spot[.] we got back to camp at 12 o'clock friday night when I found your letter of the 25th waiting for me with the dollar[.]

I went on picket yesterday and when I got back today I found that receipt but have no use for it as I have got the box pretty near empty[.] the tomatoes made us three beautiful messes[.] I must close for the present and get ready for drill[.] give my love to all enquireing friends[.] you need not knit any socks[.] I wont send for the box until we see what the Grand Army is going to do[.] I guess it is on the move[.]

Every time get hold of the snuff box I have to begin looking around to see that sis is not about to squall at me[.] I have dodged her so far though[.] I think she will find the box emty if she dont get it hid pretty soon[.] we are expecting to be payed off in two or three weeks[.] Unkle Sam owes us over

---

[86] Brigadier General Orris S. Ferry.

50 dollars a piece now[.]

      I guess I cant think of anything more to say now[.] I sent a likeness in my last letter but it was not a good one[.] I am sorry I did not get some taken at the landing[.] while there I was fat[,] well dressed[,] and had my whiskers fixed up right[,] but while we were there we was in front and had to stay close to camp and wach the rebs[.]

      Well I must stop[,] get some dinner[,] and get ready for drill[.]

Nov 3d 1862[.] Well I have got to my letter again but I dont know how long I will get to write[.] well to begin I have just got through with a big dinner and thought I would answer your other two letters[.] just tell mell he may look to get his --- kicked for failing to decide immediately as plain a matter as them pictures[.]

Fort Nansemond Va
Nov 17th 1862[87]

Well I guess I will try to scratch a few lines to let you know how things are working here at present[.] to begin I am enjoying good health at present but feel a little uncomfortable on account of a kind of pleurisy pain in the side[,] but I have had a mustard plaster on for sometime which has helped considerably[.] Laddie & hartman are in good health[.]

      Well I think from appearances we will have a little brush with the rebs tonight or tomorrow[.] nearly all the troops here have started on the direction of Blackwater[.] I have also heard several shots from heavy guns in the distance[.] three companies of us from our regt were sent out here to fort Nansemond which commands the Summitan Road to hold it and prevent an advance by that road[.] I dont know at present where the rest of the regt went as we were the first to start[.] all the afternoon we have saw in the long lines of infantry[,] artillery[,] and ambulances fileing out the Petersburgh road[,] which looks like there was something expected[.] I think likely the rebs are advanceing as our pickets were drove in the other night[.] Well I have no more to say on that subject at present as the privates know nothing until they see it come off except what they judge from appearances[.] perhaps I will have more to say about it before I start this letter so I will close for today[.]

---

[87] Fort Nansemond was located at the southwestern edge of Suffolk, between the Somerton Road and the Norfolk and Petersburg Railroad.

Thomas S. Knisley, Company G
At age 24, he enrolled Sept. 28 at Oak Forest, and mustered in as a private at Uniontown on Nov. 6, 1861. He was soon appointed "one of the corporals" for the company, which officially became fifth corporal. Knisley was present in the Peninsula Campaign; he fell sick in Sept. 1862 and was in the hospital at Suffolk, VA, where he died on Nov. 4 of "disease." (Ronn Palm Collection)

Camp Near Suffolk Va
Nov 20th 1862

Well the Reconnoisance is over and we are back in Camp[.] we returned last night[.] you will know all about the reconnoisance and more too from the papers before you get this letter so I will omit a description of it as I could not give a very good one anyhow seeing I was not along[.] I dont reckon there was as much forageing done this time as there was before from the fact that things was pretty well cleaned up[.] the other time Lash and myself came in with a quarter of a hog apiece and about half a bushel of sweet potatoes[.] we carried them 15 miles[.]

the New yorkers & Pennsylvanians are the ornryest troops in the service[.] I have saw them shoot nice fat cattle just for the liver and they would shoot all the hogs and poultry they saw whether they wanted them or not and leave them lay[.] they are more barbarous than any rebs I have saw yet except the Lousianna tigers and Georgians[.] you very seldom hear of troops from any of them four states takeing any prisoners[.] it is extermination with them[.] the Mississippians and South Carolinians are also a hard set of men[.] the New england troops are the finest looking and most agreeable in the service[.] well I have no more to say on that subject so I will get some dinner and finish afterwards[.]

I have begun to need them boots and mittens but I have been waiting to be payed off so that I could send you some money[,] but we will not get our pay now until jannary[.] I sent the other for you to use if you had any use for it[.] money is no object with me[.] I will be very thankful to get home with my life and start square with the world[.] just take good care of my horse and dont get him spoiled and I dont care if you dont have a cent of money for me[.] I expect to still send at least half I make and I want you to recolect it is for your use and not to go on interest[.] I dont want you to do another stroke of work[.] you have done your share[.] I often go home in dreams and see you worked to death[.] just get some little girl to come and live with and wait on you and dont be afraid of comeing to want for you shall always have plenty[.] let no one attempt to put harness on that horse[.] I want that job myself[.]

you need not send a very large box[.] dont send any <u>canned fruit</u>[.] it is better to send <u>dried</u>[.] canned <u>butters</u> is very nice[.] I want you to send my bible[,] Willisons afflicted mans companion[,] and my shaveing apparattus[.] send some more soda[.] the other was spoiled with the oil[.] send me enough buckwheat flour to make a mess of cakes for four men along with directions how to mix it well[.] I cant think of any more extras now so

I will quit for the present & go down and see George Orbin[.][88] I forgot[,] I want 2 or 3 bottles of Davis painkiller[.]

Crouch has just got some boots and other things from home[,] among the rest a lot of beans that I can eat[.] well I expect you can fix out the balance better than I can tell you or I will mention one thing for fear you dont know[.] dont send any doughnuts[.] I have to eat too much grease anyhow[.] you may put in about a dozen onions[.] some of these long evenings while I am on picket waching for rebs[,] mell can be picking out walnut kernels for me[.] nuts are very good & wholesome too[.] I get plenty of apples here but if you can find a nice big sound vandiver put it in[.]

well I guess I have no more to say this time[,] only I dont think we will leave here this winter[.] if we do it will be pretty soon before you will have time to get the box ready and you will see it in the papers[,] but I dont apprehend anything of the kind[.] well I will quit and get some things fixed up as I will be on guard at Division headquarters tomorrow[.] give my love to all enquireing friends[.]

of course you will know that I want the boots and mittens sent in the box[.] we have had some bad weather already[.]

Camp Near Suffolk Va
Sunday Nov 23d 1862

Well I have just got back from preaching and got dinner over so I thought I would write some[.] I have not much to say either as I just started a letter daybefore yesterday but I have got my banner read through & did not get my Advocate yet so you see I run out of employment[.][89]

I was to have worked on onc of the forts today but did not have to go until tomorrow since old peck has been in command[.] sunday has been our chief business day[.] I have never had any confidence in the man & I also believe the old divil is a coward but he is like nearly all the rest of the officers both civil and military[,] I fear we will have a big time in this country if things dont work dofferent before long[.] I see rebelion has begun at home and if it goes on very extensively it is bound to begin in the army[.] all that thousands

---

[88] Private in Company C.

[89] McJunkin refers to *The Christian Banner*, published by the American Tract Society, and *The Sunday School Advocate*, published in New York by The Reverend Daniel Wise.

George Orbin, Company C

Orbin was born in Fayette County, and enlisted at Uniontown on Oct. 9, 1861, and mustered in there on Oct. 31. He was 21 years old with gray eyes, dark hair, a fair complexion, stood 5'10", and was a farmer. He began serving with the color guard shortly after his enlistment. He became color bearer at the end of July 1862 until early Sept. 1863, when his health gave out. On Sept. 6, 1863, Orbin carried the regimental color, being the first to enter the evacuated Fort Wagner, in Charleston, SC. It is noted that Orbin was deemed unfit for further field service on Sept. 19, 1863, because of sickness and was apparently going to be transferred to the Invalid Corps, having been disabled by chronic diarrhea for six months. In the remarks, it was stated: "He is a meritorious and deserving soldier and was in the battles of Williamsburg & Fair Oaks, Va, and Kinston, Whitehall, Goldsboro, N.C. He also participated in the siege and capture of Ft. Wagner, S.C." But the transfer was never made. Orbin was sent north to a general hospital on Jan. 21, 1864. He returned to the regiment in Sept./Oct. 1864, and mustered out with the unit in Pittsburgh on Nov. 22, 1864. after the war, Orbin became a minister and pastored a church at 169 Knox Avenue, in the Knoxville area of Pittsburgh. (History of the Old Flag)

here need is a little sign of backing from home[.] Patriotism is nearly played out in the army[.]

in my other letter I wrote for that box[.] it might be you would not get it so I will mention it in this one[.] in the first place I want my boots and mittens[.] send my bible[,] willisons afflicted man's companion & my shaveing apparattus[,] 2 or 3 bottles pain killer[.] send a can of thick cream fixed so that the stopper wont come out and spill it[.] I expect you will think I have gone clar fool but you need not be alarmed about it spoiling before it gets here[.] I have had no milk of any kind this summer and only 2 or 3 qts since I left home[.] I have had it in my head to send for a can of cream all summer[.] put in about a doz onions[.] dont put in any canned fruit as it is no better than stewed and takes up room for nothing[.] if you can get a chunk of homemade cheese put it in but dont go to the store and get it like you did last spring[.] we have any amount of that kind here now[.]

well I have no more to say at this time[.] I believe only you needent send a very large box and nail a hoop around each end[.] express it to Suffolk Va via Fortress monroe[.] be particular in directing it as the 85th N.Y. also belongs to our brigade[.]

We have got ready now to have our regular meetings[.] we had preaching in our new church today at 11 for the first[.] we just got it finished last evening[.] I will describe it[.] we got two new hospital tents and went to the woods and split pine trees and put legs to them[.] it is a cheap church but our congregation is small and we could not afford a better one but it is good enough[.] Cols Howell & Purviance were both at our meeting today[.]

I want you to write what has become of Allmon & Watkins[.] they have both quit writeing to us[.] I have not heard from either for a long time[.] tell Haman I think it is time for him to be writeing to me[.]

you appear to think I ought to come home on a furlough but I guess it is hardly worth while[.] I think the conservatives will bring the war to a close before long and then I can stay when I come for I still live in hopes that God will spare me to get home[.] but I would go now very quick if I could get to[.] I dont look for a furlough until the regt is disbanded[.] I frequently go home in my sleep[.] I was in the neighbourhood last night and took dinner at Pattersons[.] I had a very nice dinner and enjoyed my visit very much[.] sis and you were both there but did not have that little ugly piece of humanity along so I did not see it[.] Jim was also at home[.] we had a nice time[.] I have never saw either of them young monsters yet but had the promise of it sometime ago[.]

they say girls are very plenty in the north[.] the next time you write I want you to describe one as I would like to know what kind of animals they are and what they look like[.] if you can ketch one just put it in that box and send[.] I have saw nothing but soldiers and munitions of war for so long that

I have forgot what everything else looks like[.] they say the children are all born with knapsacks on their backs and muskets in their hands in the north now[.] tell sis that is the kind I want her to have the next time and to send it on to Suffolk to take my place as I have got tired of the business[.]

we dont get our pay until jannary[.] we will then have six months due[.] I will have to send this letter without a stamp[.] wills folks are all well[.] I looking for Miltons picture in their next letter[.] the last I heard from you was that receipt dated oct 29th[.] this is my 3d letter since[.]

[undated 1862 letter]

Well mother as I am writeing haman a letter I guess I will put in a note to you[.] I started you a letter today but I will want a little box as I dont think we will leave here for some time[,] and if we do it will be back to the fortress[.] I dont want a very costly one this time for fear I might not get it[.] I will mention a few little thing's that I would like to have[:] a couple of plugs sweet tobacco and a little horse leg[,] one bottle Pery Davis painkiller[,] a little paper of soda [(]I mean bakeing soda[)] [.] you know I was a great hand for snuff[.] I want a large blacking box of snuff[.] dont send any larger box than the last one you sent last spring and fill the balance with whatever you like[.] nail it up so that it will bear a goodeal of handling[.] I want you to dry me a good many tomatoes for the next box if it is not too late for them[.] I want mell to gather me as many chestnuts & hickorynuts as he can conveniently[.] hazle nuts is not bad if they are plenty there[.] send by Adams express to Fortress monroe[.] direct the same as if it were a letter[.]

tell mell now is his time to make his fortune[.] tell him to take care of all the specie he can get as one dolar of it will be worth two or three of paper in a year or two if not sooner[.] I think the war _must_ close before spring as the soldiers are becomeing desperate[.] they cannot be kept under much longer[.] for my part[,] since I have saw the way thing's have worked for the last six months[,] if I were out of the scrape the union might go to thunder[.] the war could have been over last june easier than not if them in power had have tended to their business but as I am in for it I intend to do my duty[.]

I forgot to tell you to start the receipt in a letter as soon as you start the box[.] I guess I have no more to say[.] I have not been very well on some days but today I feel about as well as ever[.]

[undated 1862 letter]

If this fight comes off you will hear of the Bloody 85th playing a conspicuous part[.] it is I think the best regt in the grand army of the Potomac[.] the worst thing about it is it is with a few exceptions commanded by gentleman officer's and they wont do where military officers are needed[.] if the men were no better than the officers it would be very disastrous to get into a battle[.]

we have been called into line of battle several times and the majority of the company officers were so much excited they could not even give the few commands they did know[.] one night we were called out there was a good many lightning bugs flying about in the woods and one officer in Co. D. could not be made believe they were other than signals[.]

our field officers are good men for the business[.] I will name them[:] Col Howell[,] Lieut Col m'giffin[,] Major Giler[,] Adgt Beazell[.][90] And I dont think our Brigadier Gen can be beat[.] he is a plain old Duchman about 45 years of age[.] Gen Casey puts me in mind of joshua baker rideing around with his big coat and and old slouch hat[.] he is 65 years of age[,] short[,] and about as thick as a barrel[.]

preaching has about played out in our regt[.] we still have prayer meeting twice a week[,] sunday and thursday nights[.] we have very small congregations now[.] they have droped off until there is not much over a hundred in the regt that attends meeting[.]

I had thought of feching you an Austrian rifle when I come home but I have changed my mind[.] they shoot oz balls and then they kick like mules[.] if you had one it would kick you so far you would never get back[.] I think I will try to get a couple of Berdans sharp shooter's rifles[.] they are picking off the rebel gunners at a 1/2 mile every pop[.]

We were payed off last sunday two months wages but we are so far back here in the swamp that I dont expect I can send any home this time[.] if we get to any place where I can get my likeness taken I will send a few home[.] we have lost three men since we came here[,] makeing nine in all since we came out[.]

this is the 4th letter I have wrote to you without an answer[.] I will give you the Direction in full and this I think will be my last to you until I get one or two[.]

Mr. Milton E. McJunkin
2nd Brigade Casey's Division
Co. D Col. Howell's 85th P.V.
Washington D.C.

---

[90] Lieutenant Colonel Norton McGiffin, Major Absalom Guiler, and an unknown name. The adjutant of the regiment in early 1862 was Andrew Stewart, Jr.

Absalom Guiler, Major
A veteran of the Mexican War, Guiler was enrolled as major of the 85th on Nov. 4, 1861, and mustered in with that rank on Nov. 10. He served with the regiment until discharged for disability, resigning his position on May 31, 1862. (History of the Old Flag)

1863

Camp Near New Bern N. C.
Sunday Jan 4th 1863[91]

Well I guess I will try to write a few lines today to let you know how we have been getting along[.] well to begin I am enjoying good health at present with the exception of a cold[.] Laddie is in good health[.]

Well I shall try to make out a report of our expedition[.] I expect you know all about it though before this[.] well to begin[,] we left Suffolk on the 5th at 4 o'clock in the morning[.] by the way there was a cold rain descending all day & part of the night[.] we marched 23 miles & halted[,] kindled big fires[,] & lay down until daylight[,] when we started & marched through Gatesville[,] stopped for the night[,] and in the morning which was sunday the 7th marched down to the Chowan river[,] took transports & arrived at roanoke island before daylight where we lay until evening[,] when we started off again and arrived here on tuesday evening the 9th[.]

we lay here until thursday the 11th when we started off with 10 day's rations[,] marched 17 miles[,] took 3 or 4 prisoners and stopped for the night[.] 12th we went a few miles[,] killed 3 or 4 rebs[,] took 8 prisoners[,] lost 5 or 6 of our men and kept on[.] 13th went a few miles[,] was fired into by the rebel pickets[,] 3 or 4 of our men being wounded[.] we then opened up with artillery but with no effect[.]

Saturday jan 10th 1863
Well I guess I will try to write a few lines today[.] to begin

---

[91] The 85th, together with the rest of the brigade, left Suffolk on 5 December 1862. The column marched southwest to the Chowan River, where it embarked on transports for Newbern, North Carolina. The troops arrived in this city on 9 December. Major General John G. Foster, commanding the Department of North Carolina, assembled a force of 12,000 troops to march inland to interdict the railroad at Goldsboro. McJunkin briefly describes the march and the fighting at Southwest Creek, Kinston, Whitehall, and Goldsboro. See Dickey, pp. 208-15, for more details.

I am enjoying good health[.] I received that box last sunday[.] the boots are just the fit[.] I can charge through the swamps now without getting my feet wet unless I get into some like that one we charged through at Kingston[.] we were frequently in to our middle there but I think it was better for us[.] it give the balls more room to pass over us[.]

       Camp Near New Bern N. C. jan 14th 1863

Just one month ago today I was fighting rebs in a swamp near Kingston N.C.[.] on the 13th we had a fight at South west Creek[.] none was engaged but B & D of our regt[.] there was only 60 of us in both Cos[.] we charged on the 62d N.C. numbering 400[.] we drove them[,] killing 13[,] takeing 10 prisoners and one howitzer[.] we did not lose a man[.] on the 14th our Brigade along with the 9th N.J.[,] 10th C.T.[,] & 5th Mass were engaged for 5 1/2 hours when the 103d & 85th P.V. charged on them and drove them at the point of the bayonet[,] captureing 250 prisoners & 9 guns[.] men never showed more steady bravery than did the 85th P.V.[,] 103d P.V.[,] & 9th N.J.[.] on the whole expedition we took the advance all through but it is no use writeing much for the mails are very uncertain here[.] I wrote two letters[.] perhaps you got them perhaps not[.]

I will just tell you I was in the battles of South West Creek[,] Kingston[,] White Hall[,] & Goldsboro[.] Laddie was in all and proved himself a good soldier[.] there is an expedition leaves here in a few days for Charleston S.C. but I guess we will remain here[.] since writeing before we have had another change[.] our Col was promoted to Brigadier but would not accept it unless they would let him have his old regt so they let him have us[.]

       so you can direct to
Co. D 85th P.V. Howell's Brigade[,] Farry's Division
       New Bern N.C.[92]

I was glad to get them book's and that painkiller[.] through the day the heat is oppressive here and the insects are a little troublesome[.] the health is generally good[.] no more at present[.] the commandments[.]

---

[92] The troops in North Carolina were reorganized in January into the Eighteenth Army Corps. The 85th was part of the Second Brigade, Third Division, Brigadier General Orris S. Ferry commanding. Colonel Howell commanded the brigade, which also included the 56th New York, 58th and 174th Pennsylvania.

Ocean Steamer Maple Leaf
off Hilton Head S.C.
Monday feb 2nd 1863[93]

Well I guess as the boy's are all writeing I will write some too[.] well to begin
I am enjoying good health at present[.] we left Newbern yesterday week[,]
came to Beaufort[,] took transports[,] and have not been on land since[.] we
were out of sight of land for forty eight hours[.] we had a very rough sea most
of the time[.] there was considerable spueing done but the boy's are all lively
as crickets now[.] I know nothing of our destination as yet[.] we thought at
first it was Savanna & Charleston[,] but we have come to the conclusion now
that it is Vicks Burgh[,] but I think we will know before long[.] well I have
no more to say at present[.]

3d Well I will write some more & perhaps I can get it started[.] Well
our gunboats took an english vessel and feched it into the harbor[.] the rebs
got to fireing on our fleet as we passed Charleston[.] I guess they sunk one of
our gunboats but they did no harm to the fleet[.]

you will hear of the fall of Savanna in a few day's[.] the old
ironsides[94] are pluging away[.] we will land as soon as we get a foot holt[.]

Lincoln's our leader
both ambitious and long
for niggers and conquest
we're marching along[.]

Some kind of a camp in a cotton field near
Beaufort S.C. on an Island I think it is
st. Hellena Sunday evening feb 8th[95]

Well we landed this afternoon so I thought I would begin a letter[.] to begin

---

[93] On 25-26 January 1863, Foster embarked part of his command to
reinforce Major General David Hunter's troops for an attack on Charleston, S.C.
Because of friction between the two generals, Foster's troops remained on board their
transports until 8 February.

[94] McJunkin refers to the ironclads that assisted the land troops in their siege
operations. One of the vessels was named *New Ironsides*.

[95] The regiment disembarked on St. Helena Island on 8 February and
remained here until 1 April 1863.

81

I am enjoying good health at present[.] we spent two weeks on board the old
Maple Leaf[.] we got four months pay yesterday so most of the boys had their
own times last night[.] I guess our expedition has blowed up[.] the officers
are afraid of us[.] well I will close for the present[.]

Wednesday Night 11th
Well Mother as our Chaplain has been appointed to take our money home I
will send you twenty dollars[.] as I am in a hury I cant write much knews[.]
the Chaplain starts tomorrow and if I am liveing and well I expect to go over
to Hilton Head in the morning to get some pictures[.] that is if I can get
transportation[.] we are still on st. Dalena island[.] I dont know when we will
leave[.] the Ironsides are pecking away at Savannah & Charleston[.] that is
all the knews I know at present[.]

there is six regts of niggers here but they are quiting the business
every chance they get[.] the nigs all wish they were with their masters[.] they
say they had better times while they were slaves than they have now[.]

for the present direct to the 3d Brigade Farry's Division Washington
DC

the money will either be left in Brownsville or mailed there to Centreville[.]

tell Libbie it is not because I have forgotten her that I dont write oftener[,] but
for lack of time and opportunity[.] tell her if I have no bad luck she shall have
that picture now shortly as I expect to get a few taken tomorrow[,] no
preventing providence[.] I have not had a letter from any body for more than
two months[.] I heard from home once through Zaid Jordan[.] no more at
present[.]

M. E. McJunkin

Camp St. Hellena St. Hellena Island S.C.
Monday feb 16th 1863

Well I guess I will write a few lines today but if I would do right I would not
write atal but I suppose you would not care if I dident write[.]

I have only been away from Suffolk something over two months &
you have written to me once dated jan 9th & 10th[.] I have sent mother $20
with the Chaplain[.] the health of the troops is excellent[.] I was never as fat
in my life[.] I go considerable over two hundred now[.] I have as big a double
chin as mrs baker[.] I started to Hilton Head the other day to get some
pictures[.] I went a few miles down the coast to try if I could find some way

of getting over but the first thing I knew the tide came in and penned me up on a little island so I had to just kindle up a fire and roast and eat oysters until evening and then I had to strip and swim about 25 yds[.] but if we stay here I am going to try it again the first opportunity[.] I hear the big guns in the direction of Savanna this morning[.] they have been thundering away a goodeal for the last two weeks[.] you never say anything about the weather or anything else[.]

the weather here is as warm as it is there in july[.] the niggers are getting ready to plant corn and cotton[.] Oranges are ripe now but the wild ones are so sour they are not fit to eat[.] there is six regts of niggers here but I dont think they will do much good[.] they are deserting every chance[.]

well I guess I have said all I can think of[.]

I guess the war is not going to be over for about forty years so I expect mother had better sell my horse[.] I would like to have him when I come home but I expect he will be a goodeal of bother to keep so I will give you leave to do as you please with him[.] you can either sell him or keep him until I come[.] I am going home the first good opportunity[.]

no more at present[.]
Mr. Milton E. McJunkin
Co. D 85th regt. P.V.
Howell's Brigade Ferry's Division
Washington D.C.

Isle st Hellena S. C.
feb 19th 1863

Well Haman[,] it's a nice thing to be a stout man generally but it has made it a little disagreeable since payday[.] we have had our own times for the last two weeks[.] nearly every night about half the regt are tight & so of course a goodeal of fighting done & when there is a fight on hands I generally get a job of tieing a man or two & dragging them to the guard house[.] the other day they had Bill Wolf & Levi Ogle in a tent & three men standing guard over them[.] they were both pretty tight so they concluded they would not stay under guard, so Wolf snached the gun from one of the guards and run him clear out of the regt and Ogle took the guns from the other two and drove them into the tent and stood guard himself[.] so the next thing in order was the officer of the day running around hollowing where's Jeff Low & McJunkin[.] so you see all we had to do was to just go & lead them to the guardhouse & tie them[.] one thing though I can manage drunk men of our own regt without much trouble now as they have found out by experience that the quieter they keep after they get into my hands the better it will be for them[.] but enough of this[.]

Well to begin I am blessed with excellent health at present for which I am thankful[.] I have only been off duty five days in the last thirteen months[.] I have done more duty and been in more danger than any other man in our company[.] I have smelt powder nine times[.] I did allow to write you a letter and then write Will one too but I must close for the present as it is bed time[.]

20th

Well I will try to finish this letter before I go on picket[.] well I have not much to say that would be interesting to you[.] as for the climate it is as warm here now as it is there in july[.] we have oranges and figs here in abundance but they are as dear here as there for you must know I have been no place for the last 15 or 16 months but where there was enough people to make everything dear[.]

Generals Foster & Hunter had a knockdown the other day When Foster gave the old nigger Genl a complete thrashing[.] I want you to tell me in your next letter what the people there think of Hunter[.] we have a very poor opinion of him here[.] Hunter has six regts of niggers here commanded by Gen Saxton[,] but they dont like the business and are deserting every opportunity[.][96]

Well I have no more of importance to write now so I will close and write will a letter and by that time I will have to go on picket[.]

tell mother I have had no chance of getting any pictures & I dont know when I will have a chance except Genl Casey succeeds in getting us back[,] which I hope he will[.] good bye for the present[.]

direct to

Isle St Hellena S. C.
March 24th 1863[97]

Well as it is a wet day I will try to scratch a few lines[.] I was goeing to write

---

[96] For background on the friction between the two generals, see Dickey, pp. 233-38. Brigadier General Rufus R. Saxton commanded a brigade of colored troops raised in the Department of the South.

[97] Sent to Thomas A. West, East Bethlehem, PA.

some yesterday but I was sent over to Hilton Head after some prisoners[.]

to begin I am enjoying good health at[.] Laddie is in excellent health[.] Will Hartman was sent to the hospital yesterday[.] he went over in the same boat I did[.] I dont know any name for his disease[.] it is getting very common among the soldiers here[.] it is the loss of speech[.] there was about twenty from our regt went over yesterday with the same disease[.] one of them has not spoke above a whisper for about four months[.] Hartman will likely get a discharge before long[.]

I would like to know'the reason you dont kill them Copperhead's in the north[.][98] if we had them here we would hang about 400 on every Palmetto tree on the island and leave them for the buzzards[.] we'd make targets of some of the worst of them[.] Our sole object from the start was the abolition of slavery in the united states and nobody need look for peace as long as there is a slave in said bounds and woe to the dirt eaters and military officers that are found in the united states when the army is disbanded[.]

I dont know just when we will take Charleston[.] I think before a great while though[.] if I am spared until this Charleston affair is over I am going to try for a furlough and if they dont give me one I think I shall go anyhow or die in the attempt[.] I will close for the present as we are looking for a mail today[.]

Well we got a mail[.] I got a letter[,] makeing four I have got since I left Suffolk[.] two of them was from home[.] I think you will do pretty well if you continue to write a letter every two months[.] us poor soldiers have a greateal of encouragement[.]

on the 4th of last may when we started in pursuit of the rebs we was ordered to leave everything behind except our havresacks & canteens & one day's rations[.] well we never saw them after[.] when we came to harrison's landing they compelled us to take another outfit which we had no earthly use for[.] we remonstrated but they told us it was no use[.] we would be charged with them whether we took them or not so when we left they were put on a schooner & it sunk and so that outfit was lost too[.] so now it takes four months of our wages to pay for clotheing which they forced us to get & lose[.]

the way they get the balance of our money the commisary department cheat us out of our rations & we have to go to the sutler and buy things at exorbitant prices to keep from starvcing[.] there is five months pay due us now but it will take all that to pay our clotheing bill[.]

another thing that makes me a little out of humor today[.] I had to give up my old <u>Austrian</u> yesterday evening[.] I had carried it so long & it had been of such service to me that it seemed like parting with an old friend[.] I

---

[98] Copperhead was the name for a Southern sympathizer in the North.

could kill a reb 500 yards every clip[.] I have still got an <u>austrian</u> of larger calibre than the first[,] but my old one was tried and I was the only man in our co that had carried the same gun all the way through[.] I had hoped to carry it clear home[.]

I have saw more than any other man in our co[.] if their was a detail made to do some hard or dangerous duty I was allways one of the number[.] I have been in every battle or skirmish the regt or co have while there is not another man in the co but has missed some either from sickness or being on other duty at the time[.] there is a good many that have never heard a ball whistle yet nor never saw a wild reb[.]

you can tell ad if he means David W. Crumrine that he belongs to our Co and is in good health and always has been & if he means Eli he is Co. B's fifer and is a first rate little fellow[.] I will give you the picture of the palmetto leaf[.]

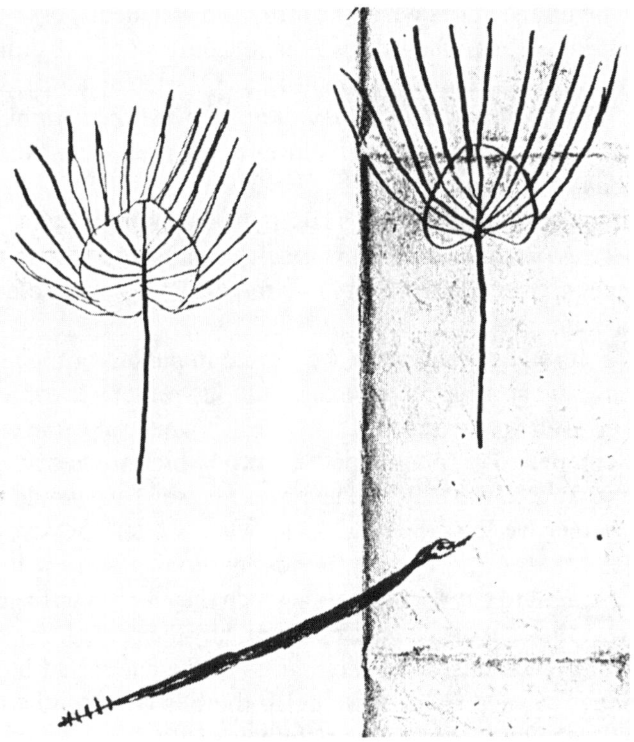

I have saw a few sights since I left home[.] I have been in six battles[,] two desperate bayonet charges[,] & several pretty brisk skirmishes to say nothing of the wood ticks[,] gallenippers[,] & body lice[.]

the weather is very warm[.] we are talking of burning Charleston[,] plowing it up[,] and sowing it with salt but some of the fellows kick against it as they want the salt to put on their fresh beef[.]

Folly Island S. C.

Sunday April 26th 1863[99]

Dear mother[:]

I received your most welcome letter of March 15th last week[.] I also received one from Nicholson & one from Mary[.] I am enjoying good health at present[.] I never felt better than since we left Virginia[.]

for the last three weeks 1300 of us have been fronting 75,000 rebs in sight of each other[,] only a narrow channel between us[.] we were in a rather precarious situation for awhile but we have now got things fixed so that it is impossible for them to land any troops on the island[.] we are looking every day for operations to begin[.] in the last three weeks I have been studying the matter over & I find but one point at which there can be a successful attack made[.] if the affair is conducted right we can reduce this place with comparatively little loss on our part and heavy loss to the enemy[.] but if hunter follows up his plan we will be defeated & our army cut to pieces[.]

but I suppose you dont know much about war & care less so I will discuss some other topics[.] Mary thinks I ought to send her my likeness[.] I think she has no right to claim either letter or likeness[.] I have been in the army for more than 1 1/2 years & she has written me one letter[.] but I will be christian like & give her a chance to get one on reasonable terms[.] more than a year ago I got a likeness taken which she was to have on the receipt of five letters & she failed to write any[,] so one went to Richmond[.] so now there is nine letters & a likeness of herself & family due before she need look for either likeness or letter[.]

I wrote you that if I was spared until this affair was over I was goeing home whether I got a furlough or not[,] but that has played out as I have not got enough money to pay my way home at present[.] if spared my time will be out in eleven months any how & then I can go home for good[.]

27th 63

well mother I expect you would rather hear how I am getting along than any other knews I could write[.] well mother[,] as a soldier for my country I have never failed to do my duty[.] I have took part in everything my co or regt has been in yet & in the last 15 months I have been off duty only 5 days[.] that is what not another man in the co can say & only 5 or 6 in the regt[.] as a

---

[99] Folly Island was south of Charleston harbor. The 85th was engaged in operations on this island from 6 April through 18 July 1863. On 26 March, the 85th became part of the Third Brigade, Second Division, Eighteenth Army Corps. The remaining units in the brigade were the 62nd and 67th Ohio, and 39th Illinois.

87

christian I have tried to do my duty but none but the man who tries it knows what it is to live a christian in the army[.]

we are persecuted less since we came into active service than while in camp at Washington[.] the boy's would often while at Goodhope[,] pick out men who in their opinion would turn out to be cowards & who brave men when we should come into battle[.] I overheard one of these conversations one day[.] I will give you part of it[.] now there's Mcjunkin[.] he'll not be of any account in battle[.] he's too d----d religious, never knew anybody that was so d----d strict but turned out to be a d----d coward[.] well I always took as little account of such talk as possible[.]

I was reminded of some of it on the 5th of may last, when we got within hearing of the musketry at Williamsburgh[.] 2 or 3 of our co sliped out of ranks & hid in the wood's (they were goodhope soldiers)[.] we had to march about a mile under fire of fort magruder & 2 or 3 redoubts[.] while marching along there, the shot, shell, grape & canister whistling over us[,] I saw some 8 or 10 more of our good hope soldiers trying to slip out of ranks[.] Lieut Michoner went to them & kept them to their places[.] I saw him point them to me & say look there at Mc your last winter's coward[.] he's the coolest man in the company[.] well mother I felt proud that I was a union soldier[.] I felt no fear although it was my first battle[.] something appeared to whisper to me that I was not to be harmed[.]

the next battle of note was Fair Oaks[.] I will tell you my feelings on that bloody field as near as I can[.] it was far the bloodiest battle I have saw yet[.] you will remember our co was on picket[.] I shall never forget the night of the 30th of may 1862[.] the whole heavens appeared to be our spread with one solid sheet of flame[.] I never heard any thunder to be compared to that & the rain fell in torrents[.] it lasted from dark until about 3 o'clock in the morning[.] Capt. Horn & myself sat at the foot of a large pine, half knee deep in water the entire night, watching the wild war of the elements & listening to the rebel cars running reinforcements into richmond[.]

between 12 & 1 o'clock I was standing at my post behind a large pine when 3 shells was thrown over into our camp[.] the word then passed down the line that a rebel brigade was seen deploying around to our right[.] I kneeled behind my tree & was peering through the bushes for the first sight of the rebel skirmishers[.] every thing was still as the grave when it appeared as if someone whispered in my ear (remember you are a union soldier[,] fear not you are safe)[.] I started up to see who had stole on me without my knoledge, but there was no one there[.] I then resumed my former position[.] some strange feeling came over me[.] I felt happy & dureing the 3 1/2 hours the balls were comeing like a hail storm, I felt no uneasiness for myself[.] I felt that I was goeing to come out of that battle unhurt[.]

Mother[,] I can say honestly I am a wiser and better man than when

John E. Michener, Companies E & K

Shown here with sideburns and gloves in hand, Michener was enrolled as a second lieutenant in Capt. Horn's company (D) on Sept. 8, 1861, at Zollarsville, and mustered in at Uniontown on Nov. 12. Then 24 years old, he served until receiving sick leave on July 25, 1862. Promoted a first lieutenant at Harrison's Landing on July 6, 1862, Michener was home at East Bethlehem, recuperating from illness. It appears that he was not officially sworn in at that rank until May 23, 1863, at Folly Island, SC. On Aug. 15, 1862, he was detailed by Gen. John Peck at Harrison's Landing to take charge of "baggage transport." From Jan. 17 through Mar. 1863, Michener served as the acting regimental quartermaster. On Aug. 22 that same year, he took command of Co. K, and was promoted captain on Dec. 3, 1863. He had charge of the skirmishers on an expedition to White Marsh Island, GA, on Feb. 22, 1864. Advancing too far, he and Cpl. James Bailey were captured. He was paroled Nov. 3, 1864, at Savannah River opposite Oakley Island. Michener was exchanged Nov. 15 for Confederate Capt. A. J. Lewis of Co. G, Powers Cavalry. A paroled prisoner of war, he mustered out and was honorably discharged on Dec. 22, 1864. One of the few officers admired by McJunkin, for his courage and bravery. (Ronn Palm Collection)

you last saw me[.] something always has & still whispers to me that I shall
return to my home[.] if I could get encouraging letters from home & enough
of them I could enjoy myself even here amid all the exposure[,] privations[,]
& hardships of a soldiers life[.] the worst enemies we have are the sneaking
cowardly traitors at home[.] it is them that are keeping us here[.] how think
you will they face <u>us</u> when we come home[.] I can assure them that in every
union soldier they will find a deadly foe[.]

    M. E. McJunkin

Folly Island S. C. Monday May 11th 1863

Dear Mother[:]

    I guess I will try to write you a few lines today[.] there is a strong sea
breeze goeing which keeps the gnats & mosquitoes away so that I can have
some chance to write. well to begin I am on picket & the butternuts over there
thinks I am an Ohio boy. so you see if they dont find out that I am one of Col.
Howell's Wildcats (as they call us) I will get to finish my letter without
exchangeing shots with them. I expect you will think I am insane or
something else[,] so I will explain the matter. well you see there is a deadly
enmity existing between the mississippians, lousianians, south carolinians,
georgians, & the Pennsylvanians & new yorkers. they seldom have a chance
at each other without makeing use of it.

    there is at present seven regt's on the island as follows, 62 & 67 Ohio,
39th Ill, 6th Conn, 4th N.H., 100th N.Y. & 85th P.V. all the picket fighting
that has been done here was in the 85th & 100th. the other troops talk with the
rebs & trade salt & coffee for tobacco & whiskey. the rebs hollowed over to
us last night, that Hooeker had gone into Richmond, with the loss of 30,000
men.[100] I think it is likely he has taken Jeffs capitol from him. we know old
Josey to be a fighting man. he would have went in to Richmond 11 months
ago if Mcclellan had not have been afraid of insulting his friend Jeff[.]

    May 12th
Well we will not be relieved until 9 o'clock so if the nats & gallenippers[101] let

---

[100] The Rebs were referring to Chancellorsville, where Major General
Joseph Hooker and the Army of the Potomac suffered a defeat at the hands of General
Robert E. Lee.

[101] Gallinipper was a name for a large mosquito.

90

Lewis Watkins, Company E

This early war photograph shows Watkins before receiving his "shoulder straps"; he wears non-commissioned officers pants and a four-button sack coat. Enrolled at Washington in Washington County at age 25, and sworn into the United States service on Wednesday Oct. 30, 1861, as a first lieutenant. He mustered in at Uniontown on Nov. 12. Began serving as acting adjutant on Jan. 1, 1863. Governor Curtin had appointed him a captain on Sept. 6, 1862, and took command of the company on Mar. 4, 1863. Officially promoted captain and mustered in on May 1, 1863, while at Folly Island, SC. In Dec. of 1863, he performed court martial duty. Watkins was given a leave of absence for 35 days to conduct the re-enlisted men of the regiment north for furlough from Hilton Head, SC, from Mar. 4 to Apr. 7, 1864. He sustained a wound at the Battle of Deep Bottom, VA, on Aug. 16, 1864, and died of his wounds Sept. 26 (also given as Sept. 4) while in the hospital at Fortress Monroe. (Ronn Palm Collection)

me alone I will try to finish my letter.

well the nats are makeing a grand charge on me.

I am enjoying reasonable health at present, but I am not quite as big as common. the hard duty along with the extreme heat & unhealthyness of the climate has pulled 30 lbs of beef off of me in the last month. the guard duty is what is takeing the beef from us. we have been on guard every other night for 1 1/2 months. the troops here are in better health & spirits than I ever saw them before. we are not as fat as we were on st Hellena but we can stand more.

I received a letter from sis on last sabbath marked No. 1. her & mell thinks I had better not come home, but I guess I will have to go anyhow, as nearly all the plagues of Egypt are here, in the shape of Alligators[,] sharks[,] swordfish[,] & I dont know how many other thing's to annoy us when we go in to bathe & then on land we have to contend with the rattlesnakes[,] copperheads[,] moccasins[,] vipers[,] & 40 other kinds that I have no names for, & about 40 different kinds of scorpions & lizzards & at least 1,000 kinds of insects, any one of which is enough to put a man crazy & then to top it out the wood ticks[,] body lice[,] stinking swamps[,] & scorching sun. why the confederacy is not worth two cents if south carolina is a sample[.]

Well I have been on the signal tower takeing a look at Charleston & whatever else might be seen, so I will tell part of what I discovered. well in the first place I seen James Island literally covered with fortifications & rifle pits. a good many are mounted with palmetto guns. I guess they must think we have no glasses over here. I could see the statue on the Calhoun monument & the clock on a steeple & could very well near tell what time it was. I guess I have wrote enough today. I got a letter from will the other day. his famly are all right. I guess we will have no fight here[.] I think if we let them alone awhile they will go away peacably[.]

I sent Tom & sis a likeness & a box of shells[.] I could get no stamps. I dont know whether they will go or not[.]

May 19th 1863 At half past two I discover that I have a furlough & am to be on board the Nelly baker by four o'clock, five miles distant. I immediately pack up & am there in good time but no time to gather any curiousities[.]

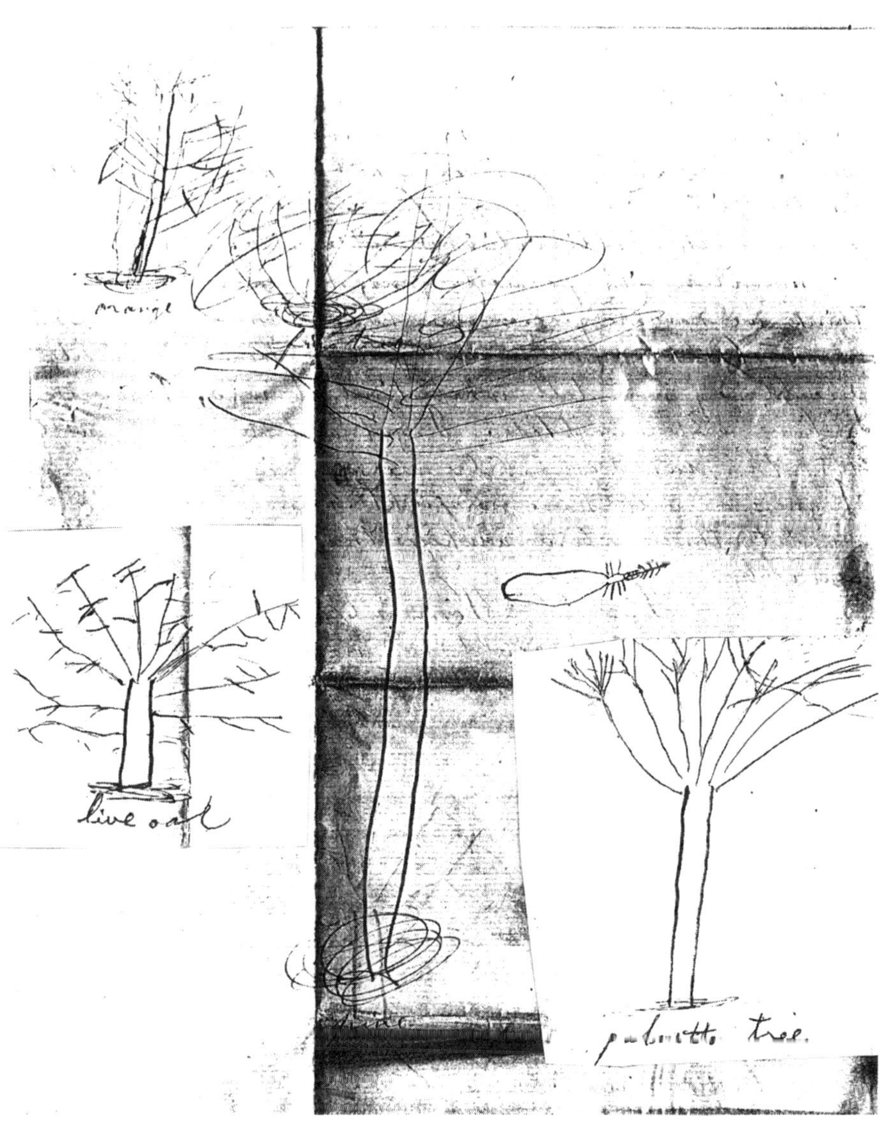

mangl
live oak
palmetto tree.

To all whom it may concern

The bearer hereof, Milton McJunkin, a private of Captain Rolla O. Phillips' company (D) of the Eighty-fifth Regt. Penna. Vol. Infantry, aged 24 years six feet three inches high, fair complexion, grey eyes, dark hair, and by profession a farmer, born in the county of Washington, and enlisted at Beallsville, in the state of Pennsylvania, on the fifteenth day of October, Eighteen hundred and sixty-one, to serve for the period of three years, is hereby permitted to go to his home in the county of Washington, state of Pennsylvania, he having received a <u>Furlough</u> from the 23d day of May 1863 to the 23 day of June 1863, <u>for good conduct in the line of duty</u>, at which time he will rejoin his company or Regiment at   or wherever it may then be, or <u>be considered a deserter</u>.

Subsistence has been furnished to the said Milton McJunkin to the 22d day of May 1863, and pay to the 28th day of February 1863 both inclusive.

> Given under my hand at Camp Peck, S. C.
> This 19th day of May 1863.
> > [s] H. A. Purviance
> > Lt. Col. Commanding 85 Regt. Penna. Vols.

[following is written across the above:]

Ration paid from May 23 to June 22/63[.] Capt. Dan S. Hart CST NY June 20/63[.] Ration from June 20th to June 24 inclusive and five days rations enroute to Hilton Head furnished by state NY soldiers depot NYork June 25, 1863 G. K. Roberts Recg Clerk

[printed form]

HEADQUARTERS, U. S. FORCES

Hilton Head, S. C. _______ June 29th__1863

Permission is granted to Milton McJunkin 85th Pa. Vols. to pass to Folly Island to rejoin his regiment.

> By order of Col. JOHN L. CHATFIELD
> [s] S. S. Stevens
> Lt. & A.A.A. Genl.

Morris Island S. C. July 17th 1863[102]

Well Mother[,] I guess I will have to write with a pencil this time as I have not been in camp since I came back[.] I have been up here in front all the time and have no ink with me[.]

well the rebs are still in Charleston. the siege is still goeing on satisfactorily. so far our loss has been the heaviest. we made four assaults on fort Waggoner and was repulsed each time with heavy loss. the 76th P.V. lost 206 men. we are working away with artillery now[.] I dont think there will be much more infantry fighting. it is generally thought that we will have possession here in 3 or 4 weeks.

I have been acting sailor for the last few day's, skedadling around through these channels in serf boats. you ought to have seen us getting out of one of them daybefore yesterday. there was five of us in the boat and we made the old thing fairly get out of the water and fly[.] we run right away from the rebs, 30 in number[.] well I must quit for the present[.]

I dont think this is a very healthy place from the amount of iron that is being scattered around. there is one continual roar of artillery and has been for a week[.] the screaming of the shells as they fly through the air has got so common that we dont pay any attention to them any more. I have written 2 or 3 letters home but received no answer yet[.]

the weather is awful warm here[.] I come pretty near goeing up the spout twice since I come back with heat[.] I have fattened up considerably since I came back[.] I weigh nearly 200 again[.]

no more at present[.]

Morris Island S.C. July 27th 1863

. . . all things are ready and the goose hang's high
Hog killer. Deer sur[:]

it is with the gratest off plasur i resume my sete to anser yor gloreus leter off the forth which i receved last weak[.] well 2 begin I will give you a deskription off Shurmen[.] he is 35, 5 ft 11 inch[.] hi giten bald & gra but brested hevvy bilt and rather dark complecshun[.]

---

[102] Morris Island was just south of Charleston harbor. The 85th conducted siege operations on this island from 18 July through 15 October 1863. In this letter, McJunkin writes of the first assault on Fort Wagner, which took place on 11 July. A second attack followed on 18 July.

    well the rebs are shelling us like blue blazes so I will cut my letter short. our loss so far as near as I can learn is about 3000 in killed and wounded. we still have 8 or 9000. if we can make out to hold our own until we get reinforcements charleston is gone up, and I have no doubt but we can. we have breast works within 200 yds of fort wagner and a mile of sumpter. we expect to commence throwing hot shot into charleston tomorrow. the north end of folly and all of morris island is literally covered with iron. there has been one continual roar of artillery for more than two weeks. well I guess thats all. there is only 4 letters due from home now.

Morris Island S.C. Aug. 5th 1863

Well Mother I will send you $25 now. if Will Hartman is there give him five dollars. if he aint there just let it rest. I will likely hear from him soon at least he promised to write.

I am in good health at present.

I came out of the trenches night before last and from the looks of my right ankle I dont think I will travel about very brisk for a few day's. the siege is progressing finely. we are still fortifying and mounting heavy guns. we have got worked right up to the rebel forts. thats all.

6th Well, all's still right.

my ankle did not get as sore as I expected[.] my foot and ankle is goodeal swelled, but I can walk about[.] I think I will be ready to go into the City with the rest of the boys[.]

Morris Island S.C. Camp
Misery   85th Regt.Co. D
U.S.A. August 16th 1863

Deer sister[:]

I receved yor lettre a male or tu ago and it is with the gratest of plasur i rite 2 inform you that i am well and about ete up with flies[,] gallinipers[,] and flee's and about cooked to bute, and hope thes fu lines may find u enjoying the same blessen. well i must quit as the old chap that is bossing this contract says we must not rite any nuse till we whip the skunks over about charleston which we will du gist whenever wc git reddy. I expect tu by this place whe the war is over and start an iren fondry[.] it is a bully centry fur iren[.] its bin ranen iren for 1 1/2 months and its gitten tu rane harder every day[.]

17th wel its rayther nisy around here to da[.] theres nigh about a thousan big guns bin hollerin aroun here sense daylite[.][103] thare maken the briks fly out of sumter like ships[.] a feller wud notarly surpose frum the wa were pepperen em at prisint that we'd soone hev the plaise but if we git it agin crismus wele be doen purty wel[.] curnel houl was sevarely kilt in the hyp las nite with a shel[.] it is not considerd dangerus[.] i murst close fur the prisint but remaneth yor affecshunate bruthern[.]

---

[103] McJunkin refers to the first bombardment of Fort Sumter.

Ross R. Sanner, Company H

Mustered in at age 19, and appointed second sergeant on Nov. 12, 1861, Sanner was promoted to first sergeant on July 1, 1862, and then first lieutenant on Aug. 1, 1862. He was wounded Aug. 21, 1863, in the neck by a sharpshooter while in the trenches in front of Fort Wagner on Morris Island. Placed on the steamer *Cosmopolitan*, Sanner was transported to the hospital at Beaufort, SC, arriving there on Aug. 27. He returned to duty on Dec. 6, 1863 (some accounts give the date as Aug. 13). Sanner was absent to conduct veteran volunteers north on furlough Feb. 25, 1864. Promoted captain May 1, 1864, then Sanner was wounded again on June 18, 1864, at Ware Bottom Church, VA, and sent to the hospital at Fortress Monroe. This wound rendered his right arm entirely useless. He was sent to recover at his home in Somerset, PA, but returned to the regiment on Aug. 1, 1864. Sanner resigned on a surgeon's certificate Sept. 22, 1864, owing to his wounds–stiffness of neck, and paralysis in the arm because of nerves being severed. (Ronn Palm Collection)

19th wel this makes the 3d days regler bumbardment[.] the hul airth has been trimblen like a shared sheap[.] thares more iren on this iland than you ever sean in awl yore wiked life[.]

our blak bruthern fites purty wel[.] thares one regt ub them in our briggade[.] ile giv u a deskripshun uv our mode uv life hear[.] wel our regt occupied the frunt trenches the uther day (we occupie the front trenches 1/3 of the time)[.] wel I went tu gunter and sez I[,] gunter les slip up to that hole and du sum sharpshuteing[.] agrede sez gunter[.] wel we crawled up very sly and got our persetion undiscuvered by the inimy[.] wel I peaps up and seas 3 rebs trien tu git a shot at some uv our sharpshuters so I pluged away at the fattest uv them but befor i cud git mi hed down fiz fiz went sum bals apast it[.] i peped over agin and seas a fat reb craulin around trien to git a better persition so i blazed awa and he jumped gist 27 ft in accordin to multiplication[.] while i wus laffen at him runnin fiz fiz fiz went sum more bals apast which reminded me that mi persition was none to the inimy[.] tu make a long story short thats the wa weve bin livein here fur nearly 2 months[.]

no more at present but remaneth the same as before[.]
Dida

Camp Misery S. C.
Near the City of Destruction
August 31st 1863

sometime ago I sent $25 home[.] if it has arrived please mail $5 to Will hartman[.] I will give you his addres in full[:]
Mr. William Hartman
1st Battalion Invalid Corps
Fort Schuyler
care Lieut. A. H. Wands
I am not certain whether Schuyler is in N.Y. or N.J. you will know and can put the state to it[.]

in the last week the 85th has lost upwards of 50 men[.] Col. Purveyance was killed yesterday. Col. Howell will hardly recover. our regt is now left with but a few d----d things at thc head of it. we have started Col. Purveyance's corps home. I thought night before last that Wilson was wounded, but he was only stunned[.] he is all right now[.] Wm. Garber of our

Joseph M. Johnson, Company I

Johnson was 28 years old when he enrolled Aug. 27, 1861, at New Salem. He mustered in as second sergeant of Capt. Weltner's company on Nov. 11. Promoted first sergeant May 23, 1862, he was again promoted on Mar. 6, 1863, to second lieutenant, and although he performed duties of that rank, he was not mustered until Sept. Johnson was wounded at Morris Island, SC, on Aug. 30, 1863. Although only a second lieutenant, Johnson commanded Co. I starting Nov. 2, 1863. He was furloughed home on Jan. 7, 1864, to attend to his sick wife and children. Wounded by a bullet in the left thigh at the Battle of Ware Bottom Church on May 20, 1864, and sent to the hospital at Fort Monroe, Johnson was furloughed home on May 31. He rejoined the regiment on July 10, 1864, and was assigned to special duty as the acting regimental quartermaster on July 13, 1864. He was honorably discharged Nov. 22, 1864. (Ronn Palm Collection)

co was killed[.][104]

     no more at present[.]

Morris Island S. C.

October 3d 1863

Well Mother, I guess I will scratch a few lines today. well to begin I am enjoying very good health at present. I have been sick none since I came back. I got my ankle hurt a little one night in the trenches & it got pretty sore, but did not disable me from doing all my duty. I had to go barefoot for nearly three months. I have only been wearing my boots about a week now. since the siege begun our regt has lost 81 men in killed and wounded. the rebs still shell us as much as ever, but since Wagner and Gregg has fell into our hands they dont do as much damage.

enclosed you will find the happy family as they appeared day beforeyesterday morning after a hard nights fatigue. Daugherty is on my right, Burson on my left.[105]

I have heard nothing from al or will since I came back. I answered both their letters. I have had some letters from Cousin Ella. I also receive one or two letters a week from my wife.[106] I want you to quit work altogether.

Folly Island S. C.

Nov. 2nd 1863[107]

Well Mother, as I have received two letters from home since I wrote any, for fear you get to thinking I have forgotten you, I will just try to scratch a few

---

[104] Lieutenant Colonel Purviance was killed on 30 August, as was William Garber. Theophilus Wilson was stunned by the nearby explosion of a shell. See Dickey, p. 278, for details of the fighting at the end of August.

[105] Alfred Dougherty and Corporal Joseph W. Burson.

[106] McJunkin was not married, so this is apparently in jest.

[107] After leaving Morris Island, the 85th camped on Black Island for a time (15-20 October), then moved back to Folly Island, where it remained from 16 October through 6 December 1863.

lines tonight, before tattoo.

well to begin I am still in the enjoyment of bully health. I can devour a considerable amount of junk and salt horse, along with any amount of other stuff such as oyster's, lizzards, sharks, and such other stuff of like character. you will be surprised to see folly island at the top so I will tell you how it is. well we are on the back track. I expect to make the round against next fall. the regt came here last thursday, but I did not arrive until last night, as I was left back to take care of the baggage and fetch it up. we just finished pitching our tents this evening.

now I will tell you why we came back here. we took Morris and black Islands, and fortified them so that the d----d, cowardly New england son's of b-----h's could hold them, and we are here now reorganiseing, expecting to do the same to jim Island after a while. I have to laugh when I talk of reorganiseing. there's the army of the potomac. they will have a little skirmish, and then spend 3 or 4 months reorganiseing. now this little band here has done more in the last four months than the army of the potomac ever done, and is in better fighting condition tonight than any army ever was.

you growl about my short letters. I wonder if this one is interesting. I always write as much as I feel like writeing. General Order's dont check me a bit. I will send you a bit of paper in this letter that General Gillmore gave me some time ago.[108] it will show you what he thinks of his little band of heroes. I will add though on my own hook that the navy has never done anything[,] only bother us. Col Howell got back yesterday. I was very glad to see him back again.

What does mary mean by not wanting ad or me to write anything only what she may see. I am sure I allow her to see anything I write home. I received a letter from ad sometime ago but have not had time to answer it yet. I want you to give me his adress in every letter. I would answer his letter tonight if I knew his adress.

well I expect I am worrying your patience already, so I will quit. you may send me some stamps in your next[.] send one of my photograph's in your next. my wife wants one and this is a poor place to get any. well I must stop scribbling[.] be a good girl. strive to enter in at the narrow gate.

Tell Mary if I get time to make them I will send her baby a string of beads in my next.

3d Wagner, Gregg Battery, Illinois[,] and the monitors have been belting away at the reb fortifications for a week, just tareing them up from the foundation.

---

[108] Brigadier General Quincy A. Gillmore relieved General Hunter as commander of the Department of the South on 12 June 1863.

[enclosure in letter of 2 November]
[Printed form]

Department of the South, Headquarters in the Field,
Morris Island, S.C., Sept. 15th, 1863.

GENERAL ORDERS.

It is with no ordinary feeling of gratification and pride, that the Brigadier General Commanding is enabled to congratulate this Army upon the signal success which has crowned the enterprise in which it has been engaged. Fort Sumter is destroyed. The scene where our country's flag suffered its first dishonor, you have made the theatre of one of its proudest triumphs.

The fort has been in the possession of the enemy for more than two years, has been his pride and boast, has been strengthened by every appliance known to military science, and has defied the assaults of the most powerful and gallant fleet the world ever saw. But it has yielded to your courage and patient labor. Its walls are now crumbled to ruins, its formidable batteries are silenced, and, though a hostile flag still floats over it, the fort is a harmless and helpless wreck.

Forts Wagner and Gregg,--works rendered memorable by their protracted resistance, and the sacrifice of life they have cost,--have also been wrested from the enemy by your persevering courage and skill, and the graves of your fallen comrades rescued from desecration and contumely.

You now hold in undisputed possession the whole of Morris Island, and the city and harbor of Charleston lie at the mercy of your artillery from the very spot where the first shot was fired at your country's flag, and the rebellion itself was inaugurated.

To you,--the officers and soldiers of this command,--and to the gallant Navy which has co-operated with you, are due the thanks of your Commander and your Country. You were called upon to encounter untold privations and dangers; to undergo unremitting and exhausting labors; to sustain severe and disheartening reverses. How nobly your patriotism and zeal have responded to the call, the results of the campaign will show, and your Commanding General gratefully bears witness.

Q. A. GILLMORE,
Brig.-General Commanding.

Folly Island S.C.
Nov. 20th 1863

Well mother, I have come to the conclusion that I must have a small Express box, as most of the boy's are sending for them. I want a couple of bottles of Davis painkiller[,] the balance in dried fruit, and butter's. I want <u>no</u> cakes at all.

I never had as good health as I have at this time, but I am out of pain killer, and it is all the medicine I ever take. in this country, a man may be in the best of health one day, and the next have none[.] just start the box at once[.] dont wait anything about it[.] just start it immediately and not be waiting to see whether the war will be over before it has time to arrive. if it gets here I will attend to it, and if it dont let it go to thunder.

I guess thats all I have to say at present.

M. E. McJunkin

    send it by Adams' express.

Port Royal S. C.
Dec. 13th 1863[109]

Well Tom, I expect you will think I am off the train track, but you see the war aint over yet. you stand a very good chance to be drafted yet before this time next year. you are a mechanic and could get from 3 to 5 dollars a day working for uncle sam and be clear of the draft[.] you could likely get in at Pittsburgh. Harry Fulmeran[,] old member of our Co discharged last summer a year, is getting 4 dollars a day, and is no mechanic either.

I wish my time was out. I think we could make our fortune pretty easy. if I live and keep my health the other 10 months of my time I wont care much how long the war lasts. I wouldent come out again to save the union as long as there was a man in the united states who had not done as much as me. you can tell mother she need not be anyway's alarmed about me soldiering any longer than 10 months more. I dont see what difference that will make to them though. Pennsylvania is not my home.

sis wrote to me that price and mctarry had made it up[,] that price had give jim a dollar and a quarter to make it up. I think money must be pretty scarce $1.25[.] I guess they have come to the conclusion to let us remain here this winter and rest.

----

[109] Sent to Thomas A. West. The 85th camped on Port Royal Island from 7 December 1863 through 22 April 1864.

Joshua B. Howell, Colonel

Just a day after his 58th birthday, Howell's demise came when riding a new horse after taking temporary command of the 3rd Division of the 10th Corps on Sept. 12, 1864. Upon leaving Corps headquarters after midnight, and checking the animal from taking a wrong road, the horse reared, tumbled over backwards and crushed the unfortunate Howell. He was put in a tent and remained there until the next morning before being attended. Taken to the brigade hospital, Howell was unconscious until his last minutes, when he roused, but was unable to speak. He died of internal injuries, a severe concussion, and a possible hemorrhage, at 10th Corps headquarters near Petersburg, VA, during the evening of Sept. 14. A field funeral was held with his brother Masons officiating, and music played by the 39th Illinois band. Soldiers of the 85th paid their respects as Howell lay under a shelter of boughs. On Sept. 17, the 85th escorted the dead Howell for delivery North. His body was embalmed and secured by his brother, Dr. T. P. Howell. Seven months later, he was named a full brigadier general from the date of his death. He was buried at Eglington Memorial Gardens at Clarksboro, NJ. (Ronn Palm Collection)

Port Royal S. C.
Dec. 27th 1863

Well I got no letters in the two last mails, and therefore ought not to write for six months, but I have a photograph to send, and therefore, will have to write.

I went up to brigade Head quarters on Christmass eve, and Genl. Howell gave me his photograph, at my request. you know he used to be our Col. and signed his name Col. on the photograph[.] it is his own hand write. he still thinks there is none like the 85th. he told me if it ever happened that we were taken out of his Brigade he would resign the star and come back to his old 85th.

I will send Col. Purviance's photograph before a great while, and as soon as I get them, one of every member of Co. D, and then I want a five dollar Album[,] Col. Purviance put first and Genl Howell next. when we get payed off again I expect I will send you some money to get the Album and about 50 of my photographs to send here.

since writeing before Genl Gillmore was married to Capt. Bragg's mother[.] the wedding came off last week.

we had a fat old christmass[,] as fat as salt junk and wormy hardtack could make it[.] some of the boys fared a little better. they got something to drink by stealing marches on the officers demijohns[.] the red fox (a member of co. D) also captured a duck, all on the sly. the happy family struck out through the country christmass night, but instead of captureing anything, came very near being captured themselves. we were very glad to get back to camp with whole hides.

I sealed up that furlough and started it, and you never wrote whether you got it or not. if you did I want you to take care of it[.] I want you to take good care of this photograph, and all others that I shall send[.]

I have wished since that I had not countermanded the order about that box, but its no difference now. there is no certainty of us staying here any length of time[.] we may stay through until spring.

Bottom Monitor

Margaret McJunkin

[undated 1863 letter]

Port Royal, Hilton head
Camp Black, 85th P. V.
Department of the South
Gordon's Division
Howell's Brigade
Abraham's Regiment
Co. D
Commanded by Captain Rolla A. Phillips
Down in Dixie
South Carolina
Hog Killer

Dear Sir[:]

it is with feelings of anxiety I set down to adress you a short epistle for your own special benefit. it was with a sorrowful heart that I heard of your affliction's. to cinvince you of my tender feeling's toward's you I have gone to the trouble of collecting some seed's to send you so that you might have an opportunity to raise your own medicine. the name of it is Vermafuge. they do say you have become wormy. the medicine help you if there is as many worms in you as there is in our hard tack.

to return to my subject[,] vermafuge is as plenty here as ragweed's are there.

Gunter has just gone to buy some more pies with the paper off an ink bottle[.] its been very wet and stormy for some days[.] the night we were on the sea, the monitor Wehawken was sunk by the storm[,] the crew all lost but three. they say the rebs are still in Charleston.

I guess you needent to be laughing at us poor devils, because we have to soldier 10 month's longer. you must recolect that the men that end this war are not born yet[.] your time to soldier comes after awhile.

take care of yourself[.] it's only two years till you'll have to come too and then it's my turn to laugh[.]

1864

Camp 85th Regt. Pa. Volunteers,
Gillmore's Command, Seymour's Division
Howell's brigade, Hilton Head Island
Port Royal, South Carolina, Department of the South
January 9th one thousand eight hundred and sixty four.[110]

Felix. Dear sir[:]

I received your wholesome epistle last night, which renewed my sorrow's on your behalf. you stated you had received the worm mixture, which you affirmed operated like Magick. for that wonderful cure I am thankful. it will gain me renown as a physician. I also sent you a prescription for the dumfumblin's, which I doubt not will have the desired effect, but, for your last contracted disease, I have nothing to offer. you state it was brought on by eating confection's. now any one who can be such a hog as to make himself sick eating them filthy animal's, there is no help for him, except his constitution is able to bear it, which I hope yours is[.]

I am also very exceedingly sorroful for the affliction's of my Dear beloved relative who you affirm, still has a desperately frightfully lame back. I feel very confident though, that I can write out a prescription that will cure it desperately. let the patient first take a cartrige box, place it on the small of the back, strapping it firmly on with the shoulder and waist belt's. then, hang a canteen and havresack, roll his overcoat neatly, and strap it on the top of the knapsack. then place the whole thing neatly between his shoulders. then, with the right hand, seize an austrian rifle, and for three years march over the Confederacy, esorcizeing himself with the spade, axe, and pick, frequently goeing through the bayonet exorcize, as also that of loading and fireing, and dodging shell's. that, I think, will relieve a lame back.

I was very sorry to hear of mother being sick. tell her if she dont take a little better care of herself, and quit acting the fool, to try to save money for me. she need never look to see me in pennsylvania again. I dont send the

---

[110] Sent to Melville McJunkin.

money for her to save for me. I want the rest of you to see if you cant treat her a little better.

Port Royal, S. C.
Jan. 17th 1864[111]

Well, sunday morning inspection is over, so I will say something about that terrible box which I received the other day. I cant contrive how you got it loaded in the waggon. the boxes the other fellows got wouldent have held over 60 such boxes as mine. its no difference now,

the other day as I was walking over the country, I found the grave of a pennsylvanian in the swamp about 1 1/2 miles from the graveyard. why he was buried there alone I cannot tell. perhaps he was a hard character and not considered fit to be put in the common grave yard, and perhaps some of his officers had a spite at him and thought they would disgrace him after he was dead.

the pages of necrology will be largely increased by the present war. literary industry will write up the biographies of most who greatly distinguish themselves, either battling for or against the nation. we shall have a deluge of memoirs[,] narratives[,] and military histories[.] every army correspondent will write about forty volumes[.] our book shelves will contain new companions to the old favourites of long ago. our libraries will dazzle with military portraits, and our curiosity drawers will hold relics of many a battle field. our great loyalty, as well as our national apreciation of heroic deeds, will cause us to venerate and worship the many, proud names that were not born to die.

but while we pay deserved respect to our Genl's and field officer's, we shall inadvertently overlook the invaluable services, the great hardship and suffering's of the common soldiers, <u>the million or more of brave, patriotic men</u>, who sacrificed the comforts of home, the proffits of business, the tenderest ties of affection, to uphold the old flag, and to conquer the enemies of a free, liberal, constitution government. the nature of all military organizations is to render the common soldier impersonal, to throw him into the cleft and chasm of battle, and if killed, simply to stop his pay and rations, or as Byron said, spell his name wrong in the newspapers.

we know something of the poor soldiers life. we have seen 100,000 and more of gallant men in the ill-stared army of the potomac, and thousands

---

[111] Sent to Thomas A. West.

109

more equally brave and heroic in this besieging army, have seen them in camp, on the march, and on the field of battle, and can testify to the severe trials, hardships, exposure and suffering to which they are inevitably allied, foot sore, overwearied, overburdened, and often (but necessarily) ill fed, under torrid heat, and freezeing cold have we seen them perform their duties, manfully and cheerfully, and we have also gone over the field of carnage, when the grass was yet wet with blood, have heard that saddest of all sounds, the wounded soldiers last sigh, and have counted thousands of tombless heroes shot and mangled beyond recognition. those dead soldiers, scattered over meadows, grainfields, orchards or in trenches and paralell's, festering in the sun, or stark and frozen by the winter's frost, with torn and clotted garments, always come back to us when we reflect upon the shocking, terrible realities of the present war, and how many hearts are saddened, how many homes are desolated by the loss of the unreturning brave.

two years ago these dead heroes were at home, on the farm, in the coal bank, in the work shop, or in the manufactory, talking of soldier life, the camp, the march, the bivouac, and jocosely saying that when this cruel war is over they would shoulder their crutch and show how fields were won. alas, they will never more return to relate campaign incidents or camp fire tales. grass is growing over their graves. the birds sing their lonely requiem and summer flowers have written their epitaphs in blossoms of red and gold. we owe an immense debt of gratitude to the rank and file of our armies. they have borne the great burthens of the war. they have fought our battles, won our victories and rolled back the accursed waves of rebellion. thousands have died on the field, or in the hospital, and many thousands more have gone home with crippled limbs, or seriously impaired health. let us not forget those brave men. let us not overlook their ill paid services. <u>they have fought the great battles of constitutional freedom between a slave oligarchy and a republican government</u>. they are the <u>unnoticed heroes</u> whom a grateful people and nation should respect and honor. other busines calls me from the desk.

I forgot to say I am enjoying good health at present[.]

Obituary

Lieut. Col. H. A. Purviance, Killed on Morris Island, Aug. 30th 1863.

Oh, thou famed and fatal fortress
On the far off southern shore
Thine shall be a name of anguish
In our bosoms ever more
Let a nation shout in triumph
O'er the crumbling of thy wall
Our poor hearts can only shudder
At the purchase of its fall.

Oh, our brother, brave and gentle
Could a thousand strongholds pay
For the one life in a moment
From his country snatched away
Who shall lead her sons to honor
With a soul so high and pure
Who shall guide their young ambition
To the glories that endure.

Only now is left the lesson
That his life or death imparts
In his country's page of glory
In the love of liveing hearts
Free from self or sordid motive
He the path of duty trod
Serveing best his kind and country
That he served from love of God.

On the heroe's wreath of laurel
Fall like dew the soldiers tears
And the mem'ry of his valor
All his goodness more endears
Oh thou famed and fatal fortress
On the far off southern shore
Thoughts of tenderness and anguish
Cling around thee evermore

January 29th 1864
M. E. McJunkin

Henry A. Purviance, Lieutenant Colonel

McJunkin admired Purviance so much that he wrote a poem commemorating the gallant lieutenant colonel. Sergeant John B. Bell noted in his diary about the demise of Purviance. "A dark day in the calendar of the 85th Regiment. . . . During the forenoon while the fire was brisk, from both sides, Lieut. Col. Purviance was killed by a shell from our owns batteries, prematurely exploding; the shell exploding immediately above him, carrying away the whole back part of his head, a fragment of the shell passing through the body near the heart, and another fragment lacerating the right arm, in a horrible manner. The remains of the Lieut. Col. were sent north while the Regiment remained on duty in the trenches, four companies of the 104th Pennsylvania Regiment acting as an escort to the dock." (Ronn Palm Collection)

Port Royal, S. C.
March 7th 1864

Well Mother, I will send G. W. Dales'es Photograph if Hunt & Rogers still have my negative. I want you to get 8 or 10 taken, and send them to me. if you can get them any time soon, I would like to have them as soon as I can get them. send in word for them the first opportunity. Mell can ride down any-time[.] I want him to go and order them as soon as he gets the letter.

George W. Dales is 18. he came out at the start, and has been a tiptop soldier. I know a great many will think from this photograph that he is a rough character, but I can testify after nearly three years acquaintance that not a truer or nobler boy lives.

Co. D nearly all reenlisted but the officers (some of them) acted the shit, and they all drew off. only three of the co. were sworn in.

Port Royal S. C.
April 1st 1864

Well Mell I sent word sometime ago for some of my <u>photographs</u> if Hunt still had   my negative. I suppose you have not had time to send them yet.

I will send a couple of dollars in this letter, and if he has the negative I want you to get 12 or 15 more and send to me.

I have not got a very good chance here to get them taken as I am on duty most of the time. they cant take very good one's here, and then they cost a goodeal more than they do there.

Gloucester Point Va.
April 27th 1864[112]

Well sis--Mary said you and Mother were cussing me for not answering your

---

[112] The 85th arrived here on 25 April. Gloucester Point is across the York River from Yorktown. Major General Benjamin F. Butler, commanding the Army of the James, concentrated many of the troops from the Department of thc South in the Yorktown area to form this new field army. Butler was expected to operate against Petersburg and Richmond as Grant and Meade attacked Lee's army. The 85th was now part of the First Brigade, First Division, Tenth Army Corps. The same four regiments that served under Howell at Charleston continued together in the brigade.

letters, so I thought I would scratch a line today to inform you that your letters dont please me as a general thing. I have frequently written for item's of knew's which was of interest to <u>me</u> and because <u>you</u> took no account of them. I suppose you never thought of it afterward.

well I guess I have not got much to write this time. knew's is very scarce now. all that is new is that we are on our way to Richmond again. we are encamped at present at Gloucester point[--] that is our Corp's, which is the 10th Army Corp's. we have a lot of d----d sap heads commanding us so I look to travel back faster than we did in 62. Howell Commands the first Brigade in the Corps' but that will give us a better chance in the retreat as we will start first.

Gold is surely God of this world of this war anyhow. it has at least placed all the biggest foolls and all the black legs in the united states in office. perhaps I have said enough on that subject for the present. if spared in five month's and eighteen day's my term of enlistment will be out.

I guess thats all. you can turn these photographs over to Mary. its no difference where they are though, so they are taken care of. My address is still Howell's Brigade, but Fortress Monroe, Va. instead of S. C.

I forgot one thing. I sent one army blanket and one new pair of sky blue pants home. the box will go to Old Fulmer's. M. E. M. is marked on both articles and my addres is written and sewed on the bundle. Tom can jump on Col some day after the box comes, when he has nothing else to do, and go over and get them.

Gloucester Point Va.
May 1st 1864

Well sis--I received your letter of the 26th this evening, and was <u>realy</u> as much <u>frightened</u> as I have ever been on meeting the <u>reb's</u>, when I opened it and found them scare-crows in it. I would like to know whose photograph's they are.

you said you were goeing to send some more. I beg of you not to do so. I have no use for them whatever. they are a <u>very</u> inferior article. I dont want such pictures as <u>they</u> are scattered over the country, so if you can find any use to put them to, keep the ballance. they will do to stick up in Mell's clearing. Im in earnest, dont send any more. I had <u>far better</u> one's taken at Hilton head.

Well I guess thats all. knews is <u>very scarce</u> here at present, and I am on guard tonight, and it has been raining all day, and we are liveing in shelter tents. we are once more in the field. we will likely have some knews sometime this summer. our regt is on the extreme right of the 10th Army

Isaac M. Kelly, Company B

Kelly was a 19-year-old student with hazel eyes, light hair, a florid complexion, and stood 5'5", when he enlisted on Feb. 26, 1864, at Greensburg. Although he enlisted as a substitute, thus receiving a $75 bounty, Kelly had seen previous service with the 100th Pennsylvania Infantry, and was noted on his muster cards as a veteran volunteer. A native of Fayette County, Kelly was wounded by a bullet in the right leg "while skirmishing at Bermuda Hundred" on May 5, 1864. He was sent to Hampton Hospital then to De Camp General Hospital at David's Island, New York Harbor, beginning on May 22. Kelly was then admitted on June 14 to Willett's Point Hospital, NY, and sent to Satterlee Hospital in Philadelphia on Aug. 9, 1864. By Sept./Oct. 1864, he was in a hospital in Pittsburgh. Kelly was, on paper, transferred to the 199th Pennsylvania Infantry on Oct. 6, 1864, and was discharged May 6, 1865, at West Philadelphia, PA, by reason of his wound in the right leg causing lameness. (Mrs. Marlene Kelley Langdon Collection at USAMHI)

Corps. they had us out on review all the afternoon yesterday. Genl Butler reviewed us in the evening. I dont know just when we will start to Richmond[,] perhaps before morning. there is some goeing awar daily some place.

> thats all[.] direct to
> Fortress Monroe Va

Bermuda Hundred Va.
May 17th 1864[113]

Well Mother[,] I had thought of not writeing until this Campaign was over, but I had a dream about you last night, which put me in the notion of scratching a few lines tonight, although I know I ought to be sleeping instead of writeing.

> well I have not time to say much, even if there was anything of importance to say. we landed at this place on the 6th[,] commenced fighting on the 7th, fought every day until today. the first 8 day's we had thing's our own way, whipped the rebs right along, but yesterday they attacked us with 50,000 men. we had but 30,000, so they whipped <u>us</u>.[114] last night our forces fell back here to our intrenchment's, all except our regt. we were left on picket. we came in tonight. if they dont attack us tomorrow, we will likely pitch into them again. two regts of our Brigade suffered severely.

Bermuda Hundred Va.
June 5th 1864[115]

---

[113]   The 85th left Gloucester Point on 4 May, then participated with the army in operations between Petersburg and Bermuda Hundred, a peninsula on the James River east of Petersburg. The regiment skirmished at Ware Bottom Church (10 May), and was generally engaged in picket duty and helping to construct entrenchments.

[114]   McJunkin refers to the Battle of Drewry's Bluff, where 18,000 Confederates under General Beauregard attacked 16,000 of Butler's troops.

[115] In this letter, McJunkin briefly relates the operations of the 85th since 17 May. The regiment was under fire much of the time. It fought again at Ware Bottom Church on 20 May. Howell's brigade captured Confederate Brigadier General R. S. Walker during the fighting.

Jacob Davis, Company E

Enrolled at age 17 at Washington, PA, on Oct. 15, 1861, and mustered in as a private at Uniontown on Nov. 12. Davis was then promoted from private to first sergeant on July 1, 1862. Promoted and mustered second lieutenant on May 1, 1863. Enrolled as first lieutenant May 5, 1864, at Gloucester Point, VA. Davis was on leave of absence from Mar. 4 to Apr. 9, 1864, escorting veteran volunteers home on furlough. In an unusual twist, Davis was discharged at expiration of term on Nov. 17, 1864, then mustered in as captain on Nov. 18, and mustered out again on Nov. 22. Shown here as a second lieutenant, Davis has a fancy kepi in hand and sports a dapper tie. (Ronn Palm Collection)

Well sis--I received your two letters some time ago--or one of them yesterday. well there is no knews here at present. nothing much goeing on[,] only fighting, and that's got to be an old thing. we have been fighting day and night for the last month. we have only missed 4 or 5 day's, but the rebs has changed the programme. instead of siegeing them--as we commenced they drove us back to our fortifications on the 16th of last month and have been siegeing us ever since.

but that's all it will amount to. our Brigade fought them a battle at Warren Bottom on the 20th. we whipped a whole Division of them, captured 2 or 3 hundred prisoners, Maj. Genl. Walker among the rest. his horse was pierced by about a hundred balls.

we are on picket about 2/3 of the time. well I guess thats all. I wish you would write to Ad for me. I dont feel much like writeing. I have not answered his last letter yet, so you can write to him and let him answer to me. write immediately and put a 50 ct shinplaster in for I am out of tobacco and wont be payed off for 2 or 3 weeks.

I want to know who is drafted in our township. I would like to know why Haman[,] Allmon & Will have quit writeing to me. I want to know what the girl's say's about them photograph's I sent home. perhaps I can get some of the boy's started to corresponding with our girl's.

little Johnny Wood's was mortally wounded on the 20th. he died in a day or two. there was not a man of our co. hurt. we have 18 men in our co. for duty. Wilson has still been lucky. he took the mump's some time ago and therefore missed a heap of this hard fighting and other duty[.] he is most well now.

I saw Jesse Harry about a week ago. the Division he is in went to Grant. they had an awful fight over on the Peninsula friday evening. it sounded to me to be of some place near Fair Oak's. it is rumored here that Grant took 15,000 prisoners and near 100 gun's.[116]

Bermuda Hundred Va.
June 19th 1864

Well I received that letter, paper, and tobacco yesterday, and was very glad to get the money and tobacco, so I thought I would let you know about it, thinking that perhaps you might do it again sometime for I dont look to be payed now until this Campaign is over, and it is hard to tell when that will be.

---

[116] McJunkin heard the Battle of Cold Harbor, a stinging Union defeat.

Joseph Welch, Company A

An 18-year-old farmer at his enlistment, he stood 5'11 1/2", with brown eyes, dark hair and a dark complexion. Born in Washington County, he enrolled at Finleyville on Sept. 13, 1861, and mustered in as a private at Uniontown on Oct. 16. Welch was present at every company muster, and re-enlisted in Feb. 1864 at Hilton Head, SC. He was killed in action at the Battle of Deep Run VA, on Aug. 16, 1864. An inventory of effects was taken at the time of his death, which showed he carried one cap, one great coat, one pair of cotton drawers, one flannel shirt, one blanket, and two pairs of socks. Here, the clean shaven youth wears a frock coat with a military vest, and sky blue trousers. A necktie and watch chain is also visible. (Ronn Palm Collection)

Grant's whole army is in this neighbour now, fighting every day. neither army can hold Peter's burgh. our brigade has lost a good many men in the last five day's. every body from that neighbourhood is all right. Jesse Harry is in good health. I have been on the sick list for about a week. I am getting all right now. I have been running about all the time, but not doing duty. I guess thats all. I will enclose Genl. Butler. he is one of my favourites.

Bermuda Hundred Va.
July 8th 1864

Well I recieved yours of the 29th a day or two ago, along with the tobacco. there is nothing new goeing on here. everything is quiet on our line. there is still a few deserter's come in every day.

if I live and keep my health, I will be a free man in 97 day's.

I guess that's all I have to say at present. since writeing before I went on duty about a week but could not stand it, so I am a convalecent again. I wish I would either get better or worse. I would sooner be bed fast than to be a convalecent.

Well I believe I shall close.

Genl Hospital, Point of Rocks, Va.
July 28th 1864[117]

Well I dont have much to do now day's so I thought I would write a few lines to pass away the time. I have received no answer for my last letter yet but I will write some anyhow.

I expect you would like to know what ail's me. it might amount to something to let it run on through. my lungs are affected some and I alway's had a heart disease. I am abel to run around every place. there is not much knews to write even if I felt like writeing. you need not answer this letter, as I expect they will send me north today. if I get north I will probably get a furlough and go home.

I guess that's all.

---

[117] Point of Rocks is located on the Appomattox River, and was the site of the Army of the James' general hospital. McJunkin was sent here on 26 July.

Oliver Sproul, Company K

This photograph of Sproul was taken later in life. When he enlisted in 1861 he was a mere 20 years old, standing 5'91/2", with blue eyes, light hair, a light complexion, and was a native of Fayette County. He joined Capt. Ludington's company enrolling at Stewart on Aug. 21, 1861, and mustering in at Uniontown on Oct. 12. By the end of June 1862, Sproul was promoted to the rank of corporal, then to sergeant in Apr. 1863. He was present for every muster until re-enlisting on Feb. 1, 1864, at age 23, while the regiment was posted at Hilton Head Island, SC. Being wounded in action at the Battle of Deep Bottom on Aug. 14, Sproul was absent in the 3rd Division Hospital ("Surgical Section") at Hampton, VA. Returning to duty, Sproul was one of the men assigned to train the 199th Pennsylvania Infantry, and on Dec. 11, 1864, was discharged for promotion in that regiment. (Ronn Palm Collection)

Belfour Genl. Hospital, Va.
July 30th 1864[118]

Well, I have made another move Northward since writeing before. I have nothing to write, so I will just give you my addres so that you can if you feel like it. my health is about the same, I am still abel to navigate. I may be sent north in a few day's and I may stay here all summer.

    my address is,

    Mr. Milton E. McJunkin
    10th Ward, Belfour Genl. Hospital
    Port's Mouth, Va.

Genl. Hospital
August 1st 1864[119]

Well, this is a business letter[.] I am here in Port's Mouth where thing's are plenty and cheap, and I am getting better and have no money to buy anything. I may stay here all summer and I may be sent north before a great while.

    I want you to write immediately and send me a dollar green back.

    I wrote daybefore yesterday and gave you my address, but for fear you dont get it I will give you my address again.

    Mr. Milton E. McJunkin
    Belfour Genl. Hospital, Ward 10
    Port's Mouth, Va.

August 16th 1864
Belfour Genl. Hospital
Port's Mouth Va.

Well, I received your letter with the money some day's ago, but have been so busy spending it that I have not had time to answer it until now. I only have

---

[118] Sent to Thomas A. West. Balfour General Hospital, in Portsmouth, Va., was a major Union medical facility.

[119] Sent to Thomas A. West.

122

a quarter left now.

I am getting along first rate so far. I find my heart is no worse than common. it was only the extreme heat that affected it more than common. my disease I believe is nothing more than a bad cough and affection of the pipe's. the diarrhea has troubled me the most for the last month, but it is getting better now.

I have give up all hope of getting North for sometime, and as I have received no pay for six months, I will have to continue drawing from home for a while. if I get north I will get a furlough and come home, but there can no furlough's be had from here. you may venture two dollar's in your next. we wont leave here for two week's anyhow, if that soon. tell Mary I will compl with her request. if Jake goes to war I will make my had qr's with her this winter.

no more at present[.]
my address is the same.

Balfour Genl. Hospital
Ports Mouth, Va. Aug. 19th 1864[120]

Well I received your last letter last night, and was glad to hear you were all getting better, for there is a prospect now of my wanting a goodeal of cooking done, now pretty soon.

the Doctor recommended me for a furlough. if it goes through I will be at home probably inside of three week's. I hope you have not failed to send them other two dollar's I wrote for, for I shall need it to buy grub along the road, if I get my furlough, and I think there is not much doubt but I will.

I have felt first rate all this week. I am able to run all over town, but that dollar you sent me was gone several day's ago, so I dont buy mutch now. well I guess that's all for the present. my address is the same.

Portsmouth Va.
Sept 4th 1864

Well mother the mail has come in <u>again</u> and not a scratch or a cent of money for me. now I want you immediately on the receipt of this letter to despatch me a two dollar greenback. I have been mad at every one of you for the last

---

Absalom Dial, Company B

Enrolled as a private at age 19 in Captain Zellar's company on Oct. 12, 1861, at Perryopolis. Appointed corporal when mustered in on Nov. 7, at Uniontown. Promoted sergeant on Apr. 10, 1862. Promoted a second lieutenant from orderly sergeant on Aug. 10, 1862. Again promoted to first lieutenant to rank from Dec. 4, 1862. He took command of the company starting June 19, 1863. Dial became sick with dysentery in Nov. 1863, although hoping to be sent north, he was directed to the "convalescent camp" at St. Augustine, FL, on Nov. 25, 1863. He rejoined the regiment on Jan. 28, 1864, from being absent sick and commanding the company starting the 31st of that month. Dial was wounded at the Battle of Deep Bottom (near Flussers' Mill, sometimes called Strawberry Plains), VA, on Aug. 16, 1864, and sent to the general hospital at Fort Monroe. In command of 85th Pennsylvania detachment from Feb. 1, 1865 to June 30, 1865, although he was absent with leave most of Jan. and June that year. (Ronn Palm Collection)

month. you know where I am, and that I have no money. if nothing happens more than I know of at present, I will likely be at home in 2 or 3 month's, if you dont keep me mad all the time, but if you use me as heretofore, I may go to Hilton Head to winter. I am what is called a Hospital Bummer at present. well I guess I am as well as when I wrote last. I have a bad cough and sometime's a goodeal of pain in my chest[.] thats all for the present[.] so mind the green back[.]

Portsmouth, Va.
Sept 6th 1864

Well, Mother, I wrote you a letter on Sunday. I was in a pretty bad humours and still am. this is a cold wet day. I always feel worse in such weather. for the last three weeks we have had a goodeal of wet weather. I have give up all hope of getting a furlough from here, so after this I want you to send me little.

I am in quite a different humor from I was a minnet ago. I have this moment received that letter with the two dollars and am very glad of it. I have been suffering for the want of money ever since I have been here. my lung's are pretty badly effected and I had nothing to buy anything to help me. the doctor sent in my name for a furlough nearly three weeks ago, but I have heard nothing from it yet. I may get it yet and I may not. no more at present.

7th[.] before sending this out I will scratch a few more lines. I wrote a very mad letter sunday for two dollar's. well you can still send it, for it will take this all to buy medicine. we get no care, or anything else here. I am very thankful I am abel to take care of myself. if I get that furlough I will come home and stay there and if I dont get it, my time is out anyhow in a little over a month, so it wont make much difference, if you send me all the money I send for.

Portsmouth, Va.
Sept 12th 1864

Well, Mother, I guess I will scratch you a few lines this morning as it is a beautiful morning, and I alway's feel better on such day's. I will give you a true statement of my case today as near as I can. there is no doubt but my

125

lung's are pretty badly effected.[121] I have only had one bad spell of pain with it, but you never saw anyone cough and spit more than I have for the last month. for 3 or 4 day's now though, my cough had been a greateal better. I think if I dont get any worse until I get home I will get well. if I had plenty of money here, it would be much better for me, for I could then buy what I need, but if I dont get home, I will likely be payed off in 2 or 3 weeks, at least we expect to be. I am looking every day for them last two dollars I sent for[.] I wish I had have said five. my ink has run out so I must quit.

Portsmouth, Va.
Sept 18th 1864[122]

I received your's of the 11th on last friday with the money and was very glad you were more punctual, for I had run out of medicine. I have just came to the ward. I have been running over town as usual. there was a lot of us moved from the Church over to the Ocean house last friday. I am now in Ward 3. you will put that on your next letter instead of 10. I want you to write every week, and send one dollar a week. I have $200 due me but cant get it at present. I dont think I am any worse or better either, but you cant tell anything about consumption[.] my new doctor examined me yesterday, and said there was only one lung affected and he thought it was not bad. I hope he is right. you may look for me anytime for my time is pretty near out. Oct 15th. no more at present.

Portsmouth Va.
Sept 23d 1864

I received yours of the 16th with the money daybefore yesterday, and was very glad to get it. I am doing myself far more good buying my own medicine than the doctor's. I cant see that <u>their</u> medicine does me as much good[.] I get a bottle of porter every day that strengthen's me, and the Cod Liver oil I think is good for the lungs. well I guess I have no more to write now, only my furlough came back the other day approved and all right, but they would not give it to me on account of my time being so near out. its not very long now until the 15th of next month.

---

[121] McJunkin had a case of consumption, known today as tuberculosis.

[122] Sent to Thomas A. West.

Portsmouth Va.
Sunday Oct 2nd 1864

Dear Mother[:]

I am sitting in my bunk this morning to try to scratch you a few line's. well to begin on thursday night I took another bad spell. I had not much idea of seeing morning for awhile, but God was merciful, as wicked as I am, and have been. my object in writeing is to let you know how thing's are. they are makeing out my discharge now. you know my time is out the 15th.

or I forgot to tell you that I had a bad spell some 4 or 5 week's ago. it lasted about a week. after that I was getting along as well as usual until this spell, and I think I am getting better of this one now.

but my object is to let you know that if Uncle Milton or Tom wishes to take a little trip and fetch me home, if liveing and able to move, I dont think they would have to wait on me[.] Whoever comes, if any one, I want them to take my money. they had better fetch right smart too. I dont know how much it would cost but that dont matter so I get home.

I may soon be over this spell, but I am so reduced that I dont think I could make the trip myself.

that's sufficient I guess[.] now Mother you will know what to do. if anyone come's they should start on receiveing this letter right away.

Go to Fortress Monroe, from there up to Portsmouth, then run up the car st where you land to the ocean house, and enquire for ward no. 3.

Balfour Genl. Hospital

Balfour Genl. Hospt. Ward 3
Oct 4th 1864

Dear Mother[:]

I thought I would write you another letter this evening, as I feel some better. I have been mending slowly ever since I took this last bad spell, but the most why I am writeing now is because I begin to feel very anxious to see someone comeing after me and I was afraid you would think it would cost too much, and so let no one come. just let Tom put Col. in his pocket, if necessary, and get here as soon as he can. O, how I wish you were a young stout woman able to stand the ride[,] the 12 hour's ride on the bay so that you could come, but that cant be, and I want to see Tom before the 15th.

Roster of Company D

William H. Horn	Captain	Resigned, 7/6/62
Rolla O. Phillips	1st Lt.	Promoted to Captain, 7/6/62; Mustered out, 12/23/64
John E. Michener	2nd Lt.	Promoted to 1st Lt. 7/6/62; Mustered out, 11/22/64
William H. Myers	1st Sgt.	Promoted to 2nd Lt. 7/6/62; Promoted to Captain, Co. G, 188th PA, 4/29/64
Howard Kerr	Sgt.	Mustered out, 12/23/64
George W. McGiffin	Sgt.	Discharged on surgeon's certificate, 3/5/63
John Horn	Sgt.	Discharged on surgeon's certificate, 7/27/62
John N. Donagho	Sgt.	Captured, 5/31/62; Died at Salisbury, 8/7/62
George S. Fulmer	Corp.	Promoted to Sgt., 9/1/62; Promoted to 1st Sgt., 3/1/64; Mustered out, 11/22/64
Harrison S. Spohn	Corp.	Promoted to Sgt., 7/6/62; Discharged on surgeon's certificate, 2/9/63
Hiram S. Myers	Corp.	Promoted to Sgt., 9/1/62; Died of disease, 2/23/64
Jacob B. Speers	Corp.	Promoted to Sgt., 4/1/63; Mustered out, 11/22/64
Thomas M. Harford	Corp.	Promoted to Sgt., 3/4/63; Promoted to Sgt. Major, 7/1/63; Transferred to Company I, 10/29/63; Mustered out, 11/22/64
Benjamin Marshall	Corp.	Wounded, 8/30/64; Discharged, 11/11/64
William W. Garber	Corp.	Killed, 8/30/63

Alexander C. Morgan	Corp.	Missing in action, 5/31/62
Isaiah Jordan	Mus.	Mustered out, 11/22/64
James T. Wells	Mus.	Discharged on surgeon's certificate, 3/18/63
William Allmann	Pvt.	Discharged on surgeon's certificate, 3/25/63
George Ames	Pvt.	Mustered out, 11/22/64
Joseph E. Ames	Pvt.	Mustered out, 12/23/64
David Baldwin	Pvt.	Captured, 8/17/64; Died in prison, 12/19/64
Robert W. Baldwin	Pvt.	Discharged on writ of habeas corpus, 11/14/61
William A. Bell	Pvt.	Discharged on surgeon's certificate, 7/8/62
John Bratton	Pvt.	Mustered out, 12/23/64
Josiah Bratton	Pvt.	Discharged on surgeon's certificate, 10/26/63
Enoch Brooks	Pvt.	Mustered out, 12/23/64
James W. Burgan	Pvt.	Died of disease, 7/15/62
Joseph W. Burson	Pvt.	Promoted to Corp., 3/1/64; Wounded, 8/16/64; Died of disease, 3/17/65
Henry Bush	Pvt.	Wounded at Morris Island; Discharged for wounds, 6/30/64
John Clendaniel	Pvt.	Wounded, 6/18/64; Discharged on War Department order, 6/10/65
Stephen Clendaniel	Pvt.	Mustered out, 12/23/64
Harvey Cox	Pvt.	Wounded 8/30/63; Mustered out, 11/22/64
Hiram Crouch	Pvt.	Died of disease, 11/20/63
Daniel W. Crumrine	Pvt.	Mustered out, 11/22/64
Israel Cumson	Pvt.	Died of disease, 6/24/62
George W. Dales	Pvt.	Promoted to Corp., 10/10/64; Mustered out, 12/23/64
Henry G. Dales	Pvt.	Discharged on surgeon's certificate, 11/6/62
Joseph A. Demuth	Pvt.	Mustered out, 11/22/64
Mahlon C. Donagho	Pvt.	Wounded 5/31/62; Discharged for wounds, 5/4/63
Alfred Dougherty	Pvt.	Deserted and returned; Discharged by War Department order, 5/12/65
George W. Fisher	Pvt.	Promoted to Hospital Steward,

3/8/64

William H. Fulmer	Pvt.	Discharged on surgeon's certificate, 10/29/62
Thomas J. Gage	Pvt.	Deserted, 12/10/61
George W. Garber	Pvt.	Died of disease, 7/18/62
Alex C. Hathaway	Pvt.	Promoted to Corp., 4/1/63; Wounded, 8/16/64; Mustered out, 11/22/64
Ben F. Hathaway	Pvt.	Promoted to Corp., 10/10/64; Transferred to Co. C, 188th PA, 6/28/65
Richard Hathaway	Pvt.	Died of disease, 3/2/63
Thomas J. Hathaway	Pvt.	Died of disease, 6/12/62
Hiram Haver	Pvt.	Wounded 8/30/63 and 6/18/64; Mustered out, 11/22/64
Jacob Haver	Pvt.	Mustered out, 11/22/64
George Heflick	Pvt.	Discharged on surgeon's certificate, 8/7/62
Elias Horn	Pvt.	Transferred to Veteran Reserve Corps, 3/16/64
Hezekiah Horn	Pvt.	Captured, 5/31/62; Exchanged 10/7/62; Mustered out, 11/22/64
Jonas Horn	Pvt.	Discharged on surgeon's certificate, 6/24/63
William H. Jackman	Pvt.	Discharged on surgeon's certificate, 9/3/62
Barnet F. Johnson	Pvt.	Promoted to Corp., 4/14/62; Promoted to Sgt., 7/1/63; Mustered out, 11/22/64
Leonidas F. Jones	Pvt.	Discharged on surgeon's certificate, 11/4/62
George Ketchem	Pvt.	Promoted to Corp., 7/6/62; Wounded, 8/16/64; Died of wounds, 9/26/64
William B. Lash	Pvt.	Mustered out, 11/22/64
Alfred R. Lucre	Pvt.	Mustered out, 11/22/64
Alexander McCay	Pvt.	Mustered out, 11/22/64
Wm. C. McCormick	Pvt.	Discharged on surgeon's certificate, 6/1/63
William H. McGiffin	Pvt.	Died of disease, 6/8/62
John McIlvain	Pvt.	Discharged on surgeon's certificate, 10/18/62

John McIlvain	Pvt.	Transferred to Co. C, 188th PA, 6/28/65
Milton E. McJunkin	Pvt.	Died of disease, 10/25/64
Oliver McVay	Pvt.	Discharged on surgeon's certificate, 9/18/62
James Meeks	Pvt.	Killed, 8/17/64
Abraham Miller	Pvt.	Promoted to Corp., 7/1/64; Wounded, 8/16/64; Died of wounds, 9/10/64
John Milliken	Pvt.	Promoted to Corp., 11/1/62; Promoted to Sgt., 10/10/64; Mustered out, 11/22/64
Jesse S. Moore	Pvt.	Died of disease, 11/9/62
Jasper Morgan	Pvt.	Died of disease, 9/22/62
Robert Pryor	Pvt.	Wounded, 8/16/64; Died of wounds, 12/17/64
Wilson Pryor	Pvt.	Discharged on surgeon's certificate, 11/17/62
Bowen Rees	Pvt.	Discharged, 11/15/64
John Rees	Pvt.	Transferred to Co. C, 188th PA, 6/28/65
William Rice	Pvt.	Discharged by War Department order, 6/10/65
William A. Rider	Pvt.	Discharged on surgeon's certificate, 12/1/62
James M. Roach	Pvt.	Discharged on surgeon's certificate, 9/16/62
Edward Roberts	Pvt.	Mustered out, 11/22/64
Eli Smith	Pvt.	Discharged on surgeon's certificate, 9/16/62
Adam Staub	Pvt.	Discharged on surgeon's certificate, 3/16/64
William L. Stull	Pvt.	Mustered out, 11/22/64
Jon. L. Sundecker	Pvt.	Died of disease, 7/12/62
Samuel O. Thomas	Pvt.	Discharged on surgeon's certificate, 7/4/63
Abraham S. Tinley	Pvt.	Promoted to Corp., 3/1/63; Wounded, 8/21/63; Mustered out, 11/22/64
Sampson Vandegrift	Pvt.	Discharged, 11/11/64
William H. Virgin	Pvt.	Mustered out, 11/22/64
Amos G. Walton	Pvt.	Died of disease, 2/29/64

Henry Walton	Pvt.	Discharged on surgeon's certificate, 6/9/63
Theophilus Wilson	Pvt.	Mustered out, 11/22/64
James Yorders	Pvt.	Discharged on surgeon's certificate, 10/7/62
Henry C. Yortz	Pvt.	Mustered out, 11/22/64

Summary of Company Statistics

Total names on roster	94
Mustered out of service	30
Resigned	1
Transferred	5
Promoted out of company	1
Killed in action	2
Wounded in action	13
Died of wounds	3
Discharged on account of wounds	3
Missing in action	1
Captured	3
Died in prison	2
Died of disease	14
Deserted	2
Discharged on surgeon's certificate	24
Discharged, other	3
Discharged on War Department order	3

REGIMENT HISTORIES
*****

The Deeds and Sacrifices of the Eighty-fifth Pennsylvania.
*****

Men Who Fought to Win
*****

Participants in a Score of Battles and in at the Finish.
*****

ANNALS OF THE WAR
*****

by S. L. McHenry,
Formerly Captain of Company K and Adjutant of the Eighty-fifth Regiment.
*****

The Eighty-fifth Regiment of Pennsylvania Volunteer Infantry, organized and commanded by Colonel Joshua B. Howell, was recruited in the four counties bordering on the Virginia line in Western Pennsylvania. It was one of several regiments that were accepted by the Secretary of War after the Pennsylvania quota then called had been filled. Colonel Howell's commission was dated August, 1861, and soon after the several companies of the regiment began drill in "Camp Lafayette," on the grounds of the Fayette County Agricultural Society in Uniontown. Early in November uniforms were received and the regiment was mustered in by Lieutenant Beach, United States Army.

Sketches of the Leaders.

Colonel Joshua B. Howell, the commanding officer, was born September 11, 1806, at Fancy Hill, the site of the family mansion of the Howells, near Woodbury, N.J. His ancestry were of Quaker stock, who came over with William Penn. He was educated at the academy in Woodbury, and in Philadelphia studied law and was admitted to the bar in Philadelphia.

Removing to Uniontown in 1828 he entered upon the practice of his profession and soon attained high rank. A man of fine presence, genial and affable in his manners, of strict rectitude and honor in all his dealings with his fellow man, he was universally beloved and admired as exhibiting the highest type of a gentleman. Although without military experience in time of war, his active, well-trained mind soon enabled him to master tactical problems. In action his courage was unsurpassed, as was demonstrated on several occasions. His death, which occurred September 12, 1864, near Petersburg, Va., caused by his horse falling upon him, was universally regretted.

Lieutenant Colonel Norton McGiffin was born in Washington, Pa., January 23, 1824. He was educated at Washington College, graduating in the class of 1841, of which General A. Baird, United States Army, was a member. Soon after leaving college he entered the law office of Judge Nathaniel Ewing, of Uniontown, Pa. The study of law was not to his liking. The declaration of war in 1846 afforded him an opportunity to develop his taste for military life, and he became one of the few representatives of Washington county in the Army of Occcupation in Mexico, joining the company of Duquesne Grays, of Pittsburgh, which was mustered as Company K, First Regiment Pennsylvania Volunteers. He served throughout the war with his company, experiencing many privations, hardships and hard fighting in the military operations of the campaign from Vera Cruz to the City of Mexico, and made for himself an excellent record for gallantry and efficiency as a soldier. After his return from Mexico he was in 1849 elected Treasurer of the county and again in 1859 was elected Sheriff. He was also elected and served as a Representative of Washington county in the Legislature of 1881. At the outbreak of the civil war he recruited a company for the three months' service in a few days, and joining the Twelfth Regiment, Pennsylvania Volunteers, under Colonel David Campbell, reported for duty at Harrisburg on the 25th of April, 1861, and was chosen lieutenant colonel of the regiment. At the close of this term of service he returned to Washington and was active in the encouragement of enlistments for the three years' service, and when the Eighty-fifth Regiment was organized he was tendered and accepted the lieutenant colonelcy. His undaunted courage and self-possession gave confidence in his leadership, which was never misplaced.

Major Absalom Guiler was a resident of Uniontown, Pa., where he was engaged in business at the time of his election as major of the regiment. He had seen service in the war with Mexico, having served as a non-commissioned officer in Company H, Second Regiment, Pennsylvania Volunteers, commanded by Colonel Roberts, where he had the reputation of being a strict disciplinarian and a good drill officer.

The first engagement of the Eighty-fifth was in the Peninsula service. The winter following enlistment had been spent in camp at Washington, which city we left on March 28, 1862, permanently assigned to Keim's, afterwards Wessell's Brigade, consisting of the Eighty-fifth, One Hundred and First and One Hundred and Third Pennsylvania and Ninety-sixth New York. On the evacuation of Yorktown the brigade, now under the command of Colonel Howell, after a memorable march through rain and mud, and a greater part of the time in hearing of the guns at Williamsburg, reached that battle-field late in the afternoon and was met by an officer of the General's staff, who inquired of Colonel Howell if he had a regiment he could detach to take the place of the Ninety-third Pennsylvania, which was about out of ammunition. The Colonel at once replied:

"Yes, sir. Forward the Eighty-fifth!" and marched off at the head of his regiment, leaving the brigade to the next highest in command.

The position to which the regiment was conducted was in the edge of a strip of woods immediately in front of Fort Magruder, and in reaching it one or two men were wounded. A brisk fire was opened and continued for some time, but darkness soon came on. A night of anxiety was spent, during which the scenes of a battle-field at night with its medley of horrible sounds were fully realized. The morning dawned at last, revealing the fact that Fort Magruder had been evacuated. The pursuit was resumed and closely followed until the Chickahominy was reached.

At New Kent Court House Lieutenant Colonel McGiffin resigned his commission, and at an election held the same day Captain H. A. Purviance was chosen in his place and First Lieutenant Lewis Walkins succeeded Colonel Purviance as captain of Company E.

Crossing to the Right Bank.

As soon as the bridges were completed the corps of General Keyes crossed to the right bank of the Chickahominy. With Casey's Division in front, daily advances were made until the picket lines were established in front of Seven Pines. Some skirmishing occurred on the 30th, and on the 31st of May a determined attack in force was made by the Confederates. The stubborn resistance made by Casey's Division is now unquestioned, and although cloud was cast upon the division by the first and hasty dispatches giving an account of the engagement, merited credit has since been given. The Eighty-fifth suffered severe loss in officers and men and was finally forced from its position by overwhelming numbers. In this engagement Lieutenant Hamilton was killed and Lieutenant Julius Smith and Captain Hooker were severely wounded.

After General Keim's death Brigadier General H. W. Wessells, of the regular army, was assigned to the command of the brigade, and after the battle of Fair Oaks the Eighty- fifth Regiment occupied the extreme left of the line at White Oak Swamp, where it remained until after the commencement of the movement to the James river. About the middle of August we arrived at Fortress Monroe, where the division of General Peck was ordered to Suffolk, Va. Companies A and F, of the Eighty-fifth Regiment, under the command of Captain Vankirk, were detailed for special duty at Point Lookout on Chesapeake Bay. Soon after reaching Suffolk a portion of Wessell's Brigade, including the Eighty-fifth, was sent on a reconnaissance.

A Movement South.

A movement south into North Carolina was next undertaken, and crossing Albemarle and Pimlico Sounds on the steamer Lane we reached Newbern, on the Neuse river. Here we joined the Eighteenth Corps, under the command of General John G. Foster, and in a few days were on the march towards Goldsboro. Following the line of the Neuse we first encountered the enemy's forces at Southwest Creek, where some pieces of artillery had been planted to command the causeway by which the creek and low ground were passed. Two companies of the Eighty-fifth Regiment, B and D, under the command of Captain Hooker, were thrown forward on the right and below the bridge and effected a crossing, when they encountered a fire of musketry and artillery. The companies returned the fire with so much energy and pressing forward at the same time, succeeded in driving the enemy from their guns. A portion of the Ninth New Jersey had also crossed the stream above the bridge, and coming up at nearly the same time the pursuit was continued. On the following morning the full force of the enemy was met, posted on the further side of a swamp in an advantageous position, covering the approaches to the bridge at Kinston. Other troops were brought up and the line of battle formed, the right resting on the Neuse river, the Eighty-fifth Regiment occupying the extreme left of the line, and while waiting for the command to advance were under a heavy fire of musketry, but could not see where it came from. Here Sergeant A. W. Pollock, of Company A, was struck and disabled by a Minie ball. When orders were given to advance the whole line moved forward across the marshy stream and over the rising ground beyond, where the fire of the enemy's artillery, as well as musketry, was met in full force. The charge, however, proved effective and the Confederates were soon in full retreat. A large number were cut off from reaching the bridge and taken prisoners. The remainder retreated across the bridge, which they fired; but our men were too quick for them, and putting out the flames followed the retreating forces through the town of Kinston, which was left in our possession. Leaving a detachment to look after the killed and wounded, the main body of our forces recrossed the river and advanced to White Hall, where a small engagement took place. At Goldsboro Railroad bridge, the objective point of the

George H. Hooker, Company B

Although only 20 years old when he enrolled in Capt. Zellar's company at Eldersville, on Sept. 7, 1861, Hooker was made a second lieutenant and mustered in at Uniontown on Nov. 15, 1861. He was promoted first lieutenant on Jan. 27, 1862, and appointed captain on May 19, 1862. Hooker was severely wounded at the Battle of Seven Pines on May 31, 1862, but back on duty with the regiment late in July 1862. Upset over the improper muster of Capt. Hughes (making Hughes senior to Hooker), Hooker submitted his resignation early in June 1863, Col. Howell reluctantly approved noting that Hooker "is a gallant and brave soldier, and a high toned gentleman and officer. I know that the motives which have influenced him in tendering his resignation are honorable, and that if his resignation is accepted, the service will not lose him–I shall regret to part with him–shall consider it a very great loss to my regiment . . . ." But it was not accepted. (Ronn Palm Collection)

George H. Hooker, Company B

On June 20, 1863, Hooker was appointed acting assistant adjutant general on Col. Howell's staff, then made acting assistant adjutant general of the 2nd Brigade (Howell's), Ferry's Division, which became the 1st Brigade, 1st Division, 10th Corps, upon arriving in Virginia in the spring of 1864. He retained that position until Aug. 1864. On Apr. 18, 1864, he was absent with leave for 30 days. He was wounded at the Battle of Strawberry Plains, VA, on Aug. 16, 1864, and sent to the general hospital at Fort Monroe, VA. Given a furlough for 30 days, Hooker was mustered out of the regiment on Jan. 3, 1865, to date from Nov. 20, 1864, having accepted appointment as assistant adjutant general of volunteers. (Ronn Palm Collection)

expedition, the enemy strongly contested the approaches to the crossing. Reinforcements having arrived, they were driven back, however, the bridge burned and its piers of solid masonry battered down by solid shot. The cavalry in the meantime had been tearing up the railroad for some miles.

A New Danger.

The object of the expedition having been accomplished the troops were recalled and the return march was commenced in a more leisurely manner. The command was absent from Newbern about thirteen days and during that time had marched one hundred and fifty miles, fought two battles, besides a number of skirmishes, captured 600 prisoners, ten or twelve pieces of artillery and a large number of small arms, stores and ammunition, destroyed the railroad bridge over the Neuse river and many miles of railroad track. On the return of General Foster from a hasty visit to Washington a reorganization of the forces in his department took place and Colonel Howell was assigned to the command of a brigade, consisting of the Eighty-fifth, One Hundred and Seventy-fourth, Fifty-eighth Pennsylvania and the Fifty-sixth New York. Our command was removed a mile or two from town on the Trent river.

Still Further South.

During the last week in January, 1863, we undertook a voyage by sea on the Ranger, Maple Leaf, Burnside and Pioneer, under sealed orders, which proved to be Port Royal harbor, S. C. Several days passed after our arrival in Broad river before the troops were landed. General Ferry's Division, in which the brigade of Colonel Howell was included, finally landed on St. Helena Island. Here we remained for some weeks, or until there was still another reorganization. On March 26 Colonel Howell was given command of a new brigade, consisting of the Eighty-fifth Pennsylvania, Sixty-second and the Sixty-seventh Ohio and the Thirty-ninth Illinois Regiments, and as soon as the preparations were completed for the naval attack on the forts in Charleston harbor this brigade, forming part of the land force designed to co- operate with the navy, was re- embarked on transports and proceeded to Stono Inlet. After nightfall on the 5th of April a part of the Eighty-fifth Regiment, with two others, under command of Colonel Howell, were towed across the inlet in surf-boats and landed on the south end of Folly Island. A rapid march was made up the beach to a point near the north end, where the main force was halted and two companies proceeded as skirmishers, examining the entire northern end of this island, which was found to be unoccupied. Returning to the main body the whole force was placed under cover of the thickly wooded shore before daybreak. In this position the force on the island was concealed from the enemy, while we had an uninterrupted view of the fleet outside the bar of Charleston harbor. About one o'clock on April 7 a line of iron-clads moved towards the entrance of the harbor. All was now excitement in our camp. The iron-clads, lying low in the water, were almost hid from our view as they passed the point of Morris Island.

About 2 P.M. the opening gun was fired from Fort Sumter, which was in full view. Soon the fire of all the forts was concentrated upon the approaching iron-clads. We waited in silence for the response which seemed long delayed, but it came at last--a deep and prolonged report--then another and another as the vessels came into line until the earth almost seemed to tremble. Two hours, possibly more, passed in this most exciting conflict, then the firing gradually ceased and the vessels were seen coming out over the bar. After they came out one of the iron-clads seemed in trouble from the gathering of other vessels about her. This proved to be the ill-fated Keokuk, which soon went down. The attack was not returned at this time, much to our disappointment. There had been no opportunity for co-operation on the part of the land forces. A disposition of the forces on Folly Island was made, a complete line of pickets being established on the side exposed to the enemy. The main force encamped near White House, an old plantation dwelling, near the middle of the island. A depot of supplies was established at the south end of the island. On the 9th Brigadier General J. Vodges, of the regular army, assumed command of all the forces on the island, and under his supervision preparations were made for the final advance on Charleston via Morris Island.

Upon the arrival of General Gilmore, who succeeded General Hunter in command of the Department of the South, it was determined to construct a battery at the north end of Folly Island, under cover of which the crossing at Light House Inlet could be effected. The batteries were constructed at night. The materials had to be brought from the landing seven miles distant on the south end of the island. So successfully was it accomplished that when on the morning of the 10th of July, about daybreak, the fringe of brushwood in front was cut away and the entire battery of forty-four guns and mortars was opened on the forts across the inlet the enemy was completely surprised.

Aid of the Infantry.

The infantry force, held in waiting in boats in Folly river, as soon as the fire slackened swept out into and across the inlet and charged the forts, taking many prisoners and following those that escaped almost to the walls of Fort Wagner. In all the operations on the island the Eighty-fifth Regiment did its full share of duty, and when the siege of Fort Wagner became a necessity it was one of the three regiments detailed for duty in the trenches, each one serving twenty-four hours in turn. This duty was of the most trying character, not only of the endurance of the men, but of their courage as well. While in the trenches they were exposed to the enfilading fire of the forts on James Island. The following is part of the record of the time, written by an eye witness: "On the morning of the 21st instant the Eighty-fifth Pennsylvania, under Lieutenant Colonel Purviance, was sent up in advance of our artillery and palisades to erect the batteries against Wagner above mentioned. It was about 3 o'clock in the morning when, with spades in hand, they had crept up to within seventy- five yards of the Confederate line, the Confederate officer in command ordered his men back into the fort and immediately Wagner opened its fire upon our Pennsylvania boys with grape and canister. The fire was ineffectual, however, and the men worked on, throwing up as fast as possible cover for themselves. Soon Fort Johnston opened fire upon them with shells and before they could secure protection killed and wounded twenty-five of the regiment. The Eighty-fifth worked on under the fire and continued their labors during the following day, never leaving their position until all had been accomplished and the battery erected."

Death of the Hero.

Within a few days after the above account was written--on the 30th of August-- Lieutenant Colonel Purviance was killed at his post of duty on the front line by the premature explosion of a shell from one of our own guns. The heroic endurance of the troops on both sides during this memorable siege has rarely been excelled. The occupants of Forts Wagner and Gregg, confined in close quarters and subjected to an almost continuous bombardment of shot and shell from the heavy guns of both army and navy, held a perilous position. The position of the besieging forces was no less trying and hazardous. Encamped on the barren sands, which served to intensify the heat, exposed night and day to a cross fire from the forts in front and on the flank for two months of the most unhealthy season, they pushed on the lines of intrenchment until almost under the walls of Wagner. Several unsuccessful attempts had been made to carry the fort by assault, the first on the 18th of July, when the gallant Colonel Shaw was killed on the parapet at the critical moment when the victory seemed won.

Preparations were in progress for a last general assault when, on the morning of the 7th of September, there being no response from the guns of Wagner a reconnoitering party was sent out, which soon discovered that the silent fort was tenantless, the garrison having quietly left it during the night in boats. The announcement was quickly made and as quickly passed along the lines that the fort was evacuated, and soon the Stars and Stripes were floating from its battlements. Battery Gregg also fell into our hands and the whole of

Morris Island was now in our possession. Fort Sumter, although apparently reduced to a mass of rubbish by our Parrott guns, still held out, its garrisoned being protected and finding safety in the bomb-proofs, rendered doubly secure by the accumulated debris of its ruined walls.

Lieutenant Colonel Henry A. Purviance, who lost his life during the siege, had been in command of the regiment most of the time since his promotion, and was greatly beloved by his command. He was the son of Parker C. Purviance, of Butler county, Pa., and was born in May, 1831. His life had been one of hard work and indomitable perseverance under many discouragements. He was a man of fine literary taste and had from his earliest years a love for books and literary work. He entered a printing office at the age of thirteen and acquired a thorough knowledge of practical printing, at the same time developing his taste for reading and study. His literary tastes finally led him into the field of journalism, and at the beginning of the war he was associated with Colonel James Armstrong in the publication of the Washington Tribune. He first entered the military service in April 1861, as a member of the company recruited by Captain McGiffin for the three months' service, which joined the Twelfth Regiment,Pennsylvania Volunteers. On his return from this service he recruited Company E, of the Eighty-fifth Regiment, of which he was chosen captain. Devoted to the cause in which he had enlisted, possessed of true courage and manliness, warm-hearted and faithful, he readily attached to himself friends who esteemed him for his many noble qualities.

At the time of Colonel Purviance's death Major Campbell was absent on duty as assistant inspector general on the staff of General Vodges. He was promoted to lieutenant colonel and soon afterwards joined the regiment which, in the meantime, was under the command of Captain L. M. Abraham, promoted to major. Major Abraham was a native of Fayette county. He had recruited Company G, which he brought into the regiment, and had served continuously with it since its organization. A man of quiet, modest demeanor, who made no pretense of possessing great military knowledge, but who did possess a large store of good common sense, which, with his unquestioned courage and determination, enabled him to act with good judgment.

Upon the withdrawal of the main body of the troops from Morris Island the Eighty-fifth was sent to Black Island, an advanced post of observation, where they built a small fort. The Eighty-fifth remained at Hilton Head until the following April, except some occasional detours, the most memorable of which was in February, when we went up the Savannah river, near Whitemarsh Island. Landing, a skirmish line was formed and a portion crossed a bridge to the main shore, where they were attacked by a superior force and driven back. Some pieces of artillery, which were planted to cover the approach to the bridge, opened fire and several members of the regiment were taken prisoners. Captain John E. Michener, of Company K, being one of the number, was taken before the commanding officer of the Confederate troops and questioned in regard to the strength of the Union forces and their intentions. The captain led the officers to believe that a large and well equipped force of the army and navy was moving upon Savannah. His artful statement, it seemed, had the desired effect, as the officers did not follow up the attack with sufficient energy to prevent the companies on the island from reaching the transports in safety.

Coming North Again.

In the reorganization of the corps it was composed of three divisions, under the command of Generals Terry, Turner and Ames. General Howell's brigade was attached to the division of General Terry.

The voyage North was made in the steamer Fulton, which landed the regiment at Gloucester Point, opposite Yorktown, Va. proceeding soon to join other forces of the Army of the James at Fortress Monroe or Hampton Roads. During the six months that remained of the three years' term of service the valor and efficiency of the regiment was shown in numerous engagements.

From the 5th of May, the date of landing at Bermuda Hundred, the Eighty-fifth was on the front line of advance from that point and had an engagement with the enemy on the 10th near Fort Darling, on the right of the line. Also, on the 16th, and again on the 20th, near Ware Bottom Church, where a general officer and a number of men were taken prisoners. Repeated attacks were made on this line by the enemy during the following weeks, notably on the 15th, 17th and 18th of June. On the 20th of June the brigade crossed the James river, taking position at Deep Bottom, but was soon recalled to its former position. Again, on the 13th of August, the division of General Terry was moved to the left bank of the James, and on the 14th had an engagement at Strawberry Plains. On the 16th, at Deep Bottom, a general engagement was brought on in which the Eighty-fifth carried the enemy's works in its front by assault. In this engagement Lieutenant Colonel Campbell, of Company K, was killed, Major Abraham was slightly wounded, Captains Watkins and Rogers were mortally wounded and Captain W. W. Kerr was taken prisoner.

A Curious Incident.

In this engagement the arrow head on top of the flagstaff was struck fairly in the centre by a Minie ball, which embedded itself there, and so remains until the present time. It is regarded as an object of great curiosity and interest. Following is a list of battles in which the regiment was engaged:

Yorktown, Williamsburg, Fair Oaks, Seven Days' Battles, Va.; Kinston, Whitehall, Goldsboro, N.C.; Morris Island, Fort Wagner, S.C.; Bermuda Hundred, Chapin's Farm, Fort Darling, Strawberry Plains and Deep Bottom, Va.

Personal mention or reference to members of the regiment in this sketch has of necessity been confined chiefly to the record of the changes occurring in officers and a brief tribute to the memory of those who lost their lives in the service. Memory recalls many familiar faces and forms among the officers and men of the regiment, who had no superiors in true soldierly character and devotion to duty, and who are deserving of the nation's highest need of praise.

Isaac M. Abraham, Company G

Abraham began his service as a captain, forming his own company. He was 43 years old when he enrolled at Smithfield on Sept. 10, 1861. He was absent sick with leave starting Aug. 4, 1862, but owing to chronic diarrhea, he needed another 20 days to recover. He returned to duty with the regiment in Sept./Oct. 1862. Abraham took command of the regiment on Feb. 24, 1863. He became sick again in Mar./Apr. 1863, and was in the hospital on Hilton Head Island, SC. Once again, Abraham took command of the regiment commencing Nov. 23, 1863. He was promoted major on Apr. 28, 1864, at Gloucester Point, VA. Abraham was among those wounded at the Battle of Strawberry Plains on August 14, 1864. He began duty on board ship exchanging prisoners of war on Oct. 28, 1864, in the area of Norfolk and Portsmouth. This duty, in which Abraham commanded 50 men and four other officers, was the guarding of some 10,000 Confederate prisoners sent from Point Lookout, MD, to be exchanged and sent to Savannah, GA. He mustered out Dec. 21, 1864. (History of the Old Flag)

144

HISTORY OF THE OLD FLAG
OF THE EIGHTY-FIFTH REGIMENT
PENNSYLVANIA VOLUNTEERS

CIVIL WAR 1861-5

By James Hadden of Uniontown

[Note by the Publishers: The History of the 85th Flag is perhaps unlike that of any other in the country, inasmuch as the flag was not only carried throughout the entire Civil War, but has also since figured in a remarkable legal battle for its possession.]

On the first day of August 1861, Joshua B. Howell, Esq., senior member of the prominent law firm of J. B. & A. Howell of Uniontown, Pa., was commissioned by the secretary of war to enlist a regiment of infantry in this locality for the term of three years for the suppression of the rebellion.

The regiment was to be known as the Eighty-fifth Pennsylvania Volunteers. Enlistments commenced immediately and ten companies, principally from the counties of Fayette, Washington, Greene and Somerset rendezvoused on the fair grounds, at Camp Lafayette, on Fayette street at the eastern part of town.

On the twelfth of October the regiment was organized by the election of the following officers: Joshua B. Howell, colonel; Norton McGiffin of Washington country, Lieut. Colonel and Absalom Guiler of Fayette, major.

A committee of ladies of Uniontown composed of Miss Mary Ewing, now Mrs. John J. Stephenson of New York city; Miss Mary Veech, now Mrs. Rev. J. T. Oxtoby, a Presbyterian minister; Miss Harriet Skiles, long since dead; Miss Sarah Beazell, now of Los Angeles, California; and Miss Rachel Smith, since Mrs. Arnold A. Plumer, of Franklin, Pa., now deceased, solicited funds with which they purchased the material for an elegant silk flag. Miss Elizabeth Hadden made it, and Major William A Donaldson gilded the stars and the figures 85 on the field. James G. Johnston, esq., subsequently editor and proprietor of the American Standard, was chosen by the committee to make the address on the occasion of the presentation of the flag to the regiment. This he did on the 18th of November, in his usual graceful and eloquent style. Col. Howell responded in an able and loyal address on behalf of this regiment, in which he forcibly expressed the appreciation and gratitude of the men who expected to follow, protect and defend the beautiful ensign which had been unfurled to the world as the emblem of political and religious liberty. He then pledged their sacred honors that rather than suffer its folds to be trailed in the dust or be returned to its native place in disgrace, they would leave their bones bleaching on the battlefields of the sunny south. How bravely and faithfully they fulfilled their vow may be learned from the subsequent history of this once beautiful and now historic flag.

Col. Howell having received orders to report at Harrisburg for active duty, the regiment took up the line of march from amp Lafayette on Wednesday, November 20th. Passion through the principal streets of town to the awaiting train, the stars and stripes floating gracefully in the front as they were proudly borne by Sergeant Joseph G. Rager, the first color-bearer of the regiment; the prancing, caparisoned horses of the officers and the bright, new uniforms of the troops as they kept step to the enlivening strains of martial music, presented a sight far surpassing in grandeur anything ever before witnessed in Uniontown.

The crowd at the railway station was immense and many brave hearts ill concealed their emotions as farewells were spoken and the train rolled away from home, families and friends. The regiment arrived at Harrisburg Thursday, November 21st, at 4 o'clock p.m., and was there presented with a regimental flag by Governor Andrew G. Curtin and immediately left for Washington, D. C., and went into camp near Bladensburg, about five miles out from the city, where it remained for a short time and then went into winter quarters at Camp Good Hope, across the east branch of the Potomac, where it was assigned to a brigade commanded by Col. Tidball, consisting of the 85th and 93rd Pennsylvania and the 59th and 86th New York volunteers. Here the troops were employed during the winter in the construction of works for the defense of Washington City.

On the 29th of March 1862, the regiment left Washington and embarked at Alexandria. With the 4th corps it proceeded to Fortress Monroe, where it joined the army of the Potomac, arriving on the 1st of April.

The 85th participated in the siege operations in front of Yorktown, and joined in the pursuit of the enemy by the Winn's mill road, the two stands of colors flying side by side cheering the brave boys on to victory. At Williamsburg they followed it, under a heavy artillery fire, to the relief of the 93rd Pennsylvania and moved on, crossing the Chickahominy near Bottom's Bridge on the 20th of May and took position a little in advance of Fair Oaks station, where the enemy made an attack at 1 o'clock p.m. on the 31st.

In this battle the faithful color-bearer was smitten down and fell into the hands of the enemy. As he fell Richard Lincoln seized the flag and as he bore it aloft with a hurrah, he too, was struck with a minie ball which severed his forefinger and shattered the flag staff. He was removed and Jacob Deffenbaugh seized the flag and bravely bore it aloft throughout the engagement.

Here the flag waved over the rifle pits on the right of the main works, a redoubt held by Hart's Battery, and here Lieut. James Hamilton and Thomas Purviance were killed and Julius A. Smith mortally wounded in fulfilling their promise. In the Seven Days' battle eighty-seven more brave boys perished in the defense of their flag.

When General George B. McClellan, with the bulk of his army, evacuated the peninsula, Keys' corps remained on duty, and this noble emblem was unfurled at Fortress Monroe.

Early on the morning of the 5th of December, the 85th, then part of Wessell's brigade, was ordered from Suffolk, Va., where it had been stationed, to Newbern, North Carolina, to reinforce General Foster, then in command of the Eighteenth corps. The glorious old banner floating in the breeze as the boys marched by the way of Gatesville to the Chowan river, where the troops embarked upon transports, and arrived at their destination on the 9th. On the 13th at South West Creek, where the enemy disputed the crossing with artillery, its waving folds beckoned the brave boys on to victory and to glory, where two pieces of artillery, five killed, a number wounded and some prisoners, rewarded the heroes. By 3 o'clock p.m. of the 14th the flag was floating in victory at Kinston, beyond the Neuse River. In this charge nine more of the 85th shed their blood in adding glory to their flag. At White Hall and at Goldsboro, where the bridge was destroyed and the railroad torn up, on the 17th, it encouraged the boys by its silent presence.

On the 1st of January 1863, the brigade moved to the south side of the Trent River, opposite the town, where, side by side with the state colors, this flag did duty in front of regimental headquarters for several weeks.

Toward the close of January the old flag again beckoned the brave boys onward to South Carolina, where General Foster was ordered to cooperate with General Hunter in his operations against Charleston, and floated at Hilton head on the 1st of February, the brigade being now under command of Col. Howell and the regiment under command of Lieut. Col. Purviance. Here the old flag stood sentry before headquarters until the 1st of April when it again led the troops to Cole's Island and then to the head of folly Island, and here floated to the breeze during the bombardment of Fort Sumter by Admiral Dupont, and while the troops were engaged in making roads, erecting defenses and placing a battery of forty-four guns.

Levi M. Rogers, Company F
Enrolled at age 23 in Rogersville, Greene County, on July 13, 1861, and mustered in as first sergeant on Nov. 11. As a second lieutenant, he took command of Co. F on June 26, 1863. Rogers was promoted first lieutenant on July 7, 1863. He suffered a wound in the left side at the Battle of Ware Bottom Church on May 20, 1864. He received a 20-day furlough to return home and recover. After recovering, he was promoted captain on Aug. 8. (Ronn Palm Collection)

Levi M. Rogers, Company F

Rogers was again wounded at the Battle of Deep Bottom on Aug. 16, 1864, being shot through the pelvis. He was sent to the hospital at Fort Monroe, where he died on Sept. 4, 1864. On Oct. 1, 1864, his brother received his effects, which were, other than the standard uniform issues: a valise, towel, razor and strap, one glass, two books, slippers, gloves, dictionary, pocket bible, a photo album, and ambrotypes and a considerable list of additional items. (Ronn Palm Collection)

On the 20th of August, the old flag was posted over the advance trenches on Morris Island. On the left were the guns of James Island and of Fort Johnson; in front those of Sumter, Gregg and Wagner; and on the right, those of Fort Moultrie. In the terrible ordeal through which the troops were compelled to pass in this siege, sixteen of the brave boys of the 85th gave up their lives, among the number being Lieut. Col. Purviance, and thirty-three shed their blood beneath the folds of the flag they loved and were determined to defend. The flag itself being tattered by the bursting of a shell almost within its folds. The casualties and sickness here became so alarming that Surgeon Hamlin, Medical Inspector of the department, reported that unless Wagner should soon fall, the troops would not be in condition to longer prosecute the siege. The 85th went upon the outworks with an aggregate strength of 451 and on the last day, the 2nd of September, it could muster but 270 fit for duty. After a concentrated bombardment of 40 hours from land and sea, Fort Wagner was evacuated and victory once more perched upon this noble ensign which was the first to enter the evacuated fort.

In the early part of December, the 85th was ordered to Hilton Head where together with its inseparable companion, the state colors, the old flag decorated the regimental headquarters, until 22nd of February, 1864, when it once more waved over its heroic defenders as they marched to White Marsh Island, near Savannah where, encountering a superior force, two more of the 85th were wounded and Capt. John E. Michener taken prisoner.

In April the stars and stripes floated over the narrow neck of land between the James and the Appomattox where on the 20th of May they led the gallant charge in which the fortifications and rifle pits were retaken from which Butler's forces had been driven. Here the rebel General Walker was wounded and taken prisoner. Two more of the noble band of defenders here gave up their lives, and the blood of twenty-five more of the 85th was spilled that victory might once more perch upon the banner to which they had sworn allegiance.

On the 16th of June Lee's advance crossed the James at Fort Darling, and early the following morning, made an attack on the picket line in front of Howell's brigade. The fighting became very heavy and the old flag of the gallant 85th waved over the lifeless bodies of seven more who had followed it so faithfully from victory to victory, and here the earth drank the precious blood of ten of its devoted followers.

On the 20th this glorious emblem led the marching troops of Howell's brigade to Deep Bottom and returned to camp and its peace upon the line on the 25th.

On August 14th this battle scarred banner floated gloriously in advance as Terry's division gallantly charged upon the earthworks of Longstreet and Hill at Strawberry Plains, and although advancing over an open plain, and exposed to a galling fire from the enemy, that glorious ensign beckoned its brave followers onward until one earthwork after another was captured and Terry was in full possession. Here twenty-one more of the heroic followers of the old flag sacrificed their blood upon the altar of their country, Lieut. William T. Campbell being among the killed and Major Abraham among the wounded, thus placing the indomitable 85th under the command of Lieut. Col. Campbell. In the several engagements which now followed in rapid succession at this place the 85th crowned itself with glory, having taken a number of prisoners and three stands of colors, at the cost of nine killed and fifty-four wounded, five of whom, mortally, and one taken prisoner, Capt. Lewis Watkins and Capt. Levi M. Rogers being among the mortally wounded.

This was the bloodiest and fiercest battle through which the 85th was called to pass, and was known as the battle at Deep Bottom and was within then miles of the Confederate capital. In the charge of the 16th the two stands of colors were carried well to the front and ten of the color company (Co. C) were killed in one dash. The flagstaff of the state colors was pierced by a minie ball, between the hand of color bearer Alex Ross and the staff holder, and another lodged in the spear head, where it flattened itself and remained embedded.

The 85th being withdrawn from the north side of the James on the 20th, the old flag was allowed to float in peace over the resting camp until the 24th, when it was hoisted over the rifle pits on the south of the Appomattox. It next floated for two weeks over Fort Morton, a fourteen-gun battery. It then joined the van in the movement across the James with the 10th and 18th corps and proudly waved over the fall of Fort Harrison and the capture of a long line of earthworks at Chapen's Farm.

Having twice advanced to within three miles of the rebel capital, this glorious emblem of freedom floated defiantly in the very face of the enemy's stronghold, and was with Terry in the recovery of the ground lost by Kantz's cavalry.

The indomitable 85th lost their brave colonel by an accident while in front a Petersburg. While returning from an entertainment given by some officers Col. Howell's horse fell upon him, inflicting injuries from which he died September 14, 1864. His body was taken by his brother to Woodbury, New Jersey, for interment.

The term of enlistment of the 85th having about expired and the brave boys having a deep sense of having faithfully satisfied the claims of their country, all the acting 1st sergeants of the regiment formed themselves into a committee to send in a request for an honorable discharge from the service, but to their disappointment the papers were disapproved at corps or division headquarters, and were returned as such about 12 o'clock the same night. The following day 1st Sergeant John G. Stevens took the papers to Gen. Grant's

Edward Campbell, Lieutenant Colonel

Campbell enrolled in Captain Purviance's company in Uniontown on Sept. 21, 1861, and mustered in there on Nov. 12, as a second lieutenant in Co. E. He was 23 years old. He was posted in Uniontown on recruiting service from Dec. 14, 1861, until Mar. 1862. On May 15, 1862, he was promoted captain of the company. Campbell was next appointed major and received a commission as such on Mar. 2, 1863, to date back to Sept. 6, 1862. In May/June 1863, he was serving as acting assistant inspector general of Stono Department of South Carolina by order of Gen. Israel Vogdes. On July 21 1863, he was assigned to detached service as chief of staff for Gen. Vogdes at Folly Island, SC. A request was made on Aug. 3, 1863, to have Campbell returned to the regiment as it was short of field officers and where he might be more useful. He was returned to the regiment on July 10. After Lieutenant Colonel Henry Purviance was killed on Morris Island, Campbell was elevated to that grade on Sept. 8, 1863, and officially mustered in with that rank on Oct. 16. Detached on recruiting service from Nov. 20, 1863, until May 3, 1864. He requested to be mustered out on Nov. 12, 1864, "having served three years from the date of first muster. . . ," which was done on Nov. 22. This is a postwar picture of Campbell. (Civil War Library & Museum, Philadelphia, PA)

headquarters for the purpose of submitting the same to him, but the general not being present at the time he returned with the disapproved papers. Fortunately Peter A. Johns was at this time visiting the troops with the poll book for the purpose of securing the soldiers' votes. Johns being informed of the disapproval of the request of the 85th, insisted that he should be permitted the honor of presenting the request to Gen. B. F. Butler, then in command of the 10th and 18th corps. Johns had no difficulty in securing an interview with that distinguished personage, who cheerfully approved of the request and immediately gave orders direct to Lieut. Col. Campbell, then in command of the regiment, to proceed immediately to Portsmouth for the purpose of being mustered out of the service. The lieutenant colonel had hoped that by reenlistments and recruits he might be able to keep up the organization and remain in command at the front, and could not conceal his chagrin upon receiving orders direct from his commanding officer to proceed to the rear. The loyal hearts of the brave boys swelled with glad emotion in anticipation of once more meeting their families and friends, and preparations were immediately made for their homeward march. As the troops passed regimental headquarters the two stands of colors were floating from their respective staffs. Sergeant George W. Ramage was told to secure the state flag-which was being left-which he did, pulling the staff from the ground and bore it away, with the marching regiment, and delivered it to Alex Ross, the color bearer, who took charge of both flags until the arrival of former color bearer John M. Moore at Portsmouth. Mr. Moore having sustained a sunstroke on August 16, 1864, was sent to the hospital and rejoined his regiment on their homeward march here. The marching regiment was halted before the headquarters of Gen. Terry, who expressed his surprise that the regiment had been ordered to the rear without his approval, but upon learning that the orders came directly from Gen. Butler he wisely refrained from any comment.

The regiment was next halted in front of General Butler's headquarters when the general was about to ride off and here the orders were reiterated to proceed to the rear for the purpose of being mustered out of service.

Three rousing cheers gave vent to overflowing hearts as the general rode off, with bared head nodding recognition of the expression of the regiment.

The regiment took boat opposite City Point that night, and went to Portsmouth, where it went into camp preparatory to making out the company rolls. Here a detail was made for five commissioned officers and fifty men, under command of Major Abraham, to guard 10,000 prisoners who were to be sent from Point Lookout to Savannah to be exchanged in November.

About one hundred and fifty members of the 85th reenlisted for three years further service or during the war and became known as the detachment of the 85th. They were incorporated, July 9, 1865, into the 188th P. V.'s but continued to be known as the detachment of the 85th and continued in service and were present and witnessed the surrender of Lee at Appomattox.

The regiment came on to Pittsburg where it was mustered out of service the 22nd of November, 1864. Here the briny tear coursed its silent way down the furrowed cheek of the suntanned veteran as he grasped the hand of his faithful comrade and messmate with whom he had shared the privations of war, had bivouacked of the gory field, braved the hissing missiles of the enemy and marched side by side to victory and to glory. Farewells were spoken with the full expectation that this band of noble heroes would never more assemble until in answer to the last great roll call, and the survivors of the grand old 85th, covered with honors, separated to be welcomed home, with overflowing hearts, by their families and friends.

The state colors having been returned to the state as the troops returned through Harrisonburg, the private flag was still in the custody of Sergeant John M. Moore of Washington county, who was a member of Company A and was colorbearer at the time the regiment was mustered out of service. Mr. Moore left the flag hanging on two nails in a warehouse on Second Avenue, where the regiment was temporarily quartered, from here James P. McCuen, a musician of Company F and a Uniontown boy, took the flag and brought it home the same evening; just three years and two days from the time it floated so gracefully and beautifully over the marching column as it passed from Camp Lafayette through the streets of Uniontown to the awaiting train.

On account of several officers and men of the 85th being detailed at Portsmouth, as previously stated, these were not discharged until in December. Sergeant John G. Stevens being of this number, he did not arrive home until December. Upon approaching his home he was surprised to find many of his old comrades assembled to give him a hearty welcome, among whom was James P. McCuen with the old flag, who addressed Sergeant Stevens as follows:

"Sergeant Stevens, in behalf of the survivors of the 85th regiment, Pennsylvania Volunteers I wish to place into your care and keeping this remnant of our once beautiful but now battle scarred and glory crowned flag. We have faithfully and devoutly followed and defended it through scorching sun sand fierce conflicts, through miasmatic swamps and over death-strewn battlefields. It is tattered with shell and crowned with glory. The original staff on which it so proudly floated when presented to our regiment by the loyal kindness of the ladies of Uniontown, has long since been shattered to splinters and unable to bear this memento of their loyal affection. The staff on which it now floats bears the scars of battle. The spear head still retains the minie ball that flattened itself in the vain effort to destroy the flag of our country. The lower part of this staff is shattered by being pierced by a ball from the

James McCuen, Company F
McCuen enrolled as a musician at age 17 on Nov. 19, 1861, at Uniontown, but he did not muster in until Dec. 21, at Fort Good Hope near Washington, DC. As a drummer, he was present with the regiment the entire time of service, except for a short time in Jan. 1864, when he was convalescing at the General Hospital at 65th and Vine Streets in Philadelphia. McCuen mustered out with the regiment at Pittsburgh on Nov. 22, 1864. He carried the regimental color back to Uniontown. After the war, McCuen worked as the master of transportation for the Queen and Cresent Railroad system and lived in Ludlow, KY. (History of the Old Flag)

enemy. Had it not been for your thoughtful persistence this precious relic would have been left in the distant south, would have fallen into the hands of strangers who knew nothing of its history, cared nothing for its donors and been lost to those who so highly prized it. By inheritance and conquest you are its proper and competent custodian, and I hope that so long as life lasts and your loyalty to your country remains steadfast, that your right to the custody of this priceless old flag may never be questioned nor disputed."

The following is a partial list of the battles, besides which there were innumerable skirmished in which the 85th was engaged.

Yorktown where the siege was begun April 23rd and continued until May 4th, when the place was evacuated. The battle of Williamsburg followed immediately after the evacuation of Yorktown, May 5th.

The battle of Fair Oaks and of Seven Pines occurred May 31st and June 1st. The engagements of the Seven Days' Battle, Jones' Ford and Harrison's Landing continuing from June 26th to July 2nd. The action beginning at Mechanicsville and ending at Harrison's Landing. Then followed the engagement at Suffolk the 10th of September, which was quickly followed by the engagement of Blackwater in October. The engagement at Southwest Creek occurred the 13th of December, followed by that of Kingston on the 14th and White hall on the 15th. The battle at Goldsboro Bridge occurred the 17th of December and thus closed up a long list of terrible and bloody engagements for the year of 1862.

The campaign for 1863 opened by the movement against Charleston from Hilton Head and folly Island, and proceeding to Morris Island July 10th, where the siege of Sumter, Greg and Wagner continued with unabated fury until the evacuation of these forts, September 6th, when the flag of the 85th borne by the colorbearer George Orbin, was the first to enter George Orbin, was the first to enter the evacuated fort.

The bombardment of Charleston with the famous "Swamp Angel" soon followed and White Marsh Island was occupied by the Union troops on the 22nd February 1864. The several engagements at Bemuda Hundred continued from May 6th till August 13th, and that of Deep Bottom followed on the 14th and that of Strawberry plains on the 16th. The engagements in front of Petersburg continued from the 25th of August until the 28th of September. Then followed that of Chapin's Farm from the 29th of September till the 14th of October. On the 13th of October occurred the engagement on the Darbytown road when Kautz's cavalry was routed and the lost ground recovered.

Those of the 85th who re-enlisted as veterans witnessed the surrender of Lee at Appomattox.

The following poem in memory of the engagements through which the old flag of the 85th was triumphantly carried is contributed by Wooda N. Carr, Esq., of Uniontown.

"Yorktown and Williamsburg are
name to ev'ry mem'ry dear.
Old Fair Oaks then and Charleston
too shall need no plaudits here;
At Jones' Ford and Southwest Creek
there rained both shot and shell,
And on the plains of Goldsboro where
many heroes fell.

The stubborn fight of Seven Days
made red the field of war,
The musketry of old Suffolk the flying
colors tore.
Old White Hall too will find a place
within each vet'ran's breast,
So long as valor shall remain for
aoldiery a test.

The fierce simoon that swept the field
at Gregg and Wagner too.
Brought death to many noble lads
that wore the suit of blue.
Ah, could Bermuda Hundred speak,
how many hearts 'twould cheer,
To know the prayers to heaven sent
by dying comrades here.
Deep Bottom, where the sky was red
with never ceasing fire,
Is know to fames and often told by
poets' tuneful lyre.
On Strawb'ry Plains and Chapin's
Farm was battle face to face.
To gain the higher ground beyond
and hold the vantage place.

Far famed is glorious Petersburg,
and only they can know,
That "war is hell" in all its forms,

who faced the southron foe.
A hist'ry like of blood and tears, the
world ne'er furnished forth,
As when the sons of Southland met
their brothers of the North."

The following persons had the honor of bearing the colors of the 85th regiment during its service in defense of their country: Joseph G. Reager, Co. B, from the time it was presented to the regiment, November 18th until he was discharged on surgeon's certificate April 27, 1862, now living at Suterville, Pa.

Richard Lincoln, Co. I, at Fair Oaks 20th May, 1862, wounded.

Jacob Deffenbaugh, Co. I, carried the flag from the 27th April, through the battles of Yorktown, Williamsburg, Fair Oaks, Seven Days, Suffolk, Blackwater, Southwest Creek, Kingston, White Hall, Goldsboro, Folly Island and Morris Island. Mr. Deffenbaugh carried the colors through twenty-five engagements and pressing to the front would call to the boys to "keep up with the flag." He is now living in Walton, Kansas.

George Orbin was Co. C, colorbearer from last of July 1862 till first of September 1863. He is now preaching the gospel in Pittsburg. It was he who carried the flag triumphantly into the evacuated fort of Wanger.

Alexander Ross, Co. A, was colorbearer from May 1st, 1864, and was bearing the flag when the staff was pierced by a ball and another was stuck in the spearhead. He carried it through Deep Bottom, Strawberry Plains, front of Petersburg, Chapin's Farm and Darbytown Road, and was colobearer when the regiment was mustered out of service. He is now living at Economy, Pa.

Walter C. Craven, Co. C, was also colorbearer with Alexander Ross in front of Petersburg, Chapin's Farm and Darbytown Road. He is now living at Wilkinsburg, Pa.

John M. Moore was colorbearer from October 1st, 1863, until mustered out of regiment November 22, 1864. He carried the old flag in all the engagements in front of Bermuda Hundred, Petersburg, Chapin's Farm and Darbytown Road. He now lives at Parish, N.Y.

At a political meeting held in Pittsburg in 1872, many of the members of the old 85th regiment met together and decided to organize an association of the surviviors of their regiment. In accordance with which circulars were mailed to all whose addresses could be obtained inviting their cooperation, and designating Uniontown as the place and the 30th of May, 1873, as the time for the first meeting and urging that a permanent organization be effected. In response to these invitations a goodly number of the comrades of the 85th met in the court house an the time and place designated and an association to be known as the Eighty-fifth Pennsylvania Regimental Association was organized by the election of the following officers, to wit: Major I. M. Abraham, president; _____________________, vice president; Jacob Davis, secretary; _____________________, treasurer; _____________________, color bearer.

At this meeting the old flag was presented to view by Sergeant John G. Stevens and called forth rounds of applause from the veterans who now viewed it for the first time since they had followed it through trying scenes which its tattered folds brought fresh to memory. It was borne in the procession by Sergeant Stevens to Oak Grove cemetery where the graves of those who had fought in the defense of their country were decorated by their surviving comrades.

The following year, 1874, the 85th Regimental Association met at Brownsville, in October, and the old flag again greeted the veterans, under the care of James Swearer, a member of Company C, and a resident of Brownsville. In 1875, the Association met at Waynesburg and the flag again greeted its old defenders, and Sergeant James E. Sayers of Waynesburg was elected colorbearer, and took charge of the flag.

In 1876, the Association met at Washington where the old flag again added interest to the deliberations of the meetings.

In 1877 the Association met at Monongahela City and the old flag gave enthusiasm to the veterans as they rehearsed the exciting scenes through which they had passed.

In 1878 the Association met at Connellsville.

In 1879 there was held at Uniontown a reunion of old soldiers of the war of the rebellion. The 85th Regimental Association joined in this reunion and also held a meeting of the association.

In 1880 the Association met at Greensboro. While here the flag was hidden and much excitement prevailed lest it be surreptitiously carried away.

In 1881 the Association met at Cannonsburg and George S. Fulmer was elected colorbearer and took charge of the flag for the coming year.

In 1882 the Association met at Pittsburg and Alex Ross, the old colorbearer, when the 85th was in active service, was elected colorbearer and assumed the duties of caring for the old flag for the coming year.

In 1883 the Association again met at Pittsburg and Alex Ross was reelected to the office of colorbearer, which duties he faithfully performed.

In 1884 the Association met at Washington. Oscar F. Lyon was elected colorbearer and took charge of the flag.

In 1885 the Association met at Cannonsburg. Here James T. Speer was elected colorbearer and the flag was put in his care for the coming year.

In 1886 the Association met at Pittsburg and Corporal William E.

James E. Sayers, Company F

Enrolling in the regiment on July 18, 1862, at Waynesburg, Sayer had been born in Greene County and was an 18-year-old student at the time. He mustered in at Harrisburg on Aug. 8, 1862. Being only 18, Sayer's father had to give permission for his son to enlist, which he did. In Apr. 1863, he served as an orderly for Colonel Howell, and in Aug./Sept. 1863, he was detailed for duty as a sharpshooter. On Nov. 20 of that same year, he was sent back to Pennsylvania on recruiting service until Apr. 1864. He was promoted sergeant in Sept./Oct., then to first sergeant on Nov. 1, 1864. When the regiment returned to Pennsylvania to be mustered out, Sayers went with it, but because he had enlisted later, he was not entitled to his discharge and sent back to the detachment still serving in the field. He was forwarded to Harrisburg as a straggler and charged $5.10 for transportation, then rejoined the detachment on Dec. 1, 1864, and served with them when assigned to the 199th Pennsylvania. He mustered out on May 14, 1865, near Richmond, VA, "by way of favor." (USAMHI)

Chick was elected colorbearer and took charge of the flag.

In 1887 the Association met in Washington.

In 1888 the association met at Pittsburgh and John B. Beall took possession of the old flag as colorbearer.

1889 the Association met at Scottdale and John G. Stevens was elected colorbearer and once more the old flag was placed in his custody.

1890 the Association met at Uniontown and Sergeant John G. Stevens was reelected colorbearer.

1891 the Association met at Waynesburg and John G. Stevens was again reelected colorbearer.

1892 the Association met at Wilkinsburg October 13th, and Seargeant John G. Stevens was reelected for the fourth term in succession as colorbearer. This was the last time the flag was exhibited by the Association until at Uniontown in 1899 when Sergeant Stevens exhibited it again.

1893 the association met at California.

1894 the Association met at Pittsburg.

1895 the Association met at Scottsdale.

1896 the Association met at Brownsville.

1897 the Association met at Uniontown.

1898 the Association met at Monogahela City.

1899 the Association met at the Uniontown in the opera house and the flag once more greeted its old defenders.

1900 at Brownsville.

1901 at Washington.

On the 4th day of March, 1898, a petition was filed praying the court that a preliminary injunction be served on Sergeant John G. Stevens and others, forbidding the removal of the flag from its present location and to present said flag to the Eighty-fifth Regimental Association. After a hearing of the case, in which the history of the flag was rehearsed, his honor, Judge Mestrezat, issued the preliminary injunction and the defendant allowed a hearing on Saturday, March 12, at 2 p.m. to file an answer to the bill of complaint.

On Saturday, March 12, the defendant came into court and requested that the preliminary injunction be made permanent, thus placing the case on the regular equity list.

The demurrer was filed through his counsel, W. G. Guiler, March 18, in which the defendant demurs to the whole of plaintiff's bill, and by agreement of counsel the time for filing an answer was extended to April 1.

At a special meeting of court held Monday evening, April 4, evidence was taken on the part of the defense, and respondent, Sergeant John G. Stevens, gave in his testimony and a history of the flag from its presentation to the regiment by the ladies of Uniontown, until the present time. Court then adjourned until Tuesday afternoon, April 5, to hear the argument on the demurrer. The counsel for the respondent rehearsed the history of the flag, which now occupies a conspicuous place in the court room and stated that it was the wish of the respondent to put the glorious old battle-marred emblem in a glass case and place it in the custody of the Fayette county historical society, from whence it cold be brought out on the occasion of every reunion of the survivors of the regiment, and at the same time be safe from the desecrating hand of the relic seekers. A number of letters were read from survivors of the regiment concurring in the foregoing desire.

Lieut. George S. Fulmer, at this time president of the Eighty-fifth Regimental Association, made an eloquent and touching address to the court in favor of the claimants. His honor then earnestly advised the contesting parties to meet together and adjust their differences amicably and keep such sacred matters out of the courts and from unfriendly criticism.

The plaintiffs were then permitted to amend the style of their suit and defendant given until on or before the 30th of April to file an answer, which was done Thursday, April 28, in which the respondent filed objections.

A hearing was held before his honor. Judge E. H. Reppert, the 8th of December, 1898, at 2 o'clock p.m. at which W. G. Guiler, Esq., argued the case for the defendant and Edward Campbell, Esq., for the plaintiff, and briefs were submitted to the court for its consideration.

On March 2, 1900, Judge Reppert handed down his decision of the finding of the facts and conclusion of law in the case. His honor stated that no assignment, transfer of conveyance of the title to said flag from the surviving members of the regiment to the plaintiff association had ever been made or by any of them, by vote, resolution or otherwise, at any meeting held by the plaintiff association. And gave as conclusion of law that the plaintiff association having shown no title to the flag in question its bill must be dismissed, and issued the following decree: "This matter came on to be heard and was argued by counsel; and now March 12, 1900, upon consideration, it is ordered, adjudged and decreed that the bill filed in this case be dismissed at the plaintiff's cost."

The case was appealed to the superior court sitting at Pittsburg and was argued on April 18th, and on the 24th of May his honor, Judge Beaver, delivered the opinion of that court affirming the common pleas court of Fayette country, remarking that it was quite clear that the members of the Eighty-fifth Regimental Association could not transfer thereunto more than their own interest in the flag, and even if this had been done, it would not have vested in the association more that the undivided one fifth interest therein. His honor further remarked:

"We fully sympathize with the members of this association in their desire to see their battle-scarred and tattered standard in safe keeping. The defendant, however, has apparently on the same desire. He seems to have good cause for his anxiety in regards to the safety of what remains of the flag. It is not denied that on one occasion, when he first allowed it to pass out of his possession, as he supposed temporarily, for a legitimate purpose the flag was mutilated and practically destroyed. To use his own expressive language in one of his answers as witness to a question of counsel, 'When they borrowed that flag from me, the field was all there and the stars were all there in it and there was a piece of a bullet imbedded in the stem and in the spear a bullet was imbedded, and the stripes were all there, so that you could make out that it was a flag; and when I got it back to Scottdale nobody could make out what it was; there wasn't a star in it, nor a single white stripe on it. Half of the bullet was picked our of the spear and I wouldn't have had that done for all the flags in the country.'"

"It is not ours to dictate or even suggest the final disposition to be made of this flag, but the efforts of the court below to secure a safe and permanent place for its custody are entirely commendable."

A motion for a reargument in the case was filed October 11, and an order of the court refusing the same was entered October 18th, thus throwing the case entirely out of the courts.

ROSTER OF THE SURVIVORS
OF THE
Eighty-Fifth Regiment, Pennsylvania Volunteers, 1902

Field And Staff.

Name	Rank	Address
Norton McGiffin	Lieut. Col.	Washington, Penna.
Edward Campbell	Lieut. Col.	Uniontown, Penna.
James B. Treadwell	Major	Somerset, Penna.
John B. Laidley	Surgeon	Carmichaels, Penna.
Samuel L. Kurtz	Surgeon	Reading, Penna.
Hugh W. Siddell	Asst. Surgeon	35th & Haverfort Sts., Phila., Pa.
Joseph C. Dowds	Adjutant	Ohiopyle, Penna.
S. L. McHenry	Adjutant	Dollar Savings Bank, Allegheny, Pa.
Joseph C. Dowds	Adjutant	Olean, N. Y.
John N. Pierce	Chaplain	Clinton, Mo.

John Murphy	Quartermaster	624 Grant St., Pittsburg, Pa.
William E. Beall	Quartermaster	No. 217 W. 142d St., New York City.
Boyd Crumrine	Q. M. Sergeant	Washington, Penna.
Samuel M. Walton	Q. M. Sergeant	Rices Landing, Penna.
W. L. Pershing	Q. M. Sergeant	Springfield, Ohio.
John B. Bell	Com. Sergeant	Crafton, Penna.
S. M. H. Beebout	Hospital Steward	Walls, Penna.
Henry L. Regar	Prin. Musician	Connellsville, Penna.

COMPANY A.

Harvey J. Vankirk	Captain	Washington, Penna.
S. C. McGregor	1st Lieut.	Burgettstown, Penna.
John Rowley	2nd Lieut.	Finleyville, Penna.
A. W. Pollock	1st Sergeant	Washington, Penna.
Robert Caldwell	Sergeant	Collier, W. Va.
Robert Crisswell	Sergeant	Florence, Penna.
William D. Shaw	Sergeant	Brisco, Iowas
Greer Hair	Sergeant	Liberty, Gage county, Neb.
Matthew Templeton	Corporal	Becks Mill, Washington county, Pa.
James N. Brown	Corporal	Canonsburg, Penna.
Thomas Griffith	Corporal	Claysville, Washington county, Pa.
William Milligan	Corporal	Gastonville, Washington county, Pa.
Alexander M. Ross	Corporal	Box 64, Economy, Pa.
Robert B. Thompson	Musician	Harmarville, Penna.
J. W. Ingles	Musician	Pleasant Hill, Neb.
Andrews, Joseph W.	Private	Boulder, Col.
Barr, Thomas J.	Private	Healdsburg, Sonomo county, Cal.
Briggs, Thomas	Private	South Washington, Penna.
Brownlee, Andrew	Private	Claysville, Penna.
Carothers, James	Private	Hawkins Station, Washin. Co., Penna.
Carothers, John	Private	Moronto, Jefferson county, Ohio.
Caldwell, Samuel R.	Private	Paris, Washington county, Penna.
Craig, James S.	Private	Stevensville, Texas.
Fulton, Thomas K.	Private	Canton, Ills.
Kerr, Joseph G.	Private	Morganza, Penna.
Kline, John R.	Private	Hollidays Cove, W. Va.
Lovejoy, Andrew A.	Private	Alliance, Ohio.
Morrison, William H.	Private	Paris, Washington county, Pa.
Martin, Philip	Private	Washington, Penna.
McCabe, Joseph E.	Private	Thompsonville, R. D. 41 Penna.

Jacob Richardson, Company A

Richardson, shown here in later years, enrolled at age 23 in Capt. Vankirk's company on Sept. 19, 1861, at Taylorstown. He mustered in at Uniontown on Oct. 16, 1861. Richardson was present with Co. A until falling ill on June 1, 1862, and on the surgeon's authority was sent to a hospital in Newport, Rhode Island. He returned to the regiment late in Aug. of 1862, and remained present with the outfit until the muster out. In Sept./Oct. 1864, he was assigned daily duty as the company cook. He mustered out on Nov. 22, 1864, at Pittsburgh, drawing $100 bounty due and owing $8.90 for clothing. (USAMHI)

McEwen, James H.	Private	Garnet, Kas.
Nickerson, Henry W.	Private	Pikes Peak, Ind.
Neill, John	Private	Cannonsburg, Penna.
Palmer, Joseph H.	Private	Jeannette, Penna
Patterson, John	Private	Venitia, R. D. 36 Washington Co.
Park, John	Private	Florence, Penna.
Richardson, Jacob	Private	Taylorstown, Washtinton Co., Pa.
Randolph, Wm. H.	Private	Hayes, Washington.
Shaw, Joseph	Private	Washington, R.D., 3, Penna.
Sias, W. H. H.	Private	New Stanton, Penna.
Sawhill, Thomas	Private	Claysville, Penna
Thompson, Rev. Jacob L.	Private	Passadena, Cal.
Vance Alecander H.	Privtate	Milford Seward county, Neb.

COMPANY B.

George B. Hooker	Captain	
James R. Kean	1st Sergeant	Reeder, Comanche couinty, Kas.
Samuel C. Stevenson	1st Sergeant	Scottdale, Penna.
Isaac F. Overholt	Sergeant	________________California.
Benjamin Orgin	Sergeant	Broad Ford, Fayette county, Penna.
Adam Harbison	Sergeant	Cannonsburg, Penna.
James F. Speer	Sergeant	Cannonsburg, Penna
John W. Bigler	Sergeant	White Pine, W. Va.
Menane Sharp	Sergeant	Washington, Penna.
Wm. McCollough	Corporal	Bissell, Washington country, Pa.
Jackson Crumrine	Corporal	Alton, Kas.
Cephas Dodd	Corporal	Cincinnati, Ohio.
George K. Strawn	Corporal	104 S. College street, Akrot, Ohio.
John S. Shallenberger	Musician	Bluff and Magee Strs., Pittsburg, Pa.
Eli Crumrine	Musician	Laramie, Wyoming.
Bair, James R.	Private	Deemston, Penna.
Baker, David W.	Private	Washington, Penna
Bryan, James H.	Private	Hutchinson, Kas.
Beattie, Joseph S.	Private	Mt. Pleasant, Iowa.
Cain, Matthew	Private	Cannonsburg, Penna.
Coder, Eli	Private	Dawson, Penna.
Cage, James G.	Private	Oak Forest, Penna.
Chalfant, Duncan C.	Private	Neligh, Neb.
Guthrie, John	Private	St. Francisville, Clark Co., Ma.
Gibbons, Thomas	Private	Coal Bluff, Washington Co. Penna.
Hammers, Leonard R.	Private	Nineveh, Greene county, Penna.
Kelley, Isaac	Private	Wilkinson, Washington.
Layton, Martin E.	Private	Layton Station, Penna.
Martin, Daniel	Private	Washington, Penna.

John F. Overholt, Company B
A recruit who enlisted on Feb. 25, 1864, at Greensburg. A 23-year-old teacher, Overholt was born and raised in Fayette County. He had brown eyes, black hair, a dark complexion, and stood 5'10". He was forwarded to the regiment on Mar. 21, 1864, from Pittsburgh. Briefly sick in May/June 1864, he was transferred to the 199th Pennsylvania Infantry on Oct. 14, 1864, at that time he was sick in the hospital at Bermuda Hundred, VA, and had been sent to Fort Monroe on Sept. 16. During this time he was fined for losing his canteen. On July 8, 1865, Overholt was again transferred, this time to the 188th Pennsylvania. (Ronn Palm Collection)

McCollough, J. W.	Private	Jefferson, Penna.
Magee, John	Private	Littleton, W. Va.
Newcomer, Joseph L.	Private	Broad Ford, Penna.
Overholt, John F.	Private	Grand Crossing, Sta. r, Chicago, Ills.
Reager, Joseph G.	Private	Suterville, Penna.
Ruttcorn, Presley H.	Private	Definance, Shelby county, Iowa.
Ryan, Evan	Private	Hume, Ills.
Rossell, John V.	Private	Scottdale, Penna.
Saunders, Geo. W.	Private	Pierre, South Dakota.
Smith, James	Private	Amity, (Washington R. D.) Penna.
Smith, Moses	Private	Hackney, (Washington R. D.) Penna.
Sterrett, Josiah	Private	Jacobs Creek, Westmoreland Co., Pa.
Stewart, William	Private	Rainbow, San Diego county, Cal.
Strawn, Harry J.	Private	Albion, Ills.
Strawn, Dr. Enos K.	Private	Madison, Westmoreland Co., Pa.
Strouch, Benedick	Private	Challacombe, Ness county, Kas.
Turner, Owen	Private	Hustonville, Penna.
Torrence, James	Private	Dawson, Penna.
Torrence, Joshua	Private	Dawson, Penna.
Watson, John	Private	Lippencott, Greene county, Penna.
Wright, Silas	Private	Bridgeville, Allegheny county, Pa.
Wilkes, John	Private	Perryopolis, Penna.

COMPANY C.

Major Gen. Robert P. Hughes	Captain	
Isaac R. Beazell	1st Lieut.	Brownsville, Penna.
William H. Davis	1st Lieut.	Dixon, Soloma county, Cal.
George J. Vangilder	2nd Lieut.	College avenue, Racine, Wis.
James A. Swearer	1st Sergeant	Beaver, Penna.
Wm. A. Fortner	Sergeant	2108 Sarah St., S. S., Pittsburg, Pa.
Franklin D. Condon	Sergeant	Sheridan, LaSalle county, Ills.
Walter C. Craven	Sergeant	743 Trenton Ave., Wilkinsburg, Pa.
John T. Norris	Sergeant	Promise City, Iowa.
Lewis Rimmel	Corporal	Adrian, Mich.
Bejamin F. Durbin	Corporal	40 Gum street, Pittsburg, Penna.
George W. Sherman	Corporal	California, Penna.
Balseley, William W.	Private	Connelsville, Penna.
Beatty, William	Private	90 Manhattan St., Allegheny, Pa.
Carlisle, David V. B.	Private	Hutchinson, Kas.
Cline, Thomas H.	Private	Brownsville, Penna.
Crawford, G. H.	Private	Richmond, Ind.
Doxler, James A.	Private	Woods Run, Penna.
Elliott, Charles H.	Private	75 S. Huron St., Wheeling, W. Va.
Fear, George W.	Private	Geneva, Ohio

Fields, Walton J.	Private	Bennet, Penna.
Fraiks, Andrew J.	Private	Mercer Bottom, W. Va.
Getty, William A.	Private	54 Marion St., Pittsburg, Penna.
Gould, William	Private	336 Brown St., Cincinnati, Ohio.
Harvey, William	Private	Bellevernon, Penna.
Holmes, Thomas J.	Private	Castle Shannon, Penna.
Lancaster, Thomas H.	Private	West Brownsville, Penna.
Layton, Lewis L.	Private	Fayette City, Penna.
Leighty, William	Private	Hutchinson, Kas.
Mahoney, Wm. H.	Private	Coal Center, Penna.
Mann, William	Private	Monogahela, Penna.
Maxwell, Alex J.	Private	Allenport, Penna.
Nutt, Wilson S.	Private	Perryopolis, Penna.
Orbin, Rev. George	Private	Knoxville, Pittsburg, Pa.
Richards, John M.	Private	Uniontown, Penna.
Rodeback, George	Private	Washington Ave., Beltzhoover, Pa.
Ryan, Francis	Private	Platte Creek, Neb.
Shallenberger, Eli F.	Private	Brownsville, Penna.
Shaw, Robert D.	Private	Uppermiddleto n. Penna.
Thompson, John B.	Private	Washington, Penna.
Wagoner, John S.	Private	Munroe City, Mo.

COMPANY D.

William H. Horn	Captain	Medical College, Richmond, Ind.
George S. Fulmer	1st Sergeant	Lincoln Avenue, Pittsburg, Penna.
Howard Kerr	Sergeant	Foxburg, Penna.
Jacob Speers	Sergeant	Marshalltown, Iowa.
Barnet T. Johnson	Sergeant	1209 Osage Ave., Kansas City, Kas.
John Milliken	Sergeant	Jefferson, Penna.
Abraham S. Tinley	Corporal	Bentleysville, Penna.
George W. Dales	Corporal	West Brownsville, Penna.
Samuel O. Thomas	Corporal	Burlington, Iowa.
Isaiah Jordan	Musician	714 Henry St., Oakland, Cal.
Allman, Wm.	Private	Garwood, Washington county, Pa.
Ames, Joseph E.	Private	Bellaire, Ohio.
Brooks, Enoch	Private	Dunn Station, R. D. 94, Pa.
Clendaniel, Stephen	Private	Berwick, Iowa
Cox, Harvey	Private	Afton, Iowa
Demuth, Joseph A.	Private	St. Joseph, Mo.
Fisher, George W.	Private	Anacosta, Washington D. C.
Haver, Hiram	Private	Iconium, Dakota
Haver, Jacob	Private	Griffinsville, Iowa
Horn, Jonas	Private	Ten Mile, Washington county, Pa.

Jackman, Wm. H.	Private	Applecreek, Ohio
Jones, Leonidas F.	Private	Homestead, Penna.
Lash, Wm. B.	Private	Beallsville, Penna.
Luker, Alfred R.	Private	Coal Center, Penna.
McKay, Alxander	Private	East Bethlehem, Penna.
McVey, Oliver	Private	West Union, Penna.
McCormick, Wm. C.	Private	Clarksville, W. Va.
Roberts, Edward	Private	Waynesburg, Penna.
Reese, Bowen	Private	Ten Mile, Washington county, Pa.
Reese, John	Private	Jonesburg, Mo.
Rider, Wm. A.	Private	Finleyville, Penna.
Stull, Wm. L.	Private	South English, Iowa.
Virgin, Wm. H.	Private	Clarksville, Penna.
Wilson, Theophilus	Private	Duluth, Minn.
Walton, Henry M.	Private	Washington, Penna.
Yoders, James	Private	Winterset, Iowa.

COMPANY E.

Charles E. Eckels	1st Sergeant	West Brownsville, Penna.
Wm. M. Linn	Sergeant	West Brownsville, Penna.
Henry M. Hand	Sergeant	Smith Center, Smith county, Kas.
Jacob D. Moore	Sergeant	Smithfield, Penna.
Adolphus J. Links	Corporal	Uniontown, Penna.
Henry J. McCallister	Corporal	Washington, Penna.
Hugh B. McNeil	Corporal	Dallas, Marshall county, W. Va.
Jeremiah Dawson	Corporal	Rogers, Ohio.
James M. Watkins	Corporal	Placerville, Cal.
George Fisher	Corporal	Arborville, York county, Neb.
Martin B. Pope	Corporal	Dunbar, Penna.
Robert M. Mitchell	Corporal	Bethany, Harrison county, Mo.
Axton, Matthew C.	Private	Soldiers' Home, Marion, Ind.
Byers, Thomas	Private	Uniontown, Penna.
Chase, Sherman	Private	Rockford, Ills.
Chew, Clark	Private	West Brownsivlle, Penna.
Clark, John	Private	Uniontown, Penna.
Davis, James C.	Private	Cottonwood Falls, Kas.
Fisher, Isaac	Private	
Garritt, Henry	Private	70 S. Dittaridge St., Pittsburg, Pa.
Gill, Benjamin	Private	Logansport, W. Va.
Hand, Wm.	Private	Hopewell, Washington county, Pa.
Hall, Edward M.	Private	Portsmouth, Ohio.
Hartman, Wm.	Private	Monongahela, Penna.
Hartsel, Jeremiah	Private	Uniontown, Penna.

Matthew C. Axton (center) and **Sergeant Charles E. Eckles** (left) of the 85th Pennsylvania, on the right sits J. T. Booth of the 6th U. S. Cavalry. (Ronn Palm Collection)

Matthew C. Axton was born in Fayette County, had black eyes, black hair, a dark complexion and stood 5'5" when he enrolled as a private in Co. E in the town of West Brownsville at age 21 on Nov. 5, 1861. He mustered in seven days later. In Sept. and Oct. 1863, he was on detached duty with the "boat infantry" at Morris Island, SC. He re-enlisted as a veteran volunteer on Feb. 1, 1864, at Hilton Head, SC. Assigned to the 199th Pennsylvania on Oct. 14, 1864. Axton was appointed a musician on Dec. 2, 1864. Transferred to the 188th Pennsylvania Infantry on July 8, 1865.

Charles E. Eckles was also born in Fayette County and had blue eyes, dark hair, a fair complexion, and was 5'91/2" tall upon enrollment at Brownsville on Oct. 15, 1861. He was 17 years old when mustered in as a private in Co. E. Eckles suffered a wound at the Battle of Seven Pines on May 31, 1862. He was promoted corporal in May/June 1862, and to sergeant on Sept. 1, 1863. In July 1863, he was doing duty as a courier on Folly Island, SC. In Dec. 1863, Eckles did duty as a clerk to the judge advocate of general court martial. He re-enlisted as a veteran volunteer on Feb. 1, 1864, at Hilton Head, SC. After returning from veterans' furlough, he began serving with the division ambulance corps on May 1, 1864. Assigned to the 199th Pennsylvania on Oct. 14, 1864, Eckles was promoted captain and officially transferred on Dec. 27, 1864.

Hennessey, Thomas   Private   Kingwood, W. Va.
Huff, James W.   Private   Fort McPherson, Ga.
Huston, Eli F.   Private   Dawson, Penna.
Keenan, Michael   Private   Uniontown, Penna.
Lincoln, Mordecai   Private   Uniontown, Penna.
Lucas, John P.   Private   Paoli, Kas.
Mahaffey, Wm.   Private   West Elizabeth, Penna.
Malone, Thomas W.   Private   Bellaire, Ohio.
Mayhorn, James W.   Private   Dunkirk, Ohio.
McClain, John V.   Private   Chalk Hill, Penna.
McKeag, David C.   Private   Columbus, Ohio.
Means, John R.   Private   Uniontown, Penna.
Ralston, Wesley J.   Private   Soldiers' Home, Leavenworth, Kas.
Smith, Henry   Private   Ola, Mich.
Woodward, John   Private   Pittsburg, Iowa.

COMPANY F.

John Morris	Captain	Jewell City, Kas.
Elmore A. Russell	1st Lieut.	Paris, Texas.
James E. Sayers	1st Sergeant	Waynesburg, Penna.
Zack C. Ragan	Sergeant	Waynesburg, Penna.
Isaac D. Haveley	Sergeant	
Rinehart B. Church	Sergeant	Rogersville, Greene county, Penna.
Thomas J. White	Sergeant	Soldiers' Home, Chaldren, Neb.
Thomas Hoge	Corporal	1409 O St., Washington D. C.
Hiram Weaver	Corporal	Holbrook, Penna.
Wm. N. Hoskinson	Corporal	Mankats, Jewell county, Kas.
Thomas M. Sellers	Corporal	Ottawa, Kas.
Daniel Swan	Musician	Sayre, Ark.
James P. McCuen	Musician	Ludlow, Ky.
Bryner, James	Private	Wind Ridge, Greene county, Penna.
Burk, Noah	Private	
Burrows, John B.	Private	Bristoria, Greene county, Penna.
Chapman, Charles	Private	Owassa, Mich.
Cheney, Jesse	Private	Nettle Hill, Greene county, Penna.
Church, Franklin	Private	New Virginia, Iowa.
Church, George	Private	Cameron, W. Va.
Cree, Alexander D.	Private	Waynesburg, Penna.
Davis, Benjamin	Private	Nettle Hill, Penna.
Earnest, Jacob	Private	Deep Valley, Greene county, Penna.
Fordyce, John	Private	Woodrough, Penna.
Fry, David	Private	Waynesburg, Penna
Fry, Thomas R.	Private	Horseneck, W. Va.
Garrison, Thompson	Private	Jollytown, Greene county, Penna.

Henry Pettit, Company F

Shown here standing, wearing a frock coat, and holding his forage cap, Pettit enrolled as a private at Jackson in Greene County, on Oct. 20, 1861, and mustered in at Uniontown on Nov. 11, he was 20 years old. Records show him present at every muster, although at times he reported sick from Jan. through Apr. 1864, during which time his pay was stopped $1.00 for a "mosquito bar." And though he apparently decided to re-enlist as a veteran volunteer, then changed his mind, he continued with the regiment and being daily assigned to the "Stretcher Corps" starting on May 19, 1864, and by June was serving as a nurse. He reported sick on Sept. 28, 1864, and was in the hospital at Hampton, VA. He mustered out at Pittsburgh on Nov. 22, 1864. (Ronn Palm Collection)

Gilbert, Elial	Private	Anita, Iowa.
Gladden, Wm. H.	Private	Vandercook, Ills.
Gray, Isaac	Private	New Freeport, Penna.
Henderson, Wm.	Private	Littleton, W. Va.
Huffman, Jacob	Private	Danville, Ills.
Huffman, James	Private	Oak Forest, Greene county, Penna.
Leonard, Harvey	Private	Simpson's Store, Wash. Co., Penna.
Lewis, George F.	Private	Martin's Ferry, Ohio.
McGlumphey, Harvey	Private	Waynesburg, Penna.
Mitchell, Andrew J.	Private	Nettle Hill, Penna.
Mitchell, Jonathan	Private	Rogersville, Penna.
Montgomery, John	Private	Cameron, W.Va., or Washington, Pa.
Montogomery, Wm.	Private	Fordyce, Penna.
Moore, Carl	Private	Humestown, Ills.
Moore, Samuel H.	Private	Humestown, Ills.
Ott, Ezra	Private	Littleton, W. Va.
Ott, Salem	Private	Littleton, W. Va.
Patterson, Samuel	Private	Elizabeth, W. Va.
Pettitt, George	Private	Deep Valley, Greene county, Penna.
Pettitt, Henry	Private	Lowman, W. Va.
Riggs, Peter	Private	Boardtree, W. Va.
Riggs, William	Private	Kossouth, W. Va.
Rinehart, Morgan	Private	Waynesburg, Penna.
Rinehart, Thomas	Private	Waynesburg, Pa.
Rizor, John	Private	Martin's Ferry, Ohio.
Roach, George	Private	Rocksdale, W. Va.
Rush, John	Private	Waynesburg, Penna.
Scott, Abijah	Private	Rogersville, Penna.
Scott, Lisbon	Private	Rogersville, Penna.
Seabald, William H.	Private	West Jefferson, Ohio.
Taylor, Levi	Private	Osceola, Iowa.
Terrell, George W.	Private	Wind Ridge, Greene county, Penna.
Thompson, Samuel	Private	Rogersville, Penna.
Weaver, Jacob	Private	Nettle Hill, Penna.
West, Jacob	Private	Rogersville, Penna.
Winger, John M.	Private	Kossouth, W. Va.
Wiseman, John	Private	St. Albens, W. Va.

COMPANY G.

John M. Crawford	2nd Lieut.	Greensboro, Penna.
David R. Graham	1st Sergeant	Pilot Grove, Iowa.
Robert H. Ross	Sergeant	New Geneva, Penna.
Jesse E. Jones	Sergeant	Ruble, Penna.

Rev. Marquis L. Gordon	Sergeant	Osaca, Japan.
Hiram Goodwin	Sergeant	Waynesburg, Penna.
Benjamin F. Campbell	Sergeant	Brushton, Penna.
Adam McGill	Musician	Breeds, Fulton county, Ills.
Bare, Baker	Private	Kirby, Penna.
Black, Lindsey	Private	Waynesburg, Penna.
Bovid, William	Private	Lockwood, Mo.
Cline, John L.	Private	Morgantown, W. Va.
Conrad, Alexander	Private	Shinston, W. Va.
Cumley, John G.	Private	Ottawa, Ills.
Eberhart, Martin L.	Private	Guthrie, Okla.
Eberhart, Wm.	Private	Scottdale, Penna.
Goodwin, David	Private	Elite, Greene county, Penna.
Graham, John	Private	Pierce City, Mo.
Graham, William M.	Private	Athens, Co.
Green, William P.	Private	Vermont, Ills.
Griffin, Charles A.	Private	Newport, Mo.
Harden, John P.	Private	Sylvia, Kas.
Hayden, Caleb F.	Private	
Hayden, Henry M.	Private	Hayden, W. Va.
Honsaker, Nicholas	Private	Masontown, Penna.
Hunter, Isaac	Private	Greensboro, Penna.
Husk, James	Private	Gumps, Penna.
Jenkins, Andrew J.	Private	Newburg, W. Va.
Kent, John R.	Private	Munroe, Jasper country, Iowa.
Knisely, George W.	Private	Springfield, Ills.
McGill, William	Private	Masontown, Penna.
Meredith, Enix	Private	Amblersburg, W. Va.
Moser, John T.	Private	Old Frame, Penna.
O'Neal, Henry	Private	Uniontown, Penna.
Patton, Henry B.	Private	Greensboro, Penna.
Pittock, Owen	Private	Waynesburg, Penna.
Pratt, Ashbel F.	Private	Uniontown, Penna.
Pratt, Joseph L.	Private	Uniontown, Penna.
Rush, John W.	Private	Grafton, W. Va.
Sutton, Wm. A.	Private	Soldiers' Home, Erire, Penna.
Titus, Benjamin	Private	Laruel Point, W. Va.
Wells, Thomas	Private	Holbrook, Penna.

COMPANY H.

Ross R. Sanner	Captain	Mountian Lake Boulevard
Norman B. Ream	1st Lieut.	1901 Prairie Ave. Chicago, Ills.
Ross R. Sterner	Sergeant	Bladensburg, Iowas

Joseph King	Sergeant	Kingwood, Penna.
Evans Rush	Corporal	Ohiopyle, Penna.
Dr. W. S. Mountain	Corporal	Confluence, Penna.
Reason B. Daniels	Coproral	Bell Plain, Iowa.
Noah M. Anderson	Muscician	McCracken, Penna.
Anderson, Thomas	Private	New Brigton, Penna.
Augustine, Peter S.	Private	Benedict, Neb.
Bearl, Willaim	Private	Confluence, Penna.
Burgess, Andrew J.	Private	New Brighton, Penna.
Caton, Noah	Private	Meyersdale, Penna.
Dean, Edward J.	Private	Ohiopyle, Penna.
Hann, Eli	Private	Salina, Fulton county, Ills.
Hileman, William	Private	Addison, Penna.
Hindbaugh, Jacob	Private	Glade, Somerset county, Penna.
Hyatt, Allen	Private	Connellsville, Penna.
Jennings, Jerome	Private	Ursina, Penna.
Kelson, John	Private	Draketown, Penna.
Morrison, Francis	Private	Ohiopyle, Penna.
Rush, Bryson	Private	Ohiopyle, Penna.
Rush, Lot	Private	Connellsville, Penna.
Sloan, Alfred	Private	Ashland, Ohio.
Sloan, Hiram M.	Private	Lima, Ohio.
Walker, John A.	Private	Connellsville, Penna.
Willey, Dr. Asa M.	Private	New Hampton, Mo.
Younkins, Harrison	Private	Jeannette, Penna.
Younkins, John	Private	Connellsville, Penna.

COMPANY I.

Joseph M. Johnson	2nd Lieut.	Coldwater, Okla.
Wm. H. Hackney	2nd Lieut.	6435 Stewart Ave., Englewood, Ills.
John G. Stevens	1st Sergeant	Uniontown, Penna.
Ellis B. Johnson	1st Sergeant	Charleston, W. Va.
Henry J. Molliston	Sergeant	Dawson, Penna.
Crawford H. Scott	Corporal	Dayton, Ohio
William E. Chick	Corporal	Uniontown, Penna.
Wm. E. Finley	Corporal	Uniontown, Penna.
John Bunting	Musician	Uniontown, Penna.
Adams, William	Private	Moyer, Penna.
Balsinger, Geo. W.	Private	Effingham, Kas.
Beeson, James	Private	Hopewood, Penna.
Bolen, Albert	Private	Fayette City, Penna.
Clear, Alexander	Private	Knoxville, Iowa
Deffenbaugh, Jacob	Private	Walton, Kas.

Dull, Joseph	Private	Broad Ford, Penna.
Freeman, Moses H.	Private	Marion, Iowa.
Hennessey, Cornelius	Private	Dunbar, Penna.
Johnson, Dr. Samuel E.	Private	New Salem, Penna.
Lilly, Thomas P.	Private	Grafton, W. Va.
Loughman, Thaddeus	Private	Big Spring, Ohio
Lynn, John W.	Private	New Castle, Penna.
Miller, George W.	Private	Uniontown, Penna.
Minerd, Isaac	Private	
Minerd, James	Private	Dunbar, Penna.
Minerd, Wm.	Private	Brownfield, Penna.
Morgan, Nathan	Private	Hopwood, Penna.
Ogle, Andrew	Private	Grand View, W. Va.
Ogle, Elias	Private	Scottdale, Penna.
Perry, William B.	Private	Uniontown, Pa.
Pratt, William A.	Private	60 Marion St., Pittsburg, Penna.
Thompson, John	Private	West newton, Penna.
Wymer, George	Private	Oliver, Penna.
Wynn, James H.	Private	Gastonville, Penna.

COMPANY K.

Reason Smurr	1st Lieut.	New Haven, Penna.
Oliver Sproul	1st Sergeant	Ohiopyle, Penna.
John M. Moore	Sergeant	Parish, N. Y.
Zachariah Snyder	Sergeant	Rockwood, Penna.
Wm. H. Murphy	Sergeant	Scottdale, Penna.
Slyvanus Hasson	Sergeant	Uniontown, Penna.
Jacob F. Miller	Sergeant	Pennsville, Penna
Wm. H. Showman	Sergeant	Normanville, Penna.
John C. Brown	Corporal	Uniontown, Penna.
James H. Miller	Corporal	Dunbar, Penna.
Isssac Cossel	Corporal	Morgans Hill, Penna.
Baily, David S.	Private	Broad Ford, Penna.
Boyd, Archibald	Private	Ohiopyle, Penna.
Brown, Wm. H.	Private	Michigan, N. Dakota
Campbell, James R.	Private	7124 Ellis Aven., Chicago, Ills.
Collins, Henry	Private	Dawson, Penna.
Daniels, David	Private	Ohiopyle, Penna.
Edwards, Thomas J.	Private	Connelsville, Penna.
Elder, Julias	Private	Lamberton, N. Y.
Grimm, Jacob W.	Private	Moyer, Penna.
Grimm, John C.	Private	Fairview, Penna.
Hall, Isaac L.	Private	Confluence, Penna.

Hart, George H.	Private	Elm, Fayette county, Penna.
Hauger, Levi	Private	Ursina, Penna.
Johnston, Charles	Private	Sculltown, Penna.
Johnston, Samuel K.	Private	Mill Run, Penna.
Keefer, Henry	Private	Fairchance, Penna.
Keefer, John	Private	Moyer, Penna.
Kimmel, Ludwick	Private	Normalville, Penna.
Lowrie, Jacob	Private	Berryville, Ark.
Lytle, Charles	Private	Confluence, Penna.
McMillen, Jacob	Private	2502 Sarah St., S. S., Pittsburgh, Pa.
Miller, Amzi	Private	Dunbar, Penna.
Morrison, Perry	Private	Bakersville, Wis.
Nicholson, David	Private	Normalville, Penna.
Nicholson, Samuel	Private	Confluence, Penna.
Philipi, Jacob	Private	New Lexington, Penna.
Shaw, Wm. S.	Private	Brisco, Iowa.
Stuck, Thomas	Private	Jacksonville, Mo.
Wilson, Perry B.	Private	Scottdale, Penna.

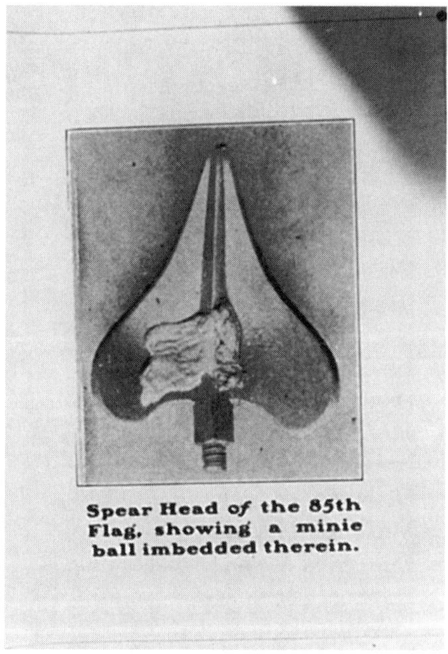

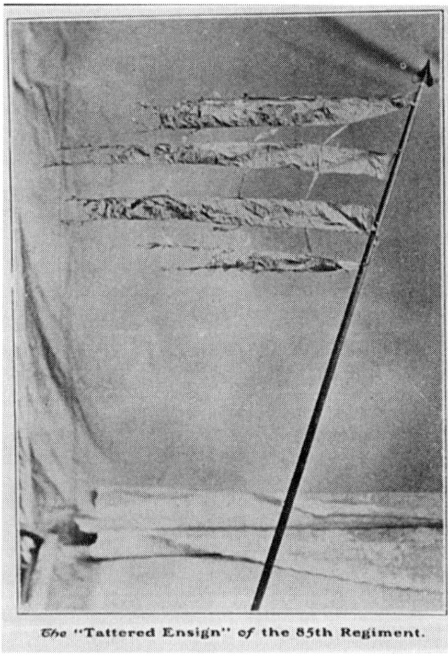

Left: The "Tattered Ensign" of the 85th Pennsylvannia. **Right**: Spearhead of the flag, showing the minie ball imbedded therein. (History of the Old Flag)

John W. Acheson, Company A

A washed out picture of Acheson. He enrolled in Capt. Vankirk's company at Washington, PA, on Oct. 1, and mustered in at Uniontown as a private on Oct. 16, 1861. The 24-year-old Acheson rose rapidly through the ranks, being promoted to first sergeant on Nov. 13, 1861, then to second lieutenant on Apr. 7, 1862. Acheson received a wound at the Battle of Seven Pines on May 31, 1862. He was promoted again to first lieutenant and transferred to Co. C on Aug. 2, 1862. Acheson was assigned to command Co. K on Mar. 1, 1863, and entitled to pay from that date. He returned to Pennsylvania on detached service for conscripts and posted at the draft rendezvous at Pittsburgh, from July 22 to Oct. 15, 1863. In Nov. and Dec. 1863, he did special duty as judge advocate to the general court martial. Acheson received promotion to captain and assistant adjutant general of U. S. Volunteers on Apr. 10, 1864, by commission from the President dated Feb. 29, 1864, and from that time no longer served with the regiment. (USAMHI)

Richard W. Dawson, Company I

Dawson enrolled at age 20 as first sergeant of Capt. Zellar's company on Aug. 13, 1861, at Uniontown, and mustered in on Nov. 7. He received promotion to second lieutenant of Co. B on Jan. 27, 1862, and then to first lieutenant on May 19. Mustered in as captain on July 21, 1862, Dawson transferred to Co. I on Aug. 12. Dawson performed duty as the acting assistant adjutant general for Gen. Henry Wessells from July 1 until Sept. 30, 1862. From July 1863 to Jan. 1864, he served as the acting assistant inspector general for Howell's brigade, and for the Department of the South from Feb. through May 1864. In mid-Sept. 1864, in addition to being the acting assistant inspector general of the 1st Brigade, 1st Division, 10th Corps, he also performed that duty for the 2nd Division. (Ronn Palm Collection)

Richard W. Dawson, Company I
While acting as aide-de-camp (Assistant Inspector General) for Gen. Adelbert Ames, Dawson was wounded during the assault on Fort Fisher, NC, on Jan. 15, 1865. He suffered a complete fracture of the left ulna by a bullet, and surgeons performed a resection. Dawson died Feb. 1, 1865, in the general hospital at Fortress Monroe, VA. (Ronn Palm Collection)

John W. Dial, Company H

Dial, who enlisted at age 24, was born in Westmoreland County, and at the time he joined the regiment, and lived in Allegheny City in Allegheny County. Dial served through the Peninsula Campaign, and came unscathed through the battle of Seven Pines where the regiment suffered 82 casualties. He remained present with the unit until re-enlisting in Feb. 1864, while the regiment was at Hilton Head, SC. At the time of his re-enlistment, he was described as having a dark complexion, dark hair, brown eyes and stood 5'8". On Oct. 15, 1864, the veterans of the 85th were attached to the 199th Pennsylvania, and after serving through the Appomattox Campaign, Dial was transferred to Co. F of the 188th Pennsylvania, which did provost guard duty in Virginia until Nov. 1865. Though a reliable soldier, Dial served as a private the entire war. In Nov. and Dec. 1864, he did daily duty as a cook. Dial is seen here wearing a sack coat with a military vest, a plug hat, and even sports a dapper tie. (Ronn Palm Collection)

George W. Downer, Company E
A 18-year-old Fayette County born farmer, that stood 5'8", with a fair complexion, grey eyes, sandy hair, and a resident of Wharton Township. He enrolled at Uniontown on September 21, 1861, and mustered in as a private on November 12. Appointed corporal on January 1, 1864. Downer re-enlist February 1, 1864, at Hilton Head, South Carolina. Beginning on August 9, 1864, he was absent sick in the hospital at Pittsburg. In November and December 1864, he was doing daily duty as a train guard at Deep Bottom, Virginia. Downer took sick again on February 12, 1865, and was sent to the hospital at Point of Rocks, Virginia. He was discharged for disease on March 26, 1865, from that hospital. The doctor noted the Downer suffered from "a hard dry cough and night sweats, accelerated pulse, emaciation,   " He was totally unfit for duty, even in the Veteran Reserve Corps.   (Ronn Palm Collection)

Charles A. Griffin, Company G
Griffin enrolled in Captain Abraham's company on Sept. 20, 1861, at Reppert's Crossroads, he was 23. Griffin mustered in at Uniontown on Nov. 6, 1861. He began doing detached service with the Signal Corps starting in Feb. 1862. He was officially transferred to the Signal Corps by Special Orders No. 24 issued by the Headquarters of the Army of the Potomac on Sept. 7, 1863. (USAMHI)

Charles A. Griffin, Company G
This photo, entitled "U.S. Signal flag–A relic of 23 battles with Grant," shows an elderly Charles Griffin (on the right) who carried the flag, and William L. Griffin–assumed to be his brother. If the photo were in color, the square on the white flag would be red. (William L. Griffin Collection)

Samuel Hendrickson, Company A

He is shown here wearing a forage cap and a frock coat with shoulder scales, backed by a United States flag. Hendrickson enlisted in Captain Vankirk's company at Thompsonville on Sept. 13, 1861. He mustered in Oct. 16 at Uniontown. He was 21 years old and stood 5'71/2", with blue eyes, light hair, and a light complexion. Hendrickson was a farmer and had been born in Thompsonville, Washington County. Absent sick beginning May 4, 1862, he was sent home on the surgeon's authority on furlough. Listed at a convalescent camp at Alexandria, VA (several accounts say Baltimore, MD), on Feb. 10, 1863, he was discharged six days' later for "valvular disease of the heart contracted in service." (Ronn Palm Collection)

Robert W. Mitchell, Company E
Born in Washington County, and 21 years old at the time of his enlistment. He enrolled at Washington, PA, on Oct. 15, 1861, and mustered in at Uniontown on Nov. 12. Mitchell was 6 foot tall, with a dark complexion, gray eyes, and dark hair. Records show him present at every muster until Sept./Oct. 1864. (Ronn Palm Collection)

Robert W. Mitchell, Company E

Mitchell re-enlisted as a veteran volunteer in Feb. 1864, and was promoted corporal on Sept. 1, 1864. On Oct. 14, Mitchell along with the remaining men of the 85th was attached to the 199th Pennsylvania. Most of 1865, he served as the company commissary, and on July 8, of that year, was transferred to the 188th Pennsylvania, and remained on provost guard duty in Virginia until Nov. 1865. (Ronn Palm Collection)

Norman Bruce Ream, Company H

Ream was born on Nov. 5, 1844, in Somerset County. His great-grandfather had fought in the Revolutionary War. Ream was an industrious young man, at age fourteen, he worked on his father's farm, taught school, made ambrotype photographs, and attended Somerset Normal School. A young hero of the regiment, Ream was a mere 16 years old (although he gave his age as 18) when he enlisted at Harnedsville on Oct. 1, 1861, and mustered in as a fourth sergeant on Nov. 12, 1861, at Uniontown. He was sent to the hospital at Harrison's Landing, VA, on August 5, 1862. At a crucial moment in the Battle of Kinston, NC, on Dec. 14, 1862, Ream urged his men forward despite swampy irregular ground and receiving heavy enemy fire. Colonel Howell noticed his gallant conduct and made him a lieutenant on the spot. He was promoted second lieutenant to date from Aug. 15, 1862. This made Ream the youngest officer in the Federal armies commissioned from the ranks—or at least it is claimed that he was. While acting as the regimental adjutant, he was severely wounded during the action at White Marsh Island, GA, on Feb. 22, 1864, the bullet passing through his upper thigh and into his groin. He received a furlough home to recover from his wound, which was extended an extra 20 days on April 20, 1864. Ream was promoted to first lieutenant on June 15, 1864, to date from May 1, 1864. He was wounded in the right leg at Ware Bottom Church, near Petersburg, VA, on June 17, 1864, and was sent to the hospital at Fort Monroe, VA. This wound injured the "flexor muscles . . . rendering locomotion both painful and difficult." He rejoined the regiment from the hospital on Aug. 15, 1864, but was discharged because of his wounds on Aug. 31, 1864. Ream kept the bullets that wounded him as souvenirs, but years later, his war wounds proved fatal. Surgery was done in 1913 to correct problems from his wounds, but his demise from the effects finally came on Feb. 9, 1915. After the war, Ream engaged in numerous business ventures in various states, the most noted being his part in founding the National Biscuit Company, known today as NABISCO. Ream married Carrie Thompson on Feb. 17, 1876, and fathered six children. (History of the Old Flag)

James M. Welch, Company A

Welch enrolled Sept. 13, 1861, at Finleyville, and mustered in at Uniontown on Oct. 16, when he mustered into Captain Vankirk's company as third sergeant. He was 28 years old upon enlistment, and was promoted second sergeant on Apr. 7, 1862, then to second lieutenant on Nov. 20, 1862. On Aug. 14, 1863, Welch penned his resignation: "As my health is impaired, and but little prospect of my recovery exists. I am obliged therefore to tender my resignation . . . ." He was discharged on "surgeon's certificate of disability" on Aug. 14, 1863, at Morris Island, SC. (Ronn Palm Collection)

Unidentified
Soldier of the 85th Pennsylvania, believed to be one of the Chase brothers. (Ronn Palm Collection)

Unidentified
A dapper man with a tie and white shirt who served with the 85th Pennsylvania. (Ronn Palm Collection)

Unidentified

Unknown soldier belonging to Co. D of the 85th Pennsylvania Infantry, who proudly
displays his company letter and regimental number on his forage cap. He wears a white
shirt, tie, vest, frock coat and sky blue trousers. (Ronn Palm Collection)

Unidentified

A soldier of the 85th Pennsylvania, possibly Coulson Coughanour of Co. K, displays his regimental number of the old 85th despite being transferred to the Veteran Reserve Corps as indicated by his light blue jacket with dark blue trim. (Ronn Palm Collection)

Unidentified

A man in civilian clothes who served with the 85th Pennsylvania. (Ronn Palm Collection)

Unidentified
Unknown soldier belonging to Co. E of the 85th Pennsylvania Infantry. (Ronn Palm Collection)

Bibliography of 85th Pennsylvania Material

Bell, John B. "Recollections of Seven Pines." *National Tribune*, 22 September 1910.

Chick, William E. "Bridges Over the Chickahominy." *National Tribune*, 7 November 1901.

__________. "Capture of Fort Gregg." *National Tribune*, 12 June 1902.

Dawson, Richard W. Papers. Duke University.

Dickey, Luther S. *History of the Eighty-fifth Regiment Pennsylvania Volunteer Infantry, 1861-1865, Comprising an Authentic Narrative of Casey's Division at the Battle of Seven Pines.* New York: J. C. & W. E. Powers, 1915.

Gordon, Donald (editor). *M[arquis] L. Gordon's Experiences in the Civil War, From His Narrative, Letters and Diary.* Boston: Merrymount Press, 1922.

Hadden, James. *History of the Old Flag of the 85th Reg't.* Uniontown: The News Standard, 1902.

Howell, Joshua B. Papers. Duke University.

__________. Diary. Glassboro (NJ) State College.

McHenry, Samuel L. "The Deeds and Sacrifices of the Eighty-fifth Pennsylvania." Philadelphia *Weekly Times*, 3 July 1886.

Milligan, William. Diary, 1861-1862. Washington and Jefferson College.

Moore, John M. "Pennsylvania's Battle Flags." *National Tribune*, 14 April 1910.

Sturgis, Isaac. Letters, June 1862; September, November 1864. Historical Society of Pennsylvania.

Sturgis, James. Letters, July 1862-August 1863. Historical Society of Pennsylvania.

INDEX

Numbers in **boldface** indicate photographs.

Remains of the flag today. (Ronn Palm Collection)

Ronn Palm has been collecting Civil War images since 1972. About 1983, he started focusing and acquiring Pennsylvania images. On June 30th, 2000, Ronn opened a museum of Civil War photographs in Gettysburg based in a historic log home circa 1802 on Baltimore Street. The museum's concentration is Pennsylvania soldiers and the feature exhibit is 260 images and artifacts concerning the Pennsylvania Bucktail regiments. In all, close to 2000 more Pennsylvania images are on display–including most of the photos found in this book. The museum will continue to expand in the future. Ronn has a special affinity for photos from his native western Pennsylvania. The museum is a tribute to the gallant and heroic soldiers of Pennsylvania. He has also been a senior editor of Military Images Magazine since its inception and has contributed his images to numerous books, publications, documentaries, and movies. Ronn often exhibits his images at Civil War shows.

Dr. Richard A. Sauers, a native of Lewisburg, Pennsylvania, received his B.A. in history from Susquehanna University, and both his M.A. and Ph.D in history from The Pennsylvania State University. He is the author of more than sixteen books, including: *The Gettysburg Campaign* bibliography (1982), *A Caspian Sea of Ink: The Meade-Sickles Controversy* (1989), the two-volume *Advance the Colors! Pennsylvania Civil War Battleflags* (1987-1991), *A Succession of Honorable Victories: The Burnside Expedition in North Carolina* (1996), *Pennsylvania in the Spanish-American War: A Commemorative Look Back* (1998), and *How to Do Civil War Research* (2000). He and his family reside in Wisconsin.

Patrick A. Schroeder has written and/or edited fourteen Civil War titles. He is a graduate of Shepherd College and Virginia Tech. Patrick has a B.S. in Historical Park Administration and a M.A. in History. He is the Historian at Appomattox Court House National Historical Park.

For a complete book and price list write:

Schroeder Publications
131 Tanglewood Drive
Lynchburg, VA 24502
www.civilwar-books.com
Email: civilwarbooks@yahoo.com

Titles Available:
* **The Pennsylvania Bucktails: A Photographic Album of the 42nd, 149th & 150th Pennsylvania Regiments** by Patrick A. Schroeder ISBN 1-889246-14-X

* **Thirty Myths About Lee's Surrender** by Patrick A. Schroeder
   ISBN 1-889246-05-0

* **More Myths About Lee's Surrender** by Patrick A. Schroeder
   ISBN 1-889246-01-8

* **The Confederate Cemetery at Appomattox** by Patrick A. Schroeder
   ISBN 1-889246-11-5

* **Recollections & Reminiscences of Old Appomattox and Its People**
   by George T. Peers ISBN 1-889246-12-3

* **Tar Heels: Five Points in the Record of North Carolina in the Great War of 1861-5**
   by the Committee appointed by the North Carolina Literary and Historical Society
   ISBN 1-889246-02-6 (Softcover)
   ISBN 1-889246-15-8 (Hardcover)

* **The Fighting Quakers** by A. J. H. Duganne ISBN 1-889246-03-4

* **A Duryée Zouave** by Thomas P. Southwick ISBN 1-889246-24-7

* **Civil War Soldier Life: In Camp and Battle** by George F. Williams
   ISBN 1-889246-04-2

* **We Came To Fight: The History of the 5th New York Veteran Volunteer Infantry, Duryée's Zouaves, (1863-1865)** by Patrick A. Schroeder ISBN 1-889246-07-7

* **A Swedish Officer in the American Civil War: The Diary of Axel Leatz of the 5th New York Veteran Volunteer Infantry, Duryée's Zouaves, (1863-1865)** edited by Patrick A. Schroeder ISBN 1-889246-06-9

* **Campaigns of the 146th Regiment New York State Volunteers**
   by Mary Genevie Green Brainard ISBN 1-889246-08-5

* **Where Duty Called Them: The Story of the Samuel Babcock Family of Homer, New York, in the Civil War** by Edmund Raus ISBN 1-889246-49-2

* **The Highest Praise of Gallantry: Memorials of David T. & James E. Jenkins of the 146th New York Infantry & Oneida Cavalry** by A. Pierson Case with new material by Patrick A. Schroeder ISBN 1-889246-17-4